ACRL PUBLICATIONS IN LIBRARIANSHIP NO. 80

Cultural Heritage
and the Campus Community

Academic Libraries and Museums in Collaboration

Alexia Hudson-Ward,
Julie Rodrigues Widholm,
and Scott Walter, *Editors*

Association of College and Research Libraries
A division of the American Library Association
Chicago, Illinois 2023

The paper used in this publication meets the minimum requirements of American National Standard for Information Sciences–Permanence of Paper for Printed Library Materials, ANSI Z39.48-1992. ∞

Library of Congress Control Number: 2022949777

Copyright ©2022 by the Association of College and Research Libraries.

All rights reserved except those which may be granted by Sections 107 and 108 of the Copyright Revision Act of 1976.

Printed in the United States of America.

26 25 24 23 22 5 4 3 2 1

CONTENTS

vii **ACKNOWLEDGEMENTS**

ix **INTRODUCTION**

1 **CHAPTER 1.** Designing a Better GLAM Alliance: Aligning Missions, Values, and Strategic Goals at the University of Oregon's Libraries and the Jordan Schnitzer Museum of Art
Adriene Lim, Jill Hartz, and Jenny R. Kreiger

15 **CHAPTER 2.** The University of Iowa Executive Leadership Academy: A Case Study in Leveraging Broad University Resources to Support GLAM Collaborations
Jane Garrity, Elizabeth Constantine, Megan Hammes, Cory Lockwood, and Lynn Teesch

33 **CHAPTER 3.** Visual Thinking Strategies and The *Framework* in the Undergraduate Classroom: Research as Inquiry and Scholarship as Conversation through the Lens of a University's Art Collection
Kayla Birt Flegal and Alexandra Chamberlain

53 **CHAPTER 4.** Pieced Together: Community Engagement Through Collaboration
Susan Dreher and Andrea Packard

63 **CHAPTER 5.** The Cultural Heritage Collaborative: Shared Mission, Expertise, and Spaces for Natural History and Library Collections
Patrick Kociolek, Robert H. McDonald, Leslie J. Reynolds, and Jennifer Knievel

73 CHAPTER 6. Restoring Indigenous Heritage: Building Community through Tribal Partnerships at the Glenn A. Black Laboratory of Archaeology
Jennifer A. St. Germain, Kelsey T. Grimm, and April K. Sievert

87 CHAPTER 7. Building Bridges: A Case Study in Community Engagement Between the Art Museum and the Library System at West Virginia University
Sally Brown and Carroll Wetzel Wilkinson

101 CHAPTER 8. Editing Wikipedia at Vanderbilt: How Library-Art Gallery Collaboration Can Benefit Learning Beyond the Classroom
Mary Anne Caton and Joseph Mella

117 CHAPTER 9. Paths to Partnership: New Models for Museum-Library Collaborations at Northwestern University
Corinne Granof

135 CHAPTER 10. Across the Square: Collaborative Paper and Photograph Conservation at the University of Washington Libraries and the Henry Art Gallery
Stephanie Lamson and Sylvia Wolf

151 CHAPTER 11. Librarians and Curators as Co-teachers: Using Collaborative, Object-Based Teaching to Motivate Student Research and Inquiry
Alexander Watkins and Hope Saska

165 CHAPTER 12. Of Primary Importance: Connecting Social Studies Teachers to Library and Museum Resources
Adrienne Scott, Pamela Nett Kruger, and Irene Korber

Contents   v

183 CHAPTER 13. Using Exhibitions for Teaching and
Learning: Collaboration Between a University Library
and Museum
Alex Regan

195 CHAPTER 14. Collection-Centered Teaching,
Learning, and Scholarship in St. John's University's
Master's Degree Program in Museum Administration
Dr. Susan Rosenberg with Alyse Hennig

209 CHAPTER 15. Collaboration and Convergence at the
Consortial Level: Museums10 and the Five College
Library Consortium
Jennifer Gunter King, Simon Neame, and Jessica Nicoll

223 CHAPTER 16. How History and a Commitment to
Social Justice Informed Library-Museum Collaboration
at Oberlin College
Alexia Hudson-Ward

239 ABOUT THE EDITORS

241 ABOUT THE AUTHORS

ACKNOWLEDGEMENTS

This book project began with a call for proposals in 2018. With high hopes and exceptional enthusiasm, Julie, Scott, and I started working on editing the chapters and coordinating the editorial process with Erin Nevius from ACRL Books. The co-editors received scores of submissions resulting in an outstanding assemblage of contributed chapters from thirty-seven authors.

Yet, circumstances superseded our intentions. And to say that life happens is an exceptional understatement.

Some of these circumstances were great. All three co-editors and several of the contributors got exciting new roles while working on the project. Several of us were tapped for new professional assignments and initiatives with national and global significance.

Concurrently, the COVID-19 global pandemic zapped all of our "bandwidth" as the co-editors and contributors turned our attention toward supporting our institutions and teams. COVID made our lives feel so upended in many ways that this book's completion hung in the balance.

Nonetheless, we persisted.

The commitment of our editors and contributors remained steadfast and unwavering. For this, I am tremendously appreciative.

Thank you to my co-editors, Julie Rodrigues Widholm and Scott Walter, for their partnership on this project, as it would not have been possible without them. I extend heartfelt appreciation to Erin Nevius, Association of College and Research Libraries (ACRL) Content Strategist and ACRL Books. They continued to believe in the importance of this project despite the many delays we faced along the way.

Many thanks to our outstanding contributors whose excitement and collegiality made getting this long-delayed book into production worthwhile. Because of you, we have an exceptional first-of-its-kind contribution to the cultural heritage community. Your openness and willingness to share your experiences with academic library-museum collaboration will be invaluable to current and future generations of librarians, curators, archivists, and administrators.

Hugs and love to my husband, Linton, for making early morning and evening tea runs to Starbucks and creating spaces in our home for me to write and edit undisturbed.

Celebrating the publication of this book is somewhat bittersweet. My mom, mother-in-law, and cat Ebony died in the four years it took to get this book completed. Several of our contributors also experienced personal impacts.

Therefore, I dedicate this book to those who supported us while we worked on this project and who are no longer with us. May our contributions inspire others in the same manner in which all of you encouraged us.

—*Alexia Hudson-Ward*

I am forever grateful to my co-editors Scott and Alexia for their patience, good humor, and resilience to complete this project over the last four years. A special thank you to Scott for connecting me to the GLAM world and thinking more deeply about new models for campus collaborations. Because higher education and our respective fields have gone through seismic change over the last few years, I look forward to seeing what new ways of thinking, connecting, and sharing come about as a response. Many thanks to my colleagues at DePaul Art Museum and now at BAMPFA for experimenting with me and to my personal crew, Timothy, Maya, and Miles, whose ongoing support for my passion for museums is greatly appreciated!

— *Julie Rodrigues Widholm*

In addition to echoing his thanks to the contributors and his co-editors, Scott would like to thank his colleagues at the DePaul University Library and the DePaul Art Museum for helping him to deepen his thinking about the opportunities for campus-wide collaboration around cultural heritage materials and collection-centered teaching, learning, and scholarship. He is also grateful for the opportunities he has had to explore similar community-based collaboration with libraries, archives, and museums in Chicago and San Diego, and looks forward to seeing how we work together to bring our shared enterprise together in the post-pandemic era in higher education.

— *Scott Walter*

INTRODUCTION

Introduction

For many decades, United States academic libraries and museums foster outstanding collaborations supporting teaching, learning, and research within their respective institutions. Much of this collaborative work was and remains deeply embedded into these colleges' and universities' organizational DNA in such a fashion that academic library-museum collaboration was primarily perceived as a common practice.

The dilemma with "common practices" within academia is that the invisible labor and caretaking required to foster progressive activities are often not documented. Consequently, identifying what skills, talents, and resources are necessary to support and advance academic library-museum collaborations have not been chronicled, which we're hoping to correct with this book.

Many academic library-museum collaborations are organically formed due to long-standing pedagogical and outreach relationships between campus librarians, archivists, and museum curators. Other collaborations were catalyzed by grant support from The Andrew W. Mellon Foundation. Irrespective of the impetus of these collaborations, the commitment to experimentation, innovation, and creativity is the proverbial red thread linking the activities presented here.

This book aims to serve as critical knowledge for the cultural heritage sector. By sharing multiple examples of successful academic library-museum collaboration, readers will learn the "secret sauce" of collaboration which is often realized only through experience. Sixteen chapters written by thirty-eight authors explore the "hows" and "whys" of academic library-museum collaboration that bring forth new dimensions of transdisciplinary objects-based pedagogy, research, and learning that are centered upon inclusive educational practices. The collaborative approaches highlighted in this book demonstrate the power of possibility when two collections-centric entities (libraries and museums) unite to enrich our collective understanding of materiality, instructional approaches, and the importance of provenance. Readers will also learn why interrogating past practices and value assignments within academic libraries and museum collections is essential to advancing culturally relevant approaches to knowledge sharing in physical and digital spaces.

CHAPTER 1

Designing a Better GLAM Alliance:
Aligning Missions, Values, and Strategic Goals at the University of Oregon's Libraries and the Jordan Schnitzer Museum of Art

Adriene Lim, Jill Hartz, and Jenny R. Kreiger

> At the University of Oregon, the UO GLAM Alliance is a creative partnership between the Jordan Schnitzer Museum of Art (JSMA) and the UO Libraries (UOL), with the purposes of helping its member institutions share resources more effectively and promote campus museums and libraries as valuable assets for research, teaching, and learning. In this chapter, the authors describe the alliance's intensive exercise in strategic planning, the ways in which the process of GLAM planning can be used for education and advocacy for libraries and museums, and how the products of planning can be used to communicate the value of these institutions to users and stakeholders.

Introduction

As academic units with long, interconnected histories on the University of Oregon (UO) campus and with several complementary collections between them, the UO Libraries and the Jordan Schnitzer Museum of Art (JSMA) joined the global GLAM (galleries, libraries, archives, and museums) movement in 2015. This was the year we began to explore our mission alignments and future collaboration strategies, using GLAM-based foundational principles and practices. Our new "GLAM Alliance" gave us a conceptual banner under which we could rally internal and cross-campus support, as we simultaneously transformed our work into a highly visible and increasingly collaborative partnership.

In 2016, we were invited to participate in an intensive GLAM summit held at the University of Miami and sponsored by The Andrew W. Mellon Foundation and the Samuel H. Kress Foundation. The summit allowed us to learn more about the experiences of other leaders who had already implemented successful GLAM initiatives at their institutions and enabled us to network with representatives of grant-funding agencies, scholars, and practitioners. Upon our return, we worked with our campus colleagues to analyze our organizations' separate strategic plans and determine synergies, intersections, and potential convergences that could be leveraged for additional institutional impact and investment. These collaborative processes were invaluable as we devised our GLAM initiatives, but they were also instrumental in our efforts to convey and demonstrate the unique value of libraries, archives, and museums to the university community. Each component of the planning process became an opportunity to bring UO stakeholders into GLAM-focused discussions.

The Context for Collaboration

There has been a strong movement in recent years toward increasing collaboration among campus GLAM organizations, partly to expand the value of services and collections these entities offer their communities and partly to demonstrate that value in an era of fierce competition for financial support. International library and museum professional associations and governmental agencies, including the Institute of Museum and Library Services (IMLS) in the United States, were key in funding and fostering the movement.[1] Non-profit entities, such as the Mellon Foundation and the Online Computer Library Center (OCLC), have invested millions of dollars in research and grant programs targeted at enhancing campus museum-library collaboration. Institutions receiving this support (including our own) are developing and testing new models of collaboration that aim to transform and enrich all participants.

In the distant past, libraries, archives, and museums were considered to be more alike than they were different. If not unified in fact, these entities were acknowledged to be carrying out similar functions and pursuing similar goals for the same relatively privileged audiences, and they interacted accordingly. Industrialization in the nineteenth and twentieth centuries created bureaucratic models that led to the separation of GLAM functions into different entities over time, encouraging a form of professional specialization and differentiation that has not been wholly beneficial for either the stewarding organizations themselves or their users.[2] To thrive in the twenty-first century, academic museums and libraries are rediscovering the commonalities in their missions, visions, and institutional values and are identifying and strengthening alignments in these areas to become better partners and advocates for each other on their campuses.[3] When such strategic alignments are in place, libraries and museums can collaborate more productively on initiatives that have the potential to benefit and transform both.[4]

Prior to joining the GLAM movement in 2015, the UO Libraries and the JSMA worked together primarily in ad hoc ways, such as the staging of a joint exhibition or the stewarding of a mutual donor's gift. Unfortunately, these efforts fell more on the traditional "cooperation" and "coordination" side of the collaborative continuum rather than true collaboration as described by Zorich, Waibel, and Erway—for example, our activities did not require any programmatic or lasting change in our organizations.[5] As the executive director of the JSMA and the dean of libraries, respectively, we did not meet regularly with each other, even though our physical offices were only minutes apart in the campus's central Memorial Quadrangle. We were collegial and supportive of one another, but prior to forming the UO GLAM Alliance, we focused mainly on advancing our units' separate missions and goals. We were also engrossed in helping our units recover from significant, across-the-board, institutional budget cuts that occurred each year from 2014 to 2018. At the same time, we were involved in meeting ambitious, unit-level fundraising goals—working with mostly separate and distinct donor bases—as part of the UO's comprehensive campaign, launched publicly in late 2014.

The organizational structure of the university made potential collaboration between our two units challenging as well. Both the JSMA and the libraries are categorized as academic units within the university's structure; however, the appointed leader of the library is an academic dean and reports directly to the provost, whereas the appointed leader of the museum is an executive director and reports to a vice provost. This difference has the real-world effect of associating our positions with different sets of groups and systems on campus. It results in fewer opportunities for us to systematically (and serendipitously) engage and learn about our units' directions, issues, and challenges. By creating the alliance, we formed a virtual structure within the university's organizational chart, one symbolizing the aspirational idea of convergence. There are now articulated reasons to engage deliberately and consistently with one another, to bring our operations and professional staff closer together, and to advocate to upper administration for our units' interdependent programs and functions. The alliance continues to maximize the positive impact of the museum and libraries, despite the arguably outdated structures still in place.

The libraries and the JSMA were always separate organizational units within the institution, as they remain now, each committed to serving our students and stewarding cultural-heritage collections, but with histories and approaches that differed from and mirrored the other in surprising ways. From its modest beginnings as a 1,000-volume library in 1882, the UO Libraries has grown into a relatively large organization, with holdings of over 3.2 million volumes in its historic main Knight Library alone and with six other branch locations, including a new, award-winning science library that opened in late 2016. As is the case with most public research libraries, the UO Libraries provide services, information, and content to meet the needs of the university's academic programs and the research interests of faculty, students, and community members. Today, people visit the physical libraries over 45,000 times each week during the fall and winter terms, and users make more than 1.5 million unique visits annually to the libraries' website. The UO Libraries has preserved an abundant scholarly legacy for future generations of inquirers and has been a member of the US federal depository program since the late nineteenth century. Over the past few decades, it has served as a technological leader on campus and incorporated advances in digital technology in all aspects of its work, especially through its two library centers, one focused on digital scholarship and one charged with enhancing educational technology and instructional design for the entire campus. The libraries' Special Collections and University Archives (SCUA) division acquires, preserves, and makes available a diverse set of primary sources for research and teaching and serves as the repository for the university's records, rare books, historic photographs, and one of the largest, historical manuscripts collections in the Pacific Northwest.

When it opened in a purpose-built building in 1933 and for much of its early history, the JSMA was not a welcoming cultural center for community members, other than for scholars specifically interested in the research of Chinese, Japanese, and Korean art. (The JSMA was the first US academic art museum to have a non-European focus.) In 2008, with a new executive director and participation from constituencies on and off campus, the museum created a new mission, vision, guiding principles, and goals that prioritized interdisciplinary, cross-campus learning and diverse community engagement. Thus, the JSMA began its successful transformation into a teaching museum focused on object-based learning and, in 2017–18, welcomed more than 9,000 UO students specifically for course-related purposes. Today, the museum is a model academic art museum and a vibrant community cultural center, with a collection of more than 14,000 objects spanning the history of art from ancient times to the present, from cultures throughout the world. Thanks in part to both federal grants and internal-grants programs, its academic partnerships across campus are extensive, involving nearly all schools and colleges of the university. One of the first academic art museums to be accredited by the American Alliance of Museums, it successfully achieved its fourth accreditation in 2011.

From its beginning, the museum shared collections with the UO Libraries. Its founding Murray Warner Collection of Oriental Art included extensive archives and lantern slides that found a caring home in the libraries' SCUA division. As the museum's collections grew, gifts of art came to the museum, while the libraries accessioned documentation, manuscripts, artists' books, diaries, and other material objects and artifacts. Through their strong partnerships with the UO Division of Equity and Inclusion, student groups, and other cultural organizations throughout the state, the JSMA and the libraries affirm diversity and inclusion in their operations and collections.

The environmental context of a museum-library partnership is important to examine so that GLAM leaders and practitioners can understand the driving forces affecting them and their institutions and can evaluate the political capital and strategic options they have available. For this reason, both the circumstances summarized in this section and the environmental scan we conducted as part of our strategic planning were crucial. We used a STEEPA scan/analysis[6] in our planning, both to educate our constituents and to gain an understanding of internal and external forces affecting our organizations. To facilitate the scan, we shared pertinent information from the disciplines of library and information science (LIS) and museum administration and read white papers and reports about liberal arts, humanities, technology, and more. As Peter Senge wrote, "An accurate picture of current reality is just as important as a compelling picture of a desired future."[7] GLAM organizations can also learn about models of organizational development and life cycles and criteria for mutually beneficial partnerships from other disciplines, such as business administration, public administration, and political science. A study of context can help GLAM leaders build a case for urgency in change initiatives, but it also helps educate everyone involved, including campus stakeholders and administrators. It informs all participants about the opportunities that exist for leveraging the current value of libraries and museums as major investments and the means by which to achieve positive change for the institution.

Collaborative Strategic Planning

Selected stages of planning and specific exercises undertaken at the University of Oregon will illustrate how the process of planning can be used by other GLAM

Chapter 1

organizations for education and advocacy, and how the products of planning can be used for communicating the value of libraries, archives, and museums to users and stakeholders.

Aligning Missions and Visions

A key concept in our planning was the explicit alignment of our units' missions and visions with the university's vision and its stated priorities. This alignment made a powerful case for the criticality of our units' missions and multidisciplinary connections to the university's overall success, enabling us to advocate successfully for more institutional and grant funding. The process of identifying our alignments in the libraries began with an appreciative inquiry exercise, a process that encourages participants to focus on the strengths and highlights of their institution and its collections. Members of the formal strategic planning council included selected UO administrators, faculty and student representatives, one donor from the libraries' Advancement Council, and members of GLAM organizations. We asked participating staff and faculty members to come to the planning table with examples of services, collections, or programs that they perceived were most aspirational for the library and museum. The museum met with its curatorial, collections, and education staff as well as faculty whose research and teaching are centered on collections that connect to those in the libraries and developed a potential list of partnership possibilities. Both the process and the product of these exercises became valuable communication and advocacy tools for the alliance that we could use across many units within the university.

Strategic planning depends upon the context of the institution's vision, on the community's desires and needs, and on the collective will and passion of the people who work there. Whether we are managing a project, working with a team to develop a proposal, or leading a large organization, we have found the most important endeavor is to develop a shared vision and shared objectives and that this in turn inspires better performance from all.

Our library and museum visions and missions are the most powerful way to express value because we must connect them purposefully to the overarching institutional mission. We use both our missions and our vision statements in every proposal we make to upper administration because they communicate a clear and compelling future to our stakeholders and, by doing so, we can share our passion and convictions. As Warren Bennis and Joan Goldsmith wrote:

> A vision is a portrait of the future to which you can commit. It is the articulation of your values. It empowers you and inspires you to do your job and contribute ideas or actions beyond yourself.... A vision

engages your heat and your spirit, taps into embedded concerns and needs, asserts what you and your colleagues want to create, is something worth going for, provides meaning to the work you and your colleagues do. By definition, a vision is a little cloudy and grand. It is living document that can always be expanded, provides a starting place from which to get to more and more levels of specificity.[8]

The JSMA's vision statement is, "We will become one of the finest university art museums in the world," while the libraries' vision is to be "a catalyst for learning, discovery, and knowledge creation, in service to the transformative power of individuals and communities." To craft our GLAM-specific vision, we convened a group of people from across the university—not only library and museum staff but also departmental faculty through our institution's senate, student representatives, and a representative from the UO development division. We talked about GLAM-related connections to the institution's mission, vision, and values and learned about stakeholders' perspectives. We asked, "What is unique about the libraries and JSMA? What are our values and how do they shape our priorities for the future? What do our users really need from us that we could provide in a seamless way? What would make us personally commit our minds and hearts to the UO GLAM Alliance over the next five years? What do you want the alliance to accomplish so that you will be committed, aligned, and proud of your association with it?"

To develop our GLAM-specific vision, we conducted an appreciative inquiry exercise, a process that focuses on the strengths of an organization. We then asked participants to come to the table with examples of organizations, services, or programs they felt were most effective and successful in their own experiences—and that this could come from any field or industry. We analyzed everyone's answers to derive themes and patterns, then used this information to draft a few competing versions of our vision and run them through faculty, administrative, and student focus groups. By doing this, we used our visioning process as a communication and advocacy tool across many groups on campus. In the end, our GLAM vision was simple but served its purpose well: "Through the UO GLAM Alliance, we will leverage our resources more effectively through shared efforts, and improve visibility and advocacy for libraries and museums as valuable assets relevant for teaching, learning, and research."

Aligning Goals and Initiatives

Academic libraries and art museums increasingly find themselves to be natural partners in furthering the goals of higher education and the missions of their universities. Higher education is faced with immense challenges: How do we prepare students for a constantly changing world, requiring new skills, creativity, and flexibility for jobs we cannot even imagine today? How can we curtail the high cost of education without affecting our goals of excellence and the breadth of our academic offerings? How do we sustain our value and resources?

Alignment becomes both a strategy and a necessity for academic museums and libraries in an era of budget reductions and shifting university priorities. This is especially timely at the University of Oregon, where we are now focused on strengthening the sciences and applied research. Alignment offers us opportunities for shared resources, experimentation, and the generation of new knowledge and greater visibility.

In reviewing mission alignments, we recognized our shared focus on student learning, scholarly research, and the dissemination of knowledge beyond the academy. We also noted a significant difference, one familiar to many academic museums across the country: academic museums also serve as our communities' art museums, extending our educational mission to K-12 populations and residents of all ages, including increasingly diverse cultures, tourists, and, more recently, social service and medical agencies, where art is used in treatment and training. Still, our educational and public service commitments were aligned at their core. We then turned to our strategic plans, which again showed an unusual degree of compatibility.

We were gratified to discover how closely we were aligned. We immediately found strong correlations among the mission documents of the university, library, and museum, as presented here:

> Institutional level: The University of Oregon is a comprehensive public research university committed to exceptional teaching, discovery, and service. We work at a human scale to generate big ideas. As a community of scholars, we help individuals question critically, think logically, reason effectively, communicate clearly, act creatively, and live ethically.

> Libraries: As an essential partner in the University's education, research, and teaching mission, the Libraries enriches the student learning experiences, encourages exploration of research, and contributes to advancements in access to scholarly resources.

> JSMA: The Jordan Schnitzer Museum of Art enhances the UO's academic mission and furthers the appreciation and enjoyment of the visual arts for the general public.

We then checked these against the mission of GLAM organizations. According to the Council for Library and Information Resources' president Charles Henry, "libraries, museums, and archives have profound and important missions in society: to increase and disseminate knowledge, to encourage civic dialog and engagement, and to support individuals in their right to access and participate in culture."[9] GLAMs are the conduits that enable the humanities to have an impact on millions of scholars, teachers, and the broader public every day.

Until recently—and as part of our summit presentation in 2016—the JSMA's institutional plan stood on four pillars:

- Bridging Cultures affirms the value of the museum's collecting and exhibitions programs and directs its activities.
- Engaging Communities assures the museum's relevance to diverse communities on- and off-campus.
- Learning Together addresses our unique role as a teaching museum, an innovative center of experiential learning, where onsite, offsite, and through virtual offerings, we transform university students into thoughtful global citizens, K-12 students into visually literate, self-directed learners, and residents of all ages and backgrounds into appreciators of cultural expression and diversity.
- Sustaining Tomorrow identifies and aims to secure the resources and growth required for a strong, practical, and visionary future and identifies our capital campaign goals.

Starting in the 2018–19 academic year, the museum's plan adopted the University's Excellence goals, interpreting them for our broad audiences. The museum's goals are to promote and enhance student access, retention, and success; enhance the impact of research, scholarship, creative inquiry, and graduate education; attract and retain high quality, diverse students, faculty, and staff; and enhance physical, administrative, and IT infrastructure to ensure academic excellence.

The libraries' strategic plan advances the major goal areas of providing significant and unique content and collections to enhance research and scholarship; improving student success through exemplary teaching, engagement, and faculty development; engaging with diverse partners to fuel discovery and create new knowledge; creating and supporting interactive learning environments to advance learning, inspire creativity, and build community; and strengthening the libraries' ability to sustain and support essential programs and resources for the university. Evident among all of these is the importance placed on student learning, faculty teaching, research, diversity, creativity, and innovation.

Examples of Program Alignments

Collaboration exhibitions and exhibition support. Object-based learning is central to both museum and library practices. The JSMA frequently borrows works from Special Collections for exhibition purposes. Both units present exhibitions, drawn from their collections and on loan that address larger university initiatives. In 2016, when the JSMA was selected as the Oregon site for the Pierpont Morgan Library's traveling exhibition First Folio! The Book that Gave us Shakespeare, the libraries lent its Andrew Marvell folio and mounted its own companion exhibition; in 2016 and 2017, both presented exhibitions that enhanced the "Common Reading," a book given to first-year students to stimulate dialog throughout the year. In 2016, students read Ta-Nehisi Coates's *Between the World and Me*; the following year Louise Erdrich's *The Round House* was chosen. Library staff regularly create bibliographies for the museum's major exhibitions to encourage visitors to learn more about topics, artists, and artworks that interest them.

While the museum has more than 25,000 square feet of exhibition space, the Knight Library presents collections objects in limited exhibit cases. Consequently, in 2011, when the libraries were close to finalizing the acquisition of author Ken Kesey's archives, the museum exhibited *Kesey's Jail Journal* and organized a panel featuring the Merry Pranksters. Museum curators and library specialists now regularly collaborate on exhibitions and research. For example, the JSMA presented a selection of *Kesey's Jail Journals* in support of the libraries' fund-raising campaign to acquire the Kesey archives, and the libraries loaned rare religious books to enhance the museum's special exhibition of Sandow Birk's *American Qur'an*.

Experiential technologies and online resources. Among the resources of the libraries are 3D printers, which are used extensively in the sciences. In its outreach to challenged populations, the museum and the Science Library work together to digitize and print reduced-sale models of sculptural works in the museum's collection that can then be touched by visitors with visual disabilities. Artists' creation of works that only exist in this format is also being explored. In the process of learning more about how academic museums and libraries serve their constituencies, we developed a deeper understanding of how both units have transformed our delivery of services. While museums have digitized their collections and placed them online (the JSMA has approximately 75 percent of its nearly 14,000-plus objects online), they are primarily focused on using actual objects for exhibition, teaching, and research purposes on site. Libraries, in contrast, have become digital humanities centers, with highly sophisticated search engines and complex metadata platforms, mostly accessible from any internet connection. Consequently, while museums have strengthened their interactions with people—students, faculty, museum professionals, visitors, etc.—libraries increasingly serve digital communities across the world. A key exception to this general observation is the "special collections" library, where objects maintain their inherent value, and JSMA outreach programs that use prints of original works of art and online curricula.

Expertise in one area results in the acquisition of work in the other. Already a repository of screenplays and other documents by alumnus James Ivory, the libraries acquired fellow alumnus James Blue's archives and films at the urging of both Ivory and the JSMA's new media curator, long a champion of Blue's experimental documentaries. Scholars researching such materials draw on the resources of both entities. Such is the case for museums and libraries at universities across the country.

Identification of Shared Values

Identifying values was most helpful because an organization's core values are what drives that entity's culture, and as we know, aspects of culture can either be positive or negative forces for change. For this exercise, we worked only with internal staff and faculty, asking them to gather in subgroups and list what were the most important, meaningful events, accomplishments, and lessons learned over the last several years and to think about why these things mattered to them. Their answers gave us insights into the culture. We then took everyone's lists away, clustered them into themes, and worked together to discover shared values from these themes. We plan to use those value statements often, inserting them into funding proposals and advocacy and marketing efforts, and turning to them as reminders when making decisions or handling difficult conflicts or situations.

Leveraging GLAM Assets in Research, Teaching, and Learning

The creation of the UO GLAM Alliance and our joint strategic goals has resulted in several successful initiatives over the past three years, all of which had to be compelling enough to inspire institutional and foundation funding, library and museum stakeholders' support, and donors' investments. One of those outcomes is "Leveraging GLAM Assets in Research, Teaching, and Learning: Faculty Fellowships to Advance Library-Museum Collaboration," supported in part by The Andrew W. Mellon Foundation with matching funds from the University of Oregon. This initiative's goal is to increase collaboration between UO Libraries and the JSMA through a program of small grants for faculty research projects that draw on the collections or expertise of both institutions. Grant funds support the JSMA's and the libraries' first joint positions: a Mellon Postdoctoral Scholar in Library-Museum Collaboration (MPS) and two graduate student employees. The MPS manages day-to-day operations of the initiative and serves as project manager for the faculty research projects, while the graduate employees provide research assistance to both the MPS and the faculty fellows. Staff of the JSMA and UO Libraries offer in-kind support for collections research and project development.

The three-year initiative comprises two year-long cycles of research grants for faculty of all disciplines and classifications (tenured, tenure-track, and non-tenure-track); grant recipients hold the title of "Mellon Faculty Fellows" for the duration of the initiative. Mellon Faculty Fellows were chosen on the strengths of their proposed projects and the potential of those projects to increase library-museum collaboration. Each of these projects deals with collections or expertise identified during strategic planning exercises as areas of alignment between UO Libraries and the JSMA, and each requires extensive support from staff at both institutions. The team assembled for each project includes a JSMA curator and a librarian to consult with the Faculty Fellow on the project's vision, content, and strategy, as well as a web developer, a metadata librarian, digital production librarians, platform experts, the JSMA Collections Manager, the MPS, and the initiative's two graduate employees. As the project manager for each Faculty Fellow, the MPS handles team communications, sets project timelines and milestones, and supervises the graduate employees.[10]

The Mellon initiative creates value for UO Libraries and the JSMA in several concrete ways. First, the experience of collaborating on the faculty projects exposes everyone involved to new ways of thinking and working. Librarians and museum curators are learning firsthand how differently their institutions approach such fundamental concerns as metadata schemas and what constitutes an "object." The Faculty Fellows, MPS, and graduate employees are learning how to translate traditional research projects into digital exhibitions, while the Digital Scholarship Services staff are adopting new technologies for displaying the Faculty Fellows' content. While the learning curve can be steep at times, the interdisciplinary project teams are finding ways to benefit from each member's expertise, and we hope that these projects serve as templates for future collections-directed collaborations.

The Mellon initiative also aligns with the university's mission on multiple levels and with UO President Michael Schill's goals of increasing research activity as well as improving student achievement and experiences. Support from the Mellon Foundation reinforces the vital role of museums and libraries in "a public research university encompassing the humanities and arts" charged to "help individuals question critically, think logically, reason effectively, communicate clearly, act creatively, and live ethically" (excerpt from UO's mission statement).

Conclusion and Next Steps

The Mellon grant has been instrumental in activating a Glam Alliance that offers the possibility of systemic change and innovative partnerships. Because the Mellon grant itself was treated as its own research project, we will learn more about the challenges and opportunities for museum-library collaboration and, perhaps, provide guidelines for success that might guide other institutions. This topic, in fact, is so central to the Mellon museum-library initiative that the Association of Academic Museums and Galleries (the only national organization solely dedicated to academic museums and galleries in the US) held a panel on the issue, chaired by Dr. Kreiger with other Mellon scholars participating annual conference in June 2019 at the University of Minneapolis.

The UO GLAM Alliance has already changed fundamental ways that our art museum and libraries work together. Staff and faculty from both organizations know more about the other's operations, priorities, and collections, and there is a growing sense of excitement about the possibilities for future research on shared collections and goals. We see this alliance and our many alignments as a successful outcome of the process of planning and of using planning products to communicate the value of our joint and separate organizations, expertise, and collections. We believe this approach has the potential to serve as a model for similar work at other organizations, especially those where there may not be a structural relationship already in existence between the museum and the library.

Endnotes

1. For descriptive overviews of developments in the GLAM movement, see Deanna Marcum, "Archives, Libraries, Museums: Coming Back Together?," *Information & Culture* 49, no. 1 (2014): 74–89; Alexandra Yarrow, Barbara Clubb, and Jennifer-Lynn Draper, *Public Libraries, Archives and Museums: Trends in Collaboration and Cooperation* (The Hague: International Federation of Library Associations and Institutions, 2008), 4–28.

2. Günter Waibel and Ricky Erway, "Think Globally, Act Locally: Library, Archive, and Museum Collaboration," *Museum Management and Curatorship* 24, no. 4 (2009): 323–35.

3. "Spanning Our Field Boundaries: Mindfully Managing Lam Collaborations," The Educopia Institute (Atlanta, GA: Educopia, 2015), 5; Sanjica Faletar Tanackovic and Boris Badurina, "Collaboration of Croatian Cultural Heritage Institutions: Experiences from Museums," *Museum Management and Curatorship* 24, no. 4 (2009): 301; Günter Waibel, *Collaboration Contexts: Framing Local, Group and Global Solutions* (Dublin, OH: OCLC Research, 2010), 6.

4. Diane Zorich, Gunter Waibel, and Ricky Erway, *Beyond the Silos of the LAMs: Collaboration Among Libraries, Archives and Museums* (Dublin OH: OCLC Research, 2008), 21–23, https://www.oclc.org/content/dam/research/publications/library/2008/2008-05.pdf; see also Sandra L. Williams, "Strategic Planning and Organizational Values: Links to Alignment," *Human Resource Development International* 5, no. 2 (2002): 217–33, for discussion of how businesses can identify and align institutional values as part of their strategic planning. Williams presents strategic alignment of values as beneficial to businesses both internally (from an human resources perspective) and externally (helps businesses differentiate themselves from competitors).

5. In *Beyond the Silos of the LAMs*, Zorich, Waibel, and Erway et al. lay out a vision of collaboration that is "transformational," not just the sum of each institution's contributions, and argue that this is the sort of collaboration that campus museums and libraries should strive to achieve. The "collaborative continuum" is described as moving from contact, cooperation, and coordination at one end of the spectrum, to true collaboration and convergence on the other end.

6. STEEPA expands the traditional SWOT environmental scan model. Instead of looking only at strengths, weaknesses, opportunities, and threats (SWOT) in a setting, planners consider social, technological, environmental, economic, political, and aesthetic (STEEPA) forces, factors, and characteristics of their environment.

7. Peter M. Senge, "The Leader's New Work: Building Learning Organizations," *Sloan Management Review* 32, no. 1 (Fall 1990): 7–23.

8. Warren Bennis and Joan Goldsmith, *Learning to Lead: A Workbook on Becoming a Leader*, 4th ed. (New York: Basic Books, 2010), see chapter 5, "Creating a Power Vision: Competency Three."

9. This quotation from CLIR president Charles Henry appeared in a news release, "CLIR Receives NEH Grant for Openlab Workshop," CLIR, August 31, 2015, https://www.clir.org/2015/08/clir-receives-neh-grant-for-openlab-workshop/.
10. More details about the University of Oregon Mellon Faculty Fellows projects can be accessed at https://library.uoregon.edu/about/mellon-faculty-fellows and https://library.uoregon.edu/about/mellon-grant-call-for-proposals.

Bibliography

Bak, Greg, and Pam Armstrong. "Points of Convergence: Seamless Long-Term Access to Digital Publications and Archival Records at Library and Archives Canada." *Archival Science* 8, no. 4 (2008): 279–93. http://link.springer.com/10.1007/s10502-009-9091-4.

Bennis, Warren, and Joan Goldsmith. *Learning to Lead: A Workbook on Becoming a Leader.* 4th ed. New York: Basic Books, 2010.

Educopia Institute, The. "Spanning Our Field Boundaries: Mindfully Managing Lam Collaborations." Atlanta, GA: Educopia, 2015.

Marcum, Deanna. "Archives, Libraries, Museums: Coming Back Together?" *Information & Culture* 49, no. 1 (2014): 74–89. https://www.jstor.org/stable/43737382.

Rosenblum, Brian. "A Report on Library-Museum Collaboration at the University of Kansas: The Spencer Museum of Art and KU Libraries." 2011.

Rosenblum, Brian, and Arienne Dwyer. "Copiloting a Digital Humanities Center: A Critical Reflection on a Libraries-Academic Partnership." In *Laying the Foundation: Digital Humanities in Academic Libraries,* edited by John W. White and Heather Gilbert, 111–26. West Lafayette, IN: Purdue University Press, 2016.

Senge, Peter M. "The Leader's New Work: Building Learning Organizations." *Sloan Management Review* 32, no. 1 (Fall 1990): 7–23.

Tanackovic, Sanjica Faletar, and Boris Badurina. "Collaboration of Croatian Cultural Heritage Institutions: Experiences from Museums." *Museum Management and Curatorship* 24, no. 4 (2009): 299–321. http://www.tandfonline.com/doi/abs/10.1080/09647770903314696.

Waibel, Günter. *Collaboration Contexts: Framing Local, Group and Global Solutions.* Dublin, OH: OCLC Research, 2010.

Waibel, Günter, and Ricky Erway. "Think Globally, Act Locally: Library, Archive, and Museum Collaboration." *Museum Management and Curatorship* 24, no. 4 (2009): 323–35. http://www.tandfonline.com/doi/abs/10.1080/09647770903314704.

Williams, Sandra L. "Strategic Planning and Organizational Values: Links to Alignment." *Human Resource Development International* 5, no. 2 (2002): 217–33. https://www.tandfonline.com/doi/abs/10.1080/13678860110057638.

Yarrow, Alexandra, Barbara Clubb, and Jennifer-Lynn Draper. *Public Libraries, Archives and Museums: Trends in Collaboration and Cooperation.* The Hague: International Federation of Library Associations and Institutions, 2008.

Zorich, Diane M., Günter Waibel, and Ricky Erway. *Beyond the Silos of the LAMs: Collaboration among Libraries, Archives, and Museums.* Dublin, OH: OCLC Research, 2008. https://www.oclc.org/content/dam/research/publications/library/2008/2008-05.pdf.

CHAPTER 2

The University of Iowa Executive Leadership Academy:

A Case Study in Leveraging Broad University Resources to Support GLAM Collaborations

Jane Garrity, Elizabeth Constantine, Megan Hammes, Cory Lockwood, and Lynn Teesch

> The University of Iowa (UI) has a long history of excellence and collaboration across the arts and humanities, but recent years have brought both challenges and opportunities for expanding upon that history. Most notably, a 2008 flood closed the university's art museum for over a decade, but construction of the new Stanley Museum of Art next to the Main Library promises to enable greater interactions between those organizations.

The leaders of the University of Iowa Libraries and Stanley Museum of Art commissioned a project in 2017 through the UI Executive Leadership Academy—Higher Ed (ELA) to investigate collaboration opportunities between their units through a GLAM lens. The ELA is an award-winning experiential leadership program for mid- to senior-level UI staff with strategic and operational responsibilities across a wide range of university functions. Strategic projects commissioned by senior leadership are intended to have high impact on the university community as well as to allow participants to stretch their current skills and develop new ones.

Members of the GLAM project team had no prior experience or familiarity with the GLAM framework but brought with them wide-ranging experience and expertise in other areas, resulting in a low-cost consultative opportunity for the project sponsors. Over the nine months of the ELA, team members reviewed the GLAM literature, found examples of best practices, and conducted interviews and ideation sessions with library and museum staff and stakeholders. They produced a robust set of recommendations for UI GLAM units to collaborate in meaningful ways:

1. Establish a formal GLAM committee that is empowered to shape an environment on campus where GLAM can flourish and be sustained.
2. Increase opportunities for collaborations across staff positions.
3. Reward and recognize staff and faculty who actively and productively collaborate in GLAM research, teaching, and service activities.
4. Identify and pursue grants and other funding opportunities that support collaborative activities across GLAM.
5. Invest in digitization and joint technologies related to accessibility and discovery.

Since the conclusion of the ELA project, Stanley Museum and UI Libraries leadership have taken steps to act on all of the above recommendations.

Overview

The University of Iowa is a public research university with 32,535 students from 114 countries and all fifty states. Founded in 1847, it is the state's oldest institution of higher education and is located alongside the picturesque Iowa River in Iowa City.

A member of the Association of American Universities since 1909 and the Big Ten Conference since 1899, the UI is home to one of the largest and most acclaimed medical centers in the country as well as the famous Iowa Writers' Workshop.

The University of Iowa has long been a nexus for arts and humanities scholarship, teaching, and outreach. The University's GLAM (galleries, libraries, archives, and museums) community encompasses the UI Libraries and Stanley Museum of Art as well as the Pentacrest Museums, UI Department of Art and Art History, Iowa Writers' Workshop, Center for the Book, Hancher Auditorium, and various institutional and departmental collections. The UI Libraries and Stanley Museum of Art hold world-class collections of African art and Dada, Fluxus, and Intermedia materials alongside Jackson Pollack's famous *Mural.* Iowa City has been termed "the Athens of the Midwest" and "Pulitzertown" and is a UNESCO City of Literature.

Collaboration across campus and beyond has been a cornerstone of UI GLAM scholarship since at least the 1920s when the "Iowa Idea" brought practicing artists and scholars together in a liberal arts environment where they could draw on each other's perspectives and led to the establishment of the nation's first master of fine arts (MFA) degree.[1] In 1968, UI professor Hans Breder founded Intermedia, the first interdisciplinary art program in the country. In 1969, the UI Museum of Art was constructed to hold UI's increasingly impressive art holdings.[2] A dispersal program also places 6,000 pieces of artwork in campus and university hospital buildings for the greater UI community to enjoy.[3]

This culture of excellence was put to the test in 2008 when a 500-year flood devastated much of the campus,[4] including the UI Museum of Art. For over ten years, UI's art collection has been stored sixty miles away at the Figge Museum in Davenport, IA. Budget cuts have delayed both construction of the new Stanley Museum building and much-needed renovations to the Main Library. However, these challenges also present opportunities to increase collaboration. Relocation of UI's artwork has prompted collection-sharing projects with schools and senior citizens statewide. Pollock's *Mural* has been restored and viewed by nearly two million people on a European and American tour.[5]

Most relevant for our project, the new Stanley Museum of Art will be located next to UI's Main Library. This prompted the Hon. James Leach, Stanley Museum of Art Interim Chair and former US Representative, and John Culshaw, Jack B. King University Librarian, to seek new "ways to increase collaboration and exposure of best-in-class collections using the GLAM lens, to heighten global awareness of Iowa City and the University of Iowa as a world-renowned mecca for the arts" by commissioning a strategic project from the UI Executive Leadership Academy-Higher Education (ELA).[6]

The ELA is an intensive nine-month experiential leadership program for mid- to senior-level UI staff and faculty with strategic and operational leadership responsibilities. It involves classroom training, executive coaching, and project and service-learning fieldwork to develop and enhance participant core competencies essential for effective, agile, and innovative leadership and build UI's leadership pipeline and organizational culture. The ELA complements other programs within the supervisory, management, and leadership development progression that makes up UI's Building University of Iowa Leadership for Diversity (BUILD) initiative, including similar programs that target health care leaders and new department chairs and associate deans. Compared to other higher education leadership development programs, such as the Big Ten Academic Alliance Academic Leadership Program or TIAA's Emerging Leaders Network, the ELA deepens networks and know-how within UI rather than focusing on networking and perspective-building across institutions. It also does not split faculty and staff. The UI's ELA program has received LEAD Awards from HR.com for three years running. Roughly 25 percent of ELA participants are promoted within two years of program completion.

Each year, the ELA invites UI senior leadership to commission visible, high-impact strategic projects that form the core of the ELA experience. Prior to selection, projects are extensively vetted to ensure that they are aligned with UI strategic pillars and have a significant impact on multiple departments/ colleges and constituencies. Team members are assigned to projects that will take them outside their comfort zones. The authors of this paper did not previously know each other and were initially unfamiliar with the GLAM framework. Instead, we were selected for our diverse goals, talents, skills, responsibilities, and experiences spanning the sciences, humanities, and management. Our areas of professional expertise include research development, technology transfer, facilities management, and wellness and human resources. Thus, ELA allowed the project sponsors to reach out beyond their organizations' walls to leverage the outside perspectives of emerging leaders across UI.

Process
Literature Review

As non-experts in GLAM, we began with a general literature review of what the term means and how it is interpreted in the community. Various roundtables and white papers provided us with a roadmap for our own review of the current state of GLAM collaborations at UI. For example, the "Collaboration Continuum"[7] defined a spectrum of collaborative activities, including initial contact, ad hoc cooperation, organized coordination, collaboration on shared creation, and convergence involving a matured infrastructure. Prior initiatives identified catalysts to drive GLAM collaboration, including a shared vision that articulates the value of GLAM institutions, a formal mandate for change and formalized collaborative administrative structures, professional incentives and flexibility to encourage staff to cross disciplinary boundaries and complete cross-sector and digital training, budgetary resources to support interdisciplinary work, and a common digital infrastructure.[8]

These lessons were reinforced by our review of specific GLAM practices and collaborations at peer institutions that are home to both large art museums and academic libraries and were either recommended by our sponsors as comparables or identified in our initial research. We learned that other universities specifically include alliances between GLAM units in their overall strategic plans.[9] Such partnerships may involve joint exhibitions and collections, development of a GLAM council, sharing of technical platforms and metadata, pursuit of joint grant opportunities, and co-location of GLAM units. University libraries and museums also collaborate with faculty on research, instruction, and outreach, expanding the ability of those faculty to reach broad audiences that might not ordinarily interact with the arts.[10]

Given UI's challenge of operating without an art museum building for over a decade, we also investigated other university's responses to changes in physical space due to renovations, budget cuts, and changes in strategic direction. We learned that digital exhibits, outreach activities, and community spaces can help engage users and connect GLAM units to the university.[11]

On-Campus Interviews with UI GLAM Faculty and Staff

We followed our review of the literature with twenty-one one-on-one, in-person interviews with Stanley Museum and Libraries staff, faculty, and stakeholders. Our goals were to better understand current activities and attitudes and to gather ideas for improvement. We asked staff to describe how they collaborate across the two institutions, to provide examples of successful collaborations, and to describe barriers to collaborations. We also asked the participants to share their top three GLAM challenges and to identify collaborative activities they would choose to implement if resources were not an issue. These interviews helped the team understand how staff work in each of the GLAM institutions and underscored the high degree of collaboration that already exists. We found that these current collaborations are typically ad hoc and come about through informal interactions, often initiated by faculty, corresponding to the cooperation phase of the "Collaboration Continuum" cited above. While interviewees recognize the benefits of such organic, naturally arising interactions, they also see a need for a more formal and visible collaboration pipeline to identify and address common goals and priorities.

Success Stories

Interviewees identified a number of existing successful collaborative projects—most between the Stanley Museum and Libraries, but others involving other units on campus. These included joint exhibits spanning the collections of both organizations and often brought in other GLAM units. For example, the exhibit "Dada Futures: Circulating Replicants, Surrogates, and Participants" is a collaboration between the Libraries, Stanley Museum, and the UI Department of English that draws on the UI Libraries' International Dada Archive,[12] a world-class collection containing about 75,000 objects.[13] The related DADA Symposium involves the pooling of time, staff, space, and resources to address a niche area with high interest from its constituents. The Shakespeare at Iowa programming involved over seventy events in one month, including a visit by one of the Folger Shakespeare Library's First Folios as part of the First Folio! The Book that Gave Us Shakespeare national traveling exhibit and work by staff in various units. A Spring 2018 Archives Crawl was a collaboration between the UI Libraries, Stanley Museum of Art, Museum of Natural History, State Historical Society, and Iowa City Public Libraries, and it brought over seventy people in a single day to view items in UI Libraries Special Collections.[14]

The Digital Scholarship & Publishing Studio,[15] housed in the UI Libraries, was mentioned by many staff as particularly generous and collegial. This group consults and collaborates with faculty and students to scan, digitize, archive, and circulate research materials in the digital humanities, enabling new lines of research and allowing researchers and students around the world to interact with UI collections, such as the Hans Breder collection, Digital Dada Library, and Fluxus Digital Collection. The UI Libraries Preservation and Conservation Department is likewise a major resource for preserving both books and artwork, and both organizations benefit from in-house paper conservation.

Challenges

Interviewees also shared frank assessments of the challenges they face in engaging in collaborative work. Several themes arose repeatedly.

Limited time for collaboration. While interviewees are enthusiastic about what collaboration can bring to the university, most find it difficult to prioritize such activities on top of their daily tasks. Planning joint projects, events, or exhibits can mean "work on top of work," and the effort needed is often disproportionate to the credit received for that effort. Notably, there is a perception among some staff that such work is not a priority for campus leaders. Due to time constraints, follow-through on both sides can be challenging. As a result, collaborations tend to be one-off and ad hoc rather than sustainable and long-term. The amount of time that individual interviewees devote to collaborative activities varies greatly, from almost none to nearly 100 percent. Some staff members, particularly in the Preservation and Conservation Department and the Digital Scholarship and Publishing Studio, are frequent connectors for collaborative and cross-disciplinary projects due to the nature of their roles.

Limited space and resources. Despite the new museum building on the horizon, space is a concern for many staff. This is exacerbated by budget cuts that have postponed renovations to the Main Library and reduced features of the nearby new art museum that would have created opportunities for organic interactions and joint events. There is a pressing need for secure, climate-controlled storage space as UI collections grow in the future. Preservation is a concern for digital media as well as physical materials. Several interviewees expressed that they would be able to do more if they had access to additional resources, such as grant funding or equipment. Current funding is largely earmarked for routine needs or urgent repairs rather than new initiatives or space.

Preconceptions. Several staff brought up false preconceptions as a factor that limits the engagement that community members have with GLAM institutions. For instance, many students and faculty still think of the library as merely a building where books are stored rather than a community of experts who can connect them to people and resources. The general public may see museums as elitist, while science and engineering students may not view the visual arts as relevant to their interests. Collaborations between GLAM institutions and the broader community may help overcome these misconceptions and draw visitors to UI's museums and libraries. There is a perception among some staff that cross-unit collaborations are not a top priority of campus leadership, given the limited funds and resources noted above.

Staff Suggestions and Ideas

Interviewees' ideas to improve GLAM collaborations at UI also shared many common themes, and some could be feasible even with resource limitations. The potential for collaboration is clearly robust on campus and highly valued by staff.

Pop-up exhibits. Quite a few staff proposed creating small pop-up exhibits across campus—in science buildings, performing arts venues, and sports venues—to reach a broader audience that might not otherwise visit the Stanley Museum or Main Library. Organizing such pop-up exhibits would also provide the opportunity for students to gain curation experience.

Create a destination for the visual arts. Although the new Stanley Museum and Main Library will not be physically connected by a corridor, there is interest in turning the nearby Gibson Square and the surrounding space into a true destination for the visual arts at UI. These spaces could host outdoor art, gathering spaces, exhibits, events, and food trucks to draw the public to both institutions.

Share staff and resources. There is a particular need for staff to coordinate the logistics of events and exhibits. Currently, this work is done by librarians, curators, and conservators as needed, but they do not have training in event planning, and it is not the best use of their skills and time. A shared coordinator position could free up GLAM specialists and avoid duplication of effort. The current number of interim and open positions among GLAM-related staff and leadership at UI creates a challenge in terms of bandwidth but also presents an opportunity to reimagine how these roles can support cross-disciplinary needs and goals.

Leverage students. Students from multidisciplinary programs on campus were cited as an opportunity area where more can be done. The UI Libraries' Department of Conservation and Preservation already relies on students for much of their work. For example, UI Libraries Special Collections hosted an exhibit where student workers each selected a work that they wished to highlight. The UI Libraries and Stanley Museum can also benefit from the strengths of students from more wide-ranging disciplines. For example, students from the Tippie College of Business Marketing Institute and the Event Planning Certificate program of the School of Journalism and Mass Communication would be able to assist with event planning and marketing while accomplishing valuable experiential learning opportunities.

Ideation Sessions

With these themes in mind, the GLAM team held two ideation sessions that were attended by twenty-five UI staff from the Stanley Museum, Libraries, and the Office of the Vice President for Research and Economic Development. These sessions were modeled on the World Café[16] and IDEO[17] brainstorming structures to encourage collaborative dialogue around four common themes raised in our interviews:

1. **Collaboration**—to enable GLAM staff on campus to prioritize collaboration more highly. How might we formalize GLAM collaboration at UI? What are the benefits and drawbacks to formal vs informal GLAM?
2. **Telling the story/engagement**—How might UI tell the story of GLAM and UI to the world and to UI organizations and leadership?
3. **Resources**—How might UI leverage existing resources across campus to support GLAM collaborations?
4. **Technology**—What are the areas of greatest need for technology and digitization to meet the needs of the future?

Participants self-organized into groups of three to five individuals and were given eight minutes to generate ideas around these prompts and write them on sticky notes. Each group then had five minutes to cluster related sticky notes to identify common themes. A facilitator from our project team sat at each table and presented their group's ideas to the whole room. Participants then moved to new tables and repeated the process twice more. At the end of the ideation session, participants voted for their top three ideas for each question by placing a sticker on the respective notes. The project team collected and recorded the day's ideas and organized them by theme and popularity.

The ideation sessions generated hundreds of ideas, more than a hundred of which received at least one vote. In the narrative below, we spotlight some of the most popular suggestions organized by the thematic areas.

Collaboration

Formalize the collections coalition. The most popular suggestion was to formalize the UI Collections Coalition or create a joint/formal team of Stanley Museum/ Libraries staff. This idea was proposed in some form in response to three of the four discussion prompts and received a total of twenty-four votes. In its current form, the UI Collections Coalition consists of staff from the UI Libraries, Stanley Museum, Pentacrest Museums, and a number of other units on campus that manage special collections. These individuals meet informally regularly, and these gatherings have led to significant collaborations and connections across UI GLAM units. The suggestion to make the Collections Coalition into a charter committee would give this group a formal charge and greater power to influence.

Formal recognition of collaborative activities. A suggestion to reward collaborative activities in faculty promotion and tenure and staff performance appraisals was particularly well-received, with nine votes. Participants believe that such formal recognition would incentivize collaboration. Moreover, job descriptions could be reworked to reflect reality and acknowledge and encourage collaborative work.

Joint strategic planning and goal-setting. Various joint strategic planning activities and resources were suggested as a means to enable this collaboration. Participants pointed out the need for GLAM units to jointly set priorities, clearly articulate shared goals, and share resources. This could be done through annual GLAM retreats at which staff could develop a clear map of existing resources and identify key players with common interests. Staff meet-and-greets with refreshments would provide a less formal avenue for relationship-building. Joint strategic planning could extend as far as restructuring.

Grant support. GLAM-specific funding was also proposed and voted on many times. In particular, participants suggested small-scale funding for Stanley Museum-UI Libraries collaboration or publication and pedagogy. The UI Obermann Center[18] was noted as a resource for funding for joint projects. Participants also noted teaching-specific funding, such as Mellon grants for teaching seminars and the Grant Wood Fellowship, as potential resources for GLAM collaboration. A common discussion theme was that many staff feel that opportunities for grants come and go because these activities are not highly valued by GLAM unit leaders and not enough support is provided to get the best possible applications out.

Telling the Story/Engagement

Shared exhibits and events. Shared exhibits were identified as both a means to tell the story of GLAM at UI and an existing resource that we can leverage. Joint collections and exhibitions across UI GLAM were proposed numerous times and received many votes. It was noted that the Stanley Museum and UI Libraries should collaborate in *all* exhibits, both digital and physical. Such co-sponsored events would build a shared audience. Some more specific suggestions were to partner with seminars and develop exhibit templates to aid with labeling and cataloging.

Collaborative teaching and degree program. The proposal to create a collaborative degree program, such as an undergraduate certificate or degree in conservation, received seven votes. A conservation internship was also well received. Staff noted that the existing curriculum at UI aligns with the most competitive conservation programs in the US. Other teaching-related suggestions were to collaborate with faculty and curriculum and reach out to science departments and other academic departments. Faculty/staff touring lectures and shared GLAM online coursework were also proposed.

Public outreach and engagement. Participants agreed strongly with the sentiment that GLAM at the UI should be free and open to the public because the UI is a state university. Coordination of K-12 resources with school trip visits and collaboration with Iowa City community events were recommended. The recent Archives Crawl was cited as a successful community event. Possible resources for GLAM outreach include county extension offices for culture and cultural artifacts as well as the UI Mobile Museum.

Communications, PR, and social media. Communications and external relations staffing at UI pales in comparison to peer institutions, and participants agree that we should hire communications staff to the level of other Big Ten schools. Other suggestions were to assign an Office of Strategic Communications staff to be proactive rather than waiting for stories and to partner Stanley Museum and UI Libraries staff for publicity. Potential topics for storytelling include giving positive publicity to existing collaborations, highlighting donors and other patrons of the arts, telling more behind-the-scenes stories, sharing the unique story of the "Iowa Idea,"[19] and sharing flood and flood recovery stories. A social media campaign was seen as a key channel to tell these stories and may involve a collaboration blog or staff blogs on the websites of GLAM units. More unique suggestions were to make a movie or game with a GLAM theme.

Resources

Create a GLAM destination. Also a major theme in interviews, ideation session participants eagerly welcomed the idea of integrating Gibson Square into a "GLAMpus" to draw people to the space around the Main Library and new Stanley Museum. The GLAMpus could include signage to direct visitors to exhibits, outdoor GLAM exhibits and events, and food trucks (analogous to a popular Science Thursday event at the UI Carver College of Medicine). Staff also suggested using the City of Literature organization to leverage outside support for GLAM at UI and in Iowa City.

Facilities and infrastructure. Participants suggested leveraging common infrastructure and creating a clear map of existing resources. HVAC and building technologies were noted as particular areas of concern for preservation. Shared off-site storage was another topic of interest. The UI Libraries and Stanley Museum may be able to leverage resources at the Old Capitol and Museum of Natural History. IT services and web design were seen as a notable area to target for integration.

Knowledge sharing. UI staff and their expertise are key resources to develop GLAM collaboration at UI. Cross-disciplinary projects and cross-attendance of professional society conferences (AAM, SAA, ALA) would allow GLAM staff to better understand each other's fields. Job-sharing (75 percent/25 percent split) between the units would also encourage more collaboration. Co-conservation and preservation are notable areas in which staff can serve as resources to each other to share collection care knowledge.

Technology

Accessibility and shared cataloging. A number of participants highlighted the need to share GLAM digital infrastructure at UI, including resource management and storage retrieval systems, such as the online catalog and Aeon reader request system. The most highly voted suggestion was to develop finding aids, describe digital items, and make data keyword searchable. Staff suggested data mapping to assist efficient systems and exploring linked data possibilities. They also proposed connecting collections through data—such as the Art Museum Collections in the Iowa Digital Library—via collection assessment tools to audit physical and digital objects.

Digitization. When digitizing collections, we need to "do it once and do it right." This includes scanning, coordinating rights assessment, and connecting IDL thumbnails to a physical location. Digitization facilities should be centrally located and centrally staffed.

Open access. Participants believe that we should make as much open access as possible (consistent with the value placed on public outreach and engagement). The proposal to create a shared public digital presence with high-quality images was very popular.

Use of technology to enhance exhibits. Participants suggested providing iPad-based evaluation in galleries. These iPads could also enable information-sharing with audiences, such as access to IDL and metadata while viewing the physical collection.

Main Recommendations

After synthesizing the various activities above, which were conducted over the course of approximately two months, the ELA team formed main recommendations for the project sponsors.

1. Establish a formal GLAM committee that is empowered to shape an environment on campus where GLAM can flourish and be sustained.

We recommend an official university charter committee comprised of faculty, staff, and students representing the Stanley Museum of Art, the Libraries, GLAM disciplines, and with representation from the Pentacrest Museums. As described by the university's operations manual, charter committees are established, modified, and disestablished by the collective action of the following three organizations, namely, The University of Iowa Student Government, the Staff Council, and the Faculty Senate, and by the president of The University of Iowa. Charter committees are established to assure that university-wide services and activities will be carried out in the best interests of education and society. The formal structure of a charter committee would empower this group to influence policy, programs, and operations related to GLAM at UI and would ensure that various stakeholder groups are heard.

The committee could either be based on or interface with and supplement existing committees on campus. Most notably, UI Collections Coalition is highly valued by UI staff. This group consists of staff who manage UI's many institutional and departmental collections, which cover historical, medical, and scientific interests in addition to the visual arts. Its mission is "to support the educational, research, and service goals of the University of Iowa by encouraging and advancing the professional care, documentation, and study of the artifacts, specimens, and documents in the various collections located in the University community, to make the collections meaningful and accessible to members of the University and the general public, and to encourage the professional growth and development of the administrators, curators, and keepers of the collections." However, the Collections Coalition currently has no official recognition or charge, which limits its ability to effect real change.

The proposed GLAM Committee should be charged with investigating and implementing many of the suggestions identified in our interviews and ideation sessions, such as:

- map out and clearly identify GLAM resources on campus;
- develop a framework for GLAM units to share physical and digital infrastructure and staff;
- identify priorities for collections on campus;
- develop plans to more fully utilize space near the Stanley Museum and Main Library as a "GLAMpus" that highlights visual arts at UI and provides gathering spaces for UI and local community members;
- identify and develop opportunities for new undergraduate and graduate degree and certificate programs, beginning with an evaluation of the feasibility of a degree or certificate program in conservation;
- envision and consider new organizational structures, reporting lines, and budgetary strategies for the future; and
- develop a GLAM strategic plan.

2. Increase opportunities for collaborations across staff positions.

More organic collaborations will arise if GLAM staff have additional opportunities and mechanisms to build relationships across units, engage in cross-training and professional development, and prioritize collaborative activities as a key aspect of their job expectations. Some specific mechanisms to do this include

- creation of joint position(s) for collections and/or events;
- combined professional development/training opportunities for libraries and museum staff;
- networking events targeting staff and faculty across the full scope of GLAM units and departments at UI;
- bi-annual meetings or retreats of GLAM staff; and
- small grants for collaborative exhibits or projects.

3. Reward and recognize staff and faculty who actively and productively collaborate in GLAM research, teaching, and service activities.

Formal recognition of collaborative activities will enable staff and faculty across all GLAM functions to more highly prioritize this work. Examples of this include

- inclusion of collaboration as a key area of responsibility in staff job descriptions;
- a formal system of merit or credit for staff who productively collaborate;
- recognition of staff contributions to collaborations in annual performance reviews;
- inclusion of collaboration in evaluation criteria for teaching, scholarship, and service in the faculty promotion and tenure process; and
- GLAM recognition program or awards.

4. Identify and pursue grants and other funding opportunities that support collaborative activities across GLAM.

Funding for the arts and humanities generally, and museums and libraries specifically, is challenging. In seeking external financial support, we recommend the UI Stanley Museum of Art and the UI Libraries look closely at public and private funders and develop new models, along with the more traditional practices and places like the National Endowment for the Arts (NEA) and National Endowment for the Humanities (NEH), for securing external funding for GLAM practices on campus.

Resources are already in place on campus to help with collaborative grant applications. These include the newly established Research Development Office in the UI Office of Vice President of Research and Economic Development, which offers one-stop concierge services for strategic collaboration and proposal development. These offices and others should be utilized to identify opportunities and collaborations on and off campus and to provide help in the submission of strong proposals that leverage UI's strengths in the arts and humanities. In our final report, our project team highlighted funding trends in the arts and identified several dozen foundations, federal, and internal grant opportunities relevant to GLAM collaborators.

5. Invest in digitization and joint technologies related to accessibility and discovery.

Digitization and improved discovery of GLAM collections enable collaborations and support UI's research, teaching, and outreach missions by making materials more available to students, researchers, and the general public. Tools linking UI's various catalogs and databases would make collaborations across GLAM disciplines and units easier by avoiding duplication of resources and allowing researchers to find materials through a single search. Specific recommendations include the following:

- Expand metadata creation, including finding aids, captions/transcripts, and item-level description for digitized items to enhance public digital presence and allow for open access.
- Utilize linked data, named entity recognition, and knowledge bases like Wikidata and crowdsourcing concepts to enrich data.
- Increase the scope of digitization for paper-based and audio/visual materials with investment in equipment, budgets, and staff.

Actions Resulting on UI's Campus

Our ELA project team presented the above findings in the form of a detailed white paper to our sponsors and the ELA cohort in May 2018 and to University Libraries and Stanley Museum staff in November 2018 at their first joint retreat.[20]

The first joint retreat was a recommendation that came from the interviews and ideation sessions as a part of our research and information gathering. Our recommendations served as a jumping-off point for a brainstorming session by the full staff of both organizations. Since that time, both units, led by original project sponsor John Culshaw and new UI Stanley Museum Director Lauren Lessing, have begun to implement our ELA team's recommendations to move their unit further along the "Collaboration Continuum," noted in the actions below:

> 1. **Establish a formal GLAM committee that is empowered to shape an environment on campus where GLAM can flourish and be sustained.** The UI Libraries, Stanley Museum, and Pentacrest Museums have jointly established a Blue Ribbon Panel on New Collaborations Across UI Galleries, Libraries, Archives, and Museums (UI GLAM). The

charge of this panel is to develop an effective and lightweight organizational framework for fostering closer collaborations among the three units, with potential to scale to others. This framework will have both institutional authority and the ability to effect change. Given institutional mechanisms for executive committees, it is unlikely that it will take the precise form our group envisioned.[21]

The Stanley Museum is also introducing the Stanley Campus Council, a student advisory board, to guide student engagement.

2. **Increase opportunities for collaborations across staff positions.** Museum curatorial staff and Special Collections librarians are collaborating to co-plan an exhibition. The Stanley Museum is hiring a curator of learning and engagement who will pursue active collaborations.[22] Further, the Blue Ribbon Panel described above is charged to identify three to five collaboration possibilities that could yield near-term results.

3. **Reward and recognize staff and faculty who actively and productively collaborate in GLAM research, teaching, and service activities.** Participation in GLAM projects is now reflected in performance evaluations for Stanley Museum staff. Collaboration is recognized as a core value of the Stanley Museum of Art.[23]

4. **Identify and pursue grants and other funding opportunities that support collaborative activities across GLAM.** The museum and library are applying for grant funding to support the creation of a shared staff position and digital resources supporting curricular use of their collections.

5. **Invest in digitization and joint technologies related to accessibility and discovery.** The Stanley Museum is working with the Iowa Digital Library to update and increase the number of museum collection objects that will be hosted on the new UI Libraries website. They are also ensuring that

> the University Archives, University Art Library, and State Historical Society of Iowa are all able to provide state and national library catalog access to the museum's publications. Tech can enhance attendees' understanding of the collection, improve accessibility for people with disabilities, and create an opportunity for play.[24]

In June 2019, UI broke ground for the new $50 million, 63,000-square-foot Stanley Museum of Art building next door to the Main Library.[25] The building is designed to be not just a gallery, but also a laboratory, an educational resource, and an incubator for interdisciplinary conversation and research.[26]

Conclusion

It is our hope that by reading how the University of Iowa utilized an internal, existing resource (UI Executive Leadership Academy) that other readers can seek for their own unique, local partnerships and develop relationships with key stakeholders in their own GLAM-related endeavors to move strategic initiatives forward.

Endnotes

1. "The 'Iowa Idea,'" University of Iowa, School of Art and Art History, last modified January 12, 2017, accessed December 5, 2019, https://art.uiowa.edu/about/iowa-idea.
2. Shelbi Thomas and Emily Nelson, "UI art museum to build on decades of brilliance," University of Iowa, accessed December 5, 2019, https://uiowa.edu/stories/ui-art-museum-50-years-brilliance.
3. Thomas and Nelson, "UI art museum to build."
4. John Schwartz, "How the University of Iowa Recovered from the 'Unfathomable' Flood That Ruined It," *New York Times* (May 10, 2019), accessed online on December 5, 2019, https://www.nytimes.com/2019/05/10/climate/iowa-floods-disasters-lessons-learned.html.
5. Schwartz, "How the University of Iowa Recovered."
6. UI Executive Leadership Academy-Higher Education (ELA), University of Iowa, https://hr.uiowa.edu/development/leadership-development/executive-leadership-academy-higher-ed.
7. Diane Zorich, Gunter Waibel, and Ricky Erway, *Beyond the Silos of the LAMs: Collaboration Among Libraries, Archives and Museums* (Dublin OH: OCLC Research, 2008), https://www.oclc.org/content/dam/research/publications/library/2008/2008-05.pdf.
8. Zorich, Waibel, and Erway, *Beyond the Silos*; Jill Deupi and Charles Eckman, "Prospects and Strategies for Deep Collaboration in the Galleries, Libraries, Archives, and Museums Sector," *Academic Art Museum and Library Summit* (January 2016); Wendy M. Duff, Jennifer Carter, Joan M. Cherry, Heather MacNeil, and Lynne C. Howarth, "From Coexistence to Convergence: Studying Partnerships and Collaboration among Libraries, Archives and Museums," *Information Research: An International Electronic Journal* 18 no. 3 (September 2013); Erica Pastore, *The Future of Museums and Libraries: A Discussion Guide* (Washington, DC: Institute of Museum and Library Services, 2009); Stephanie Allen, et al., *Collective Wisdom: An Exploration of Library, Archives and Museum Cultures* (Dublin, OH: OCLC Research, 2017); G. W. Clough, *Best of Both Worlds: Museums, Libraries, and Archives in a Digital Age* (Washington, DC: Smithsonian Institution, 2013).

The University of Iowa Executive Leadership Academy   31

9.   Deupi and Eckman, "Prospects and Strategies; J. Hartz and A. Lim, report submitted by University of Oregon: Jordan Schnitzer Museum and UO Libraries, prepared for the Academic Art Museum and Library Summit, Coral Gables, FL, November 2015; "Strategic Plan 2018–2022: The Block Museum as Frame of Mind," Northwestern University, 2018; "Strategic Plan for Gardens, Libraries and Museums 2015/16–2019/20," University of Oxford, UK, 2015.
10. J. Kelly, *Clinician's Eye*, UVA Arts, Fall 2014; V. Hartfield-Méndez and M. Tierney, The University Museum and Community Engagement, *Public* 1(1-2) (2014).
11. M. Maloney, "Museum of Toronto: Not Your Traditional Museum," *Now* (May 13, 2015); P. Gabbara, "MSU's Broad Art Museum opened 5 years ago to high hopes. It's met only some of them," *Lansing State Journal* (November 9, 2017); B. Brauer-Delaney and W. Stoepel, "New Date: Broad Art Museum Expansion Open To Public May 19-20," *MSU Today* (March 20, 2018); R. Faires, "Update: Fate of UT's Fine Arts Library Provost OKs recommendations to preserve, upgrade fifth floor," *Austin Chronicle* (April 11, 2018).
12. The International Dada Archive, The University of Iowa, http://dada.lib.uiowa.edu/.
13. Emily Nelson, "Stanley Museum of Are creating space for new era," last accessed December 5, 2019, https://www.google.com/url?q=https://now.uiowa.edu/2019/09/stanley-museum-art-creating-space-new-era
14. Special Collections and Archives, University of Iowa Libraries, https://www.lib.uiowa.edu/sc/.
15. Digital Scholarship & Publishing Studio, University of Iowa Libraries, https://www.lib.uiowa.edu/studio/.
16. The World Café Community Foundation, 2015, http://www.theworldcafe.com/.
17. IDEO, 2015, https://www.ideou.com/.
18. Obermann Center for Advanced Studies, University of Iowa, https://obermann.uiowa.edu/.
19. University of Iowa, School of Art and Art History, https://art.uiowa.edu/about/iowa-idea.
20. The full UI Executive Leadership Academy "GLAM" report, including four appendices which includes a full bibliography of GLAM-related research, questions used in the ideation sessions (which could be modified and implemented at other institutions), and a compendium of funding opportunities and links, can be accessed at https://ir.uiowa.edu/lib_ar/25/.
21. Blue Ribbon Panel on New Collaborations Across UI Galleries, Libraries, Archives, and Museums (UI GLAM), shared by Lauren Lessing, email communication, November 1, 2019.
22. Emily Nelson, "Stanley Museum of Are creating space for new era," last accessed December 5, 2019, https://now.uiowa.edu/2019/09/stanley-museum-art-creating-space-new-era.
23. "Statements of Core Values, Vision, and Mission," Stanley Museum, University of Iowa, accessed December 5, 2019, https://stanleymuseum.uiowa.edu/about/statements-of-core-values-vision-and-mission/.
24. "Statements of Core Values," Stanley Museum.
25. Emily Nelson, "UI to host ceremonial groundbreaking for Stanley Museum of Art," University of Iowa, https://now.uiowa.edu/2019/04/ui-host-ceremonial-groundbreaking-stanley-museum-art.
26. Thomas and Nelson, "UI art museum.

Bibliography

Allen, Stephanie, et al. *Collective Wisdom: An Exploration of Library, Archives and Museum Cultures*. Dublin, OH: OCLC Research, 2017.

Blue Ribbon Panel on New Collaborations Across UI Galleries, Libraries, Archives, and Museums (UI GLAM). Shared by Lauren Lessing, email communication, November 1, 2019.

Brauer-Delaney, B., and W. Stoepel. "New Date: Broad Art Museum Expansion Open To Public May 19-20," *MSU Today* (March 20, 2018).

Clough, G. W. *Best of Both Worlds: Museums, Libraries, and Archives in a Digital Age*. Washington, DC: Smithsonian Institution, 2013.

Deupi, Jill, and Charles Eckman. "Prospects and Strategies for Deep Collaboration in the Galleries, Libraries, Archives, and Museums Sector." *Academic Art Museum and Library Summit* (January 2016).

Chapter 2

Duff, Wendy M., Jennifer Carter, Joan M. Cherry, Heather MacNeil, and Lynne C. Howarth. "From Coexistence to Convergence: Studying Partnerships and Collaboration among Libraries, Archives and Museums." *Information Research: An International Electronic Journal* 18 no. 3 (September 2013).

Faires, R. "Update: Fate of UT's Fine Arts Library Provost OKs recommendations to preserve, upgrade fifth floor." *Austin Chronicle* (April 11, 2018).

Gabbara, P. "MSU's Broad Art Museum opened 5 years ago to high hopes. It's met only some of them," *Lansing State Journal* (November 9, 2017).

Hartfield-Méndez, Vialla, and Meghan Tierney. "The University Museum and Community Engagement." *Public* 1(1-2) (2014).

Hartz, J., and A. Lim. Report submitted by University of Oregon: Jordan Schnitzer Museum and UO Libraries, prepared for the Academic Art Museum and Library Summit, Coral Gables, FL, November 2015.

IDEO. 2015. https://www.ideou.com/.

International Dada Archive, The. The University of Iowa. http://dada.lib.uiowa.edu/.

Kelly, J. *Clinician's Eye*. UVA Arts, Fall 2014.

Maloney, M. "Museum of Toronto: Not Your Traditional Museum," *Now* (May 13, 2015).

Nelson, Emily. "Stanley Museum of Are creating space for new era." Last accessed December 5, 2019. https://now.uiowa.edu/2019/09/stanley-museum-art-creating-space-new-era.

———. "UI to host ceremonial groundbreaking for Stanley Museum of Art," University of Iowa, https://now.uiowa.edu/2019/04/ui-host-ceremonial-groundbreaking-stanley-museum-art.

Northwestern University. "Strategic Plan 2018–2022: The Block Museum as Frame of Mind." 2018.

Pastore, Erica. *The Future of Museums and Libraries: A Discussion Guide* (Washington, DC: Institute of Museum and Library Services, 2009).

Schwartz, John. "How the University of Iowa Recovered from the 'Unfathomable' Flood That Ruined It." *New York Times* (May 10, 2019). Accessed online on December 5, 2019. https://www.nytimes.com/2019/05/10/climate/iowa-floods-disasters-lessons-learned.html.

Thomas, Shelbi, and Emily Nelson. "UI art museum to build on decades of brilliance." University of Iowa. Accessed December 5, 2019. https://uiowa.edu/stories/ui-art-museum-50-years-brilliance.

University of Iowa. Obermann Center for Advanced Studies. https://obermann.uiowa.edu/.

———. School of Art and Art History. https://art.uiowa.edu/about/iowa-idea.

———. School of Art and Art History. "The 'Iowa Idea.'" Last modified January 12, 2017. Accessed December 5, 2019. https://art.uiowa.edu/about/iowa-idea.

———. Stanley Museum. "Statements of Core Values, Vision, and Mission." Accessed December 5, 2019. https://stanleymuseum.uiowa.edu/about/statements-of-core-values-vision-and-mission/.

———. UI Executive Leadership Academy-Higher Education (ELA). https://hr.uiowa.edu/development/leadership-development/executive-leadership-academy-higher-ed.

University of Iowa Libraries. Digital Scholarship & Publishing Studio. https://www.lib.uiowa.edu/studio/.

———. Special Collections and Archives. https://www.lib.uiowa.edu/sc/.

University of Oxford. "Strategic Plan for Gardens, Libraries and Museums 2015/16–2019/20." University of Oxford, UK, 2015.

World Café Community Foundation, The. 2015. http://www.theworldcafe.com/.

Zorich, Diane, Gunter Waibel, and Ricky Erway. *Beyond the Silos of the LAMs: Collaboration Among Libraries, Archives and Museums*. Dublin OH: OCLC Research, 2008. https://www.oclc.org/content/dam/research/publications/library/2008/2008-05.pdf.

CHAPTER 3

Visual Thinking Strategies and the *Framework* in the Undergraduate Classroom:
Research as Inquiry and Scholarship as Conversation through the Lens of a University's Art Collection

Kayla Birt Flegal and Alexandra Chamberlain

Introduction

The following case study details a collaboration between the DePauw University Libraries and the DePauw University Galleries and Collection at the Richard E. Peeler Art Center (Galleries at Peeler). Together, a representative from each of these

contributing partners (Kayla Birt Flegal, Access and Outreach Services Librarian, with Rank of Assistant Professor from the DePauw Libraries, and Alexandra Chamberlain, at the time of this research was, Assistant Director and Curator of Exhibitions and Education from the Galleries at Peeler) sought to assess student confidence in scholarly discourse through the use of the combined pedagogical theories of Visual Thinking Strategies (VTS) and The Association of College and Research Libraries (ACRL) *Framework for Information Literacy for Higher Education* (herein *Framework*) in the classroom learning environment for the course Academic Excellence Seminar (UNIV135). Together, these theories provide a shared foundation for instructional design and assessment. The VTS sessions provided a setting for students to explore Research as Inquiry and Scholarship as Conversation, two frames outlined in ACRL's *Framework*. Pre- and post-VTS session surveys gave the authors feedback directly from the students, while observations based on VTS and the *Framework* rubrics during the VTS sessions provided data as well.

Through this partnership, the DePauw University Libraries and the Galleries at Peeler were able to support their individual missions, as well as the mission of the university, giving evidence to the necessity of both academic endeavors and to the success of students across disciplines.

The Setting
DePauw

DePauw University is an undergraduate liberal arts university located in Greencastle, Indiana, comprised of approximately 2,200 FTE students. The institution values encouraging its students to strive to examine topics through various, if not seemingly disparate, lenses. In its 2017 revised mission statement, DePauw University states that it "develops leaders the world needs through an uncommon commitment to the liberal arts."[1] More specifically, the University points out that through its role as a liberal arts institution, its "diverse and inclusive learning and living experience, distinctive in its rigorous intellectual engagement and its global and experiential learning opportunities, leads to a life of meaning and means. DePauw prepares graduates who support and create positive change in their communities and the world."[2] Because of its size and its goals in providing a distinctive liberal arts education to explore and engage a diverse curriculum, the DePauw University Libraries and Galleries at Peeler are uniquely situated to be the collaborators for cross-disciplinary campus partnerships.

DePauw University Libraries

As many libraries have already noted, the DePauw University Libraries is seeing a decline in check-outs of physical research materials and an increase in digital resource use. This increase in digital resources and their use does not necessarily mean there is an increase in students' use of research reference services (offered readily) nor does it indicate an increase in student research confidence. What librarians have anecdotally noted, and faculty have reported, is a frequent disconnect between students' understanding of what research requires and what the students are capable of accomplishing. Libraries and librarians are situated to address students' research needs beyond access to resources, and this includes the students' conception of and confidence in research.

The DePauw University Libraries serves as the academic "center" of the university—much like the fitness center is for the body, the library is an interdisciplinary center for the mind. This is exemplified by the libraries' central location in an academic quad as well as its dedication to being a student-centered space. The libraries' mission is to support the academic curriculum and co-curriculum of the university, as well as the research interests of faculty and students. The mission of the DePauw University Libraries indeed leaves out the importance of the holistic understanding of research the greater library community recognizes (for example, ACRL's *Framework for Information Literacy*). With this in mind, Birt Flegal realized an opportunity to promote the spoken and unspoken mission(s) of the library while encouraging students to find their research voices.

Galleries at Peeler

Similar to the DePauw University Libraries, the Galleries at Peeler also support the academic curriculum and co-curriculum but are often assumed to only support that of the fine arts. In this misunderstanding, the authors saw an advantageous partnership: to bridge two entities that are able to work interdisciplinarily by nature to promote student learning.

Like the DePauw University Libraries, the Galleries at Peeler often experience a disconnect in regard to campus utilization of its resources. The Galleries at Peeler is the university museum for DePauw. Housed in The Richard E. Peeler Art Center, it is the educational mission of the galleries and collections to inspire and engage diverse audiences through its collections, exhibitions, and public programming, and to stimulate the spirit of inquiry through a variety of learning styles. The team at Peeler is dedicated to providing educational programming that enhances the cultural life of the immediate community by contributing to the enrichment of students, faculty members, and the general public. While it quickly became the strength of the gallery staff to connect exhibits and collections across disciplines and throughout the community, they often found the existence of the galleries themselves fell under the radar, specifically in useability for faculty and staff for the benefit of their students. On a campus of over 2,700 individuals, prior to the 2016–2017 academic year, the Galleries at Peeler typically only saw between 1,000 and 2,000 visitors per semester. In a step toward fulfilling and acting on the teaching aspect of its mission, in spring 2016, the

Galleries at Peeler created a new position among the gallery staff: assistant curator of exhibitions and education (promoted to assistant director and curator of exhibitions and education in fall 2018). This position was tasked with two roles primarily: (1) develop more educational opportunities in which the collection and exhibitions on display could be utilized throughout campus and community, and (2) work toward establishing a better relationship with the audience of the Galleries at Peeler, thus raising visitation statistics. It is worth noting here that within three years of the creation of this position, visitorship with the Galleries at Peeler increased by almost 60 percent.[3]

The Galleries at Peeler hosts approximately ten exhibitions per year in about 10,000 square feet of space. These primarily consist of traveling exhibits, student shows, faculty shows, artist solo/group shows, and exhibitions curated from the university's permanent art collection. The staff maintain a programming focus to be as interdisciplinary as possible in order to reach across campus disciplines. Housing the university collection of approximately 3,700 objects, the Galleries at Peeler offers teaching and research opportunities through exhibitions and collections objects alike.

Looking ahead, the gallery program is in a strong position to develop deeper, more meaningful relationships with campus and community. Leveraging the vastly improved collection for exhibitions and undergraduate research, teaching, and learning, as well as campus and curricular partnerships, as evidenced by this partnership with the DePauw University Libraries and UNIV 135 course, the Galleries at Peeler are, at long last, poised to do great things with the very tools and treasures at its disposal.

UNIV135

The course description for UNIV135 states, "This course is designed to support students in their development as learners through readings, reflective writing, and class discussion. Topics covered include active reading, taking good notes, preparing for exams, and time management. Students will be encouraged to explore their strengths as scholars, to address their weaknesses and to become more engaged in the learning process." Students self-identify for the course, and the course is often recommended to struggling students by their academic advisors. Struggling, in this case, can mean emotionally or academically as an undergraduate student to the extent that it is affecting their academic performance. Students can be referred to the UNIV135 course as incoming first-years or can self-select the course as a sophomore or junior; seniors are not allowed to take the course. The course also tends to attract international students as a course that will aid in acclimating to the US collegiate learning environment. In fall 2018, the course was composed of three upperclassmen (sophomores and juniors) and eleven first-years; four students identified as international students.

A unit of the course covers research strategies, which typically involves meeting with a librarian to discuss research and access to resources. But it was recognized there was something impeding students from engaging in research with confidence. Students did not seem to acknowledge that research begins with inquiry and scholarship is an ongoing conversation, of which they are a part. Instead, students felt that the research process was an insurmountable task and often mentioned anecdotally being overwhelmed by the assignment. This caused the students to procrastinate their research assignments and complete them in more of a "crisis mode," completing the bare minimum requirements and turning in "something" rather than producing work of which they were able to be proud. While knowing what resources are available is important, for this course in particular, it was deemed a priority to instead focus on how undergraduates see themselves as valid researchers who can complete assignments with confidence.

Instructional Model
The *Framework*
ACRL's *Framework* is a basis of assessment and professional goals for instruction librarians at the university level. Built around six conceptual frames, the *Framework* outlines learning practices and learner dispositions to establish expectations and outcomes for each frame. For the basis of this research, the authors have focused on two frames: Research as Inquiry and Scholarship as Conversation. Research as Inquiry posits that research is a repetitive process that requires students to continually ask questions of increasing complexity. Scholarship as Conversation supports the importance of sustained scholarly discourse.

The *Framework* posits the flexibility of the interconnected core concepts in relation to the rigidity of standards. The core concepts, or frames, give practitioners areas of information literacy competency with varying degrees of aptitude. This allows librarians to create scalable lessons according to the needs of the students. Research as Inquiry builds upon asking increasingly complex questions to refine their research topic and scope while considering information from multiple sources to synthesize into a cohesive argument. For the UNIV135 students, this meant approaching research as merely asking questions. As practice, Birt Flegal had the students write down a basic list of questions regarding a topic for a research project they had to complete. Students brainstormed for ten minutes. Following this, students paired up and partner A had one minute to introduce their topic to partner B; then partner B had three minutes to ask questions about partner A's topic. Then they switched roles. This afforded students to hear other questions they might not have thought of when contemplating their topic.

Scholarship as Conversation encourages learners to seek out voices from various areas and have the agency to respond to these voices. Students mentioned they did not have the authority to speak to topics they were assigned for research projects in various courses. When pressed, students merely said they were not knowledgeable enough in the topic, or sometimes they were not even vaguely interested, so they did not have anything to contribute. The lack of confidence in this area was directly addressed by the students in UNIV135 through the sessions with Chamberlain using the pedagogical theory Visual Thinking Strategies, asking simple questions to establish authority.

Visual Thinking Strategies

Visual Thinking Strategies (VTS) is a research-based teaching method focused on a teacher-facilitated discussion surrounding carefully selected images for a student-centered discussion discovery process to take place. "VTS uses art to teach visual literacy, thinking, and communication skills—listening and expressing oneself. Growth is stimulated by several things:

- Looking at art of increasing complexity
- Answering developmentally based questions
- Participating in peer group discussions, carefully facilitated by teachers."[4]

In its original form, VTS asks three questions during a session with students/ visitors in which all feedback and conversation happens out loud and in dialogue with each other:

1. What's going on in this picture?
2. What do you see that makes you say that?
3. What more can we find?

For the purposes of this case study, the authors slightly tweaked the format of the traditional VTS to assist in the observational need of the authors and further the classroom-based nature of UNIV 135. Students in each session were encouraged first to write their personal answers to the VTS prompts above without discussion with one another. After allowing the students some time to reflect and write, the authors then facilitated a discussion following the traditional VTS format. The authors found that allowing those students who do not initially speak in front of their peers the opportunity to collect their thoughts prior to others speaking allowed for more conversation to take place among the entire group instead of quieter individuals simply nodding in agreement with the loudest voice in the room.

Additionally, the written component provided the authors with an increased understanding of students' reactions to the sessions, outside of body language observed throughout the process. For example, many of the written responses received at the second session voiced the applicability and use of close looking and increased attention to detail throughout other academic courses. Students throughout these sessions were also willing and understanding in listening to others' personal reactions to the works on display, and rather than focusing on the negatives in their opinions being different, showed excitement in seeing how someone else was interpreting the same information they were given. The authors realize that these findings could only come about through the utilization of both written responses and traditional VTS methods as well as a constant observation of participants' body language throughout the session.

Case Study
Preparation
The authors worked together in the past utilizing a VTS exercise in the spring 2018 iteration of UNIV 135. Realizing its potential, the authors met before the start of fall 2018 to design another VTS visit for the upcoming class. Together they designed a two-stage process to quantify how VTS can help support student confidence, building in the research process.

In choosing works for the two sessions of VTS for the UNIV 135 fall 2018 course, Chamberlain made a short list of works from the collection that provided some built-in narrative structure for any onlookers—i.e., no works of abstraction were considered. Together, the authors decided on a photo by Robert Doisneau for the first session and a photo by Sonja Hinrichsen for the second session.

FIGURE 3.1. Sonja Hinrichsen, *Big Circle (from "Snow Drawings")*, 2009, 2009.11.1.5, DePauw University Permanent Art Collection, with permission from the artist.

While both chosen works used photography as their medium, each presented a wholly different narrative to unpack and explore for the students. Doisneau's black and white *Le Petit Balcon*, 1953, depicts a bar scene with several individuals gazing toward but not directly at the photographer. Hinrichsen's *Big Circle (from "Snow Drawings")*, 2009, presents a drastically different scene (figure 3.1).

In full, contrasting color, Hinrichsen shows viewers a landscape, covered in snow, but disturbed by the presence of someone, or something, creating a meditative path of concentric circles out from the photographer.

To track student responses and classroom discussion during the VTS sessions, a rubric was created. The authors looked at various rubrics that had already been created according to the two frames from the *Framework* as well as VTS. The rubric for this project included areas of assessment for the in-class discussion of the artwork. The rubric was adapted from Smita Avasthi's "Student Learning Outcomes with Rubrics for Performance Indicators for Community College Students" and the VTS rubric outlined by Yenawine. The rubric for this case study includes assessment of observations and basic interpretation, multiple interpretations and probing questions, open-ended questions, investigative inquiry, and conversational inquiry. The rubric gives the instructors a way to record the students' comments and interactions with each other in academic discourse.

The authors also conducted a student self-assessment at the beginning and end of the semester to evaluate students' perceived confidence in participating in academic discourse, adapted from a 2008 Carnegie Mellon University Assessment Task Force survey. The survey includes Likert-scale questions regarding

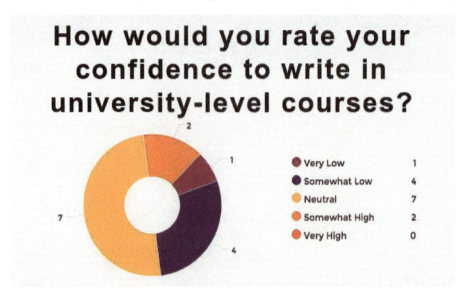

FIGURE 3.2. Student responses from question 1 of the pre-survey given at the beginning of the semester, fall 2018.

confidence in the areas of university-level writing, course participation, research, and comfort in visiting museums. The authors also gathered information on intended major(s) and first language(s). Together, Birt Flegal and Chamberlain hypothesized the self-assessments would show an increase in confidence over the course of the semester. Figures 3.2-3.8 show the responses in the pre-survey given to the UNIV 135 students at the beginning of the semester.

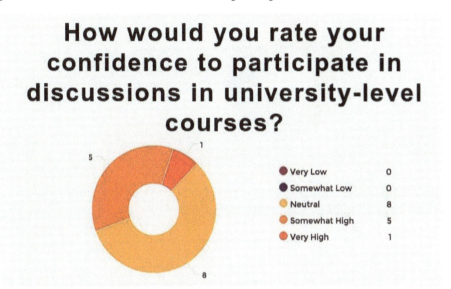

FIGURE 3.3. Student responses from question 2 of the pre-survey given at the beginning of the semester, fall 2018.

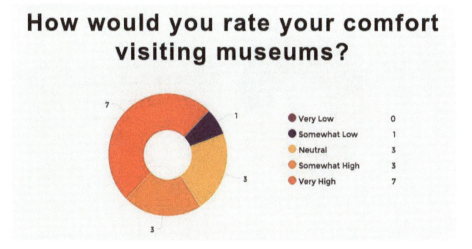

FIGURE 3.4. Student responses from question 3 of the pre-survey given at the beginning of the semester, fall 2018.

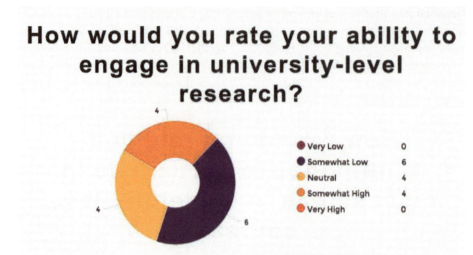

FIGURE 3.5. Student responses from question 4 of the pre-survey given at the beginning of the semester, fall 2018.

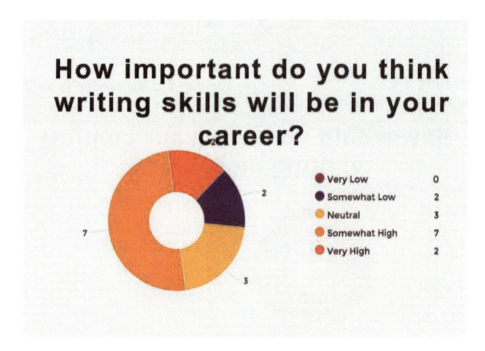

FIGURE 3.6. Student responses from question 5 of the pre-survey given at the beginning of the semester, fall 2018.

FIGURE 3.7. Student responses from question 6 of the pre-survey given at the beginning of the semester, fall 2018.

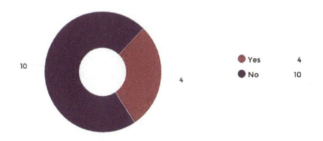

FIGURE 3.8. Student responses from question 7 of the pre-survey given at the beginning of the semester, fall 2018.

Session 1, Sept. 9, 2018

For the first session, Birt Flegal introduced Chamberlain with a short explanation of the interdisciplinary opportunities with fine arts and the Galleries at Peeler. Chamberlain transported Robert Doisneau's *Le Petit Balcon* to the classroom for the students to encounter. The work in question was placed flat on a table. Because of the small room and lack of viewing space, the students were encouraged to come up to the table for closer viewing.

44   Chapter 3

After a few minutes of simply gazing at the work, worksheets were distributed to each student with the following VTS questions:

- What's going on in this work?
- What do you see that makes you say that?
- What more can we find/what other questions do you have?

During this time, they were encouraged to remain quiet and simply write down their thoughts in regard to the work and questions in front of them. VTS intentionally does not require much direction, other than the three questions above. In this way, students can take inspiration from the artwork as unobstructed as possible. The next phase was for students to share their observations. Chamberlain led the discussion while Birt Flegal took notes and made observations on student responses and participation using the rubric.

Throughout the session, students were exhibiting reticence when asked the three VTS questions. When students did speak, there was a lack of probing questions. Students made observations and occasional interpretations of the observations but spoke with a distinct lack of confidence, often including a qualifier to their comments ("…but maybe not." "I'm probably wrong…" etc.). Three students of the thirteen who were present offered no comments at all during the session.

The authors gathered the students' written responses at the conclusion of the first session in order to review and anecdotally assess. The written responses to the three posed questions revealed a depth of thought and engagement that was not present in the verbal discussion. Multiple students noted the direction of the audience's attention, the predominance of white males, and the varying representations of gendered behavior in the picture. It is of note that the two students who did not speak at all during the verbal session wrote multiple responses for each of the questions posed on the written portion of the VTS session. The authors were able to conclude from the written responses that the students did, indeed, engage with the artwork but seemed to struggle with engaging with their peers' comments and questions in discussion.

Preparation for Session 2

Prior to the second VTS session, which would take place at the end of the semester, the students in UNIV135 were given an introduction to the library and its resources. While many of the students likely already visited the library and/ or had a class that met with a librarian, it was important to make sure all the students had similar introductions to the library spaces and services available. During this session, Birt Flegal, in librarian mode, introduced concepts related to the *Framework* that would also help the students in other courses that included a research component. For one of the activities, the students were given a worksheet with three large boxes in which they were to brainstorm broad, general/generic, and specific terms related to their research projects. In this exercise, Birt

Flegal encouraged the students to be creative, to visualize their topics, and write down words that described what they were seeing. Some students were more receptive to the process than others, and that was evident in their responses on the worksheet. The results from this exercise somewhat coincided with the results from the first VTS session. Some students were active in the discussion while others remained silent; but the written responses revealed engagement with the activity and, beyond that, a growing sophistication and comfort in the students' research vocabulary (asking more open-ended questions, beginning preliminary outlines, etc.).

The authors had hoped that because the students were subsequently introduced to research and VTS the class would increase in involvement and participation in the discussion portion during the second VTS session that would take place at the end of November 2018.

Session 2, November 29, 2018

Next, during the second VTS session, the UNIV135 students visited the Peeler gallery storage area (instead of the VTS session happening in the UNIV135 classroom) for Chamberlain to lead the class in a discussion on the second photograph: Sonja Hinrichsen's *Big Circle (from Snow Drawings)* (figure 3.1 previously). This second session followed much in the same manner as the first; however, this time, being in a different setting, the work in question was presented on an easel at eye level for the students to gaze upon. Initially, the authors saw a definitive difference in this session compared to the first. Students who did not participate in the first session started participating in the second. Following a few moments in which students were encouraged to silently look at the work and write their answers/thoughts to the VTS questions posed on a sheet in front of them, Chamberlain led the class in a traditional VTS session with the following questions:

1. What's going on in this work?
2. What do you see that makes you say that?
3. What more can we find/what other questions do you have?

In the same manner as the first session, Birt Flegal made observation notes, both concerning spoken word and body language from the students, while Chamberlain spoke with the class. From Birt Flegal's notes and the recollections of the authors, there is evidence that more students engaged with the artwork, but there were more expressions of confusion by the piece than with the Doisneau photograph previously. Hinrichsen's piece is more abstract and there are no human forms present. The creativity of possible interpretations was somewhat lacking, but the discussion did reveal a greater maturity of thought and process. Students' creativity in interpreting the piece seemed hampered, but there was an increase in the students' conversations with each other about their respective comments and observations according to the rubric Birt Flegal used to track student discussion.

The written responses from the second VTS session reflected the discussion more accurately than the written responses from the first VTS session. This time, the students wrote what they shared verbally, potentially revealing greater confidence in their thought process, confidence that allowed them to share openly in class. As a better way to assess student engagement and confidence, the authors also added a component to the end of the session by asking the students to write on their worksheets a possible research question inspired by the work of art. The students were prompted to think about their majors or interests to help inspire their research questions. Elicited responses varied from basic questions on the location of the photograph to extremely reflective questions regarding weather patterns, communication theories, confirmation bias, and even a question involving a physics equation regarding human destruction noting that "in physics, everything is created in a vacuum," and "This image conveys effort, the effort of (possible) deforestation, (possible) crop production, as well as the concentric path traveled by the person. The effort humans put into attempting to mend what they have broken. What is the path of human destruction?"

Remainder of the Semester
Assessment of Impact

For the second session, the students' written responses more closely reflected the class discussion. The authors also noted that all students present (two were absent) spoke during the second session, and each student presented their observations and cited evidence from the photograph to support their comments. This increase in engagement and sophistication of discussion cannot be directly related only to VTS activities as each student participated in other courses and experiences throughout the semester that influenced their research confidence; yet their collective growth could indicate success in the activity. During the second VTS session in November, the authors were able to observe the students listening and responding to each other as fellow researchers—having a research conversation that reflects the knowledge practices and dispositions of ACRL's *Framework* frame, Scholarship as Conversation.

During the first session with the Doisneau photograph, the students were repeatedly encouraged to contribute to the conversation, and the written responses from the first session were notably shorter as compared to the written responses from the second session. The rubric and notes from the second session reveal that the students were more forthcoming and open to sharing their observations and interpretations. Students also started building off each other's comments and ideas in a way they did not display during the first session, even with a more abstract photograph. The amount of thoughtful written text on the worksheets from the first session in September compared to the second session in November is notable and should be recognized as evidence of the ability of VTS to increase the students' research confidence.

Students were given a post-VTS survey at the conclusion of the fall 2018 semester, the same survey that was given at the beginning of the semester before the first VTS session. Students self-reported an increase in their confidence to write, discuss, and research at the university level. The following figures show the responses in the post-survey given to the UNIV 135 students at the end of the semester.

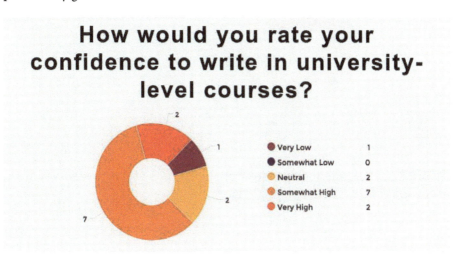

FIGURE 3.9. Student responses from question 1 of the post-survey given at the end of the semester, fall 2018.

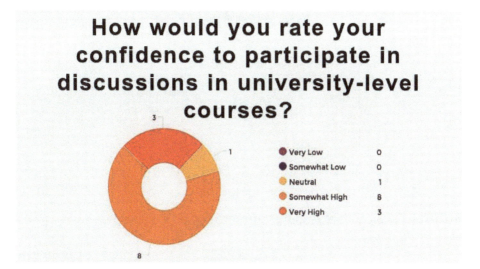

FIGURE 3.10. Student responses from question 2 of the post-survey given at the end of the semester, fall 2018.

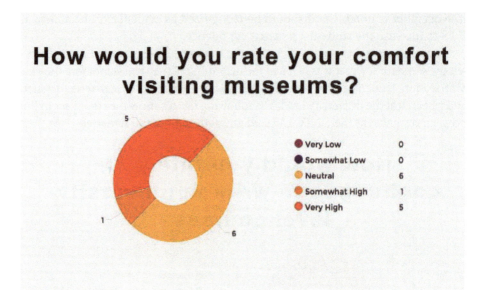

FIGURE 3.11. Student responses from question 3 of the post-survey given at the end of the semester, fall 2018.

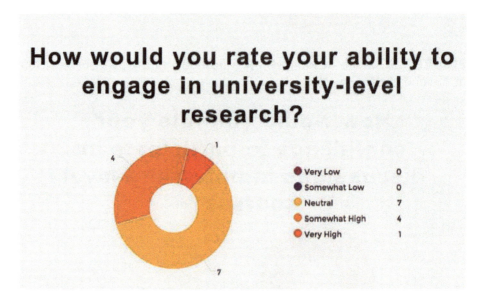

FIGURE 3.12. Student responses from question 4 of the post-survey given at the end of the semester, fall 2018.

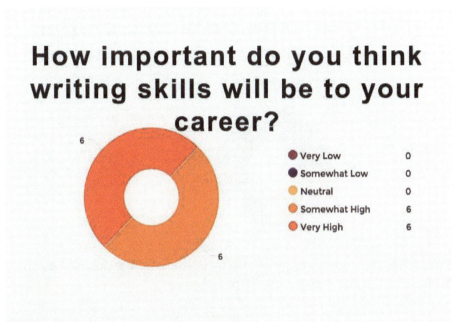

FIGURE 3.13. Student responses from question 5 of the post-survey given at the end of the semester, fall 2018.

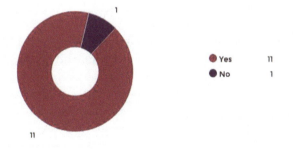

FIGURE 3.14. Student responses from question 6 of the post-survey given at the end of the semester, fall 2018.

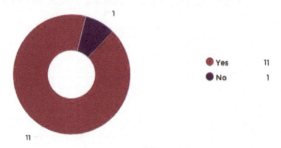

FIGURE 3.15. Student responses from question 7 of the post-survey given at the end of the semester, fall 2018.

Next Steps

Moving forward, the authors plan to continue in these research endeavors, albeit at different universities. Together, they plan to widen their pool of feedback and student responses in order to build upon the knowledge gained from this first iteration. In learning from this first experience, the authors plan to implement a few new strategies in future semesters:

- Establish a more transparent lens for the students around the connection between VTS sessions, the research process, and how the methodology of a VTS practice can work together well for the benefit of the researcher.
- Inclusion of a Research section in the UNIV 135 final portfolio reflection. This portfolio requires the student to reflect on their semester and what areas of scholarship they improved upon and on which they still need to work. Current sections include Time Management, Note-taking, Environment, etc. The Research section would ask students to write about their research process and encourage the students to look at how they used, or could use, VTS to help with the research process.
- Formalize a method of assessment of students' written responses during the VTS sessions. This way, the authors can gather more accurate data to support their research.
- Since the fall 2018 iteration, the authors have included a free-response question on the pre- and post-surveys regarding the research process. The authors noted there was not much data being collected from the students that indicated a change in the students' research processes.

Out of this, the authors hope to encourage DePauw University, and others like it, to continue to actively utilize their campus resources as spaces for curricular-based collaboration. Academic museums and libraries serve a similar purpose: to provide access and interpretation to their collections. Our respective collections are often perceived as passive, but it is through this type of collaboration that we are recognized as active assets to the overall university goals concerning student success. Together, academic museums and libraries share a vested interest in appealing to both students and universities by establishing themselves as spaces that actively support students' participation and contribution to scholarly discourse.

Endnotes

1. "Mission and Vision," DePauw University, 2017, retrieved January 19, 2020 from https://www.depauw.edu/about/mission-and-vision/.
2. "Mission and Vision," DePauw University.
3. The authors would like to make a note that due to university financial restructuring that took place at the conclusion of the spring 2019 semester, the role of assistant director and curator of exhibitions and education no longer exists at the Richard E. Peeler Art Center at DePauw University.
4. Philip Yenawine, *Visual Thinking Strategies: Using Art to Deepen Learning across School Disciplines* (Cambridge, MA: Harvard Education Press, 2014).

Bibliography

Association of College and Research Libraries. *Framework for Information Literacy for Higher Education.* 2016. http://www.ala.org/acrl/standards/ilframework.

DePauw University. "Mission and Vision." 2017. Retrieved January 19, 2020. https://www.depauw.edu/about/mission-and-vision/.

Ferlazzo, Larry. "Response: The Best Ways to Engage Students in Learning." *Classroom Q & A with Larry Ferlazzo* (blog), December 6, 2014. Accessed December 18, 2018. http://blogs.edweek.org/teachers/classroom_qa_with_larry_ferlazzo/2014/12/response_the_best_ways_to_engage_students_in_learning.html.

Hailey, Dabney. "Visual Thinking, Art, and University Teaching Across Disciplines." *About Campus* 19, no. 4 (September/October 2014): 9–16.

Joel Smith Media. VTS: Visual Thinking Strategies. Accessed December 18, 2018. https://vtshome.org/.

Meeks, Amanda, Larissa Garcia, Ashley Peterson, and Alyssa Vincent. "Create: Adapting the Framework to Studio Art Disciplines." *C&RL News* (November 2017): 554–59.

Milbourn, Amanda. "A Big Picture Approach: Using Embedded Librarianship to Proactively Address the Need for Visual Literacy Instruction in Higher Education." *Art Documentation: Journal of the Art Libraries Society of North America* 32, no. 2 (2013): 274–83. https://doi.org/10.1086/673517.

Moeller, Mary, Kay Cutler, Dave Fiedler, and Lisa Weier. "Visual Thinking Strategies = Creative and Critical Thinking." *The Phi Delta Kappan* 95, no. 3 (2013): 56–60. http://www.jstor.org/stable/23611815.

Nelson, Amelia. "Visual Thinking Strategies from the Museum to the Library: Using VTS and Art in Information Literacy Instruction." *Art Documentation: Journal of the Art Libraries Society of North America* 36 (Fall 2017): 282–92.

Ravas, Tammy, and Megan Stark. "Pulitzer-Prize-Winning Photographs and Visual Literacy at The University of Montana: A Case Study." *Art Documentation: Journal of the Art Libraries Society of North America* 31, no. 1 (2012): 34–44. https://doi.org/10.1086/665334.

Thomas, Elizabeth, Nancy Place, and Cinnamon Hillyard. "Students and Teachers Learning to See. Part 1: Using Visual Images in the College Classroom to Promote Students' Capacities and Skills." *College Teaching* 56, no. 1 (2008): 23–27. http://www.jstor.org/stable/27559348.

Volk, Steven S., and Liliana Milkova. "Crossing the Street Pedagogy: Using College Art Museums to Leverage Significant Learning Across the Campus." In *A Handbook for Academic Museums: Exhibitions and Education*, edited by Stefanie S. Jandl and Mark S. Gold, 88–115. Edinburgh & Boston: Museums Etc., 2012.

———. *Transfer: Learning In and Through the Academic Art Museum to A Handbook for Academic Museums: Advancing Engagement.* Edited by Stefanie S. Jandl and Mark S. Gold, 28–63. Edinburgh & Boston: Museums Etc., 2015.

Waibel, Günter. "Library, Archive, and Museum Collaboration." OCLC Research. Last modified November 30, 2011. Accessed December 18, 2018. https://www.oclc.org/research/activities/lamsurvey.html.

Xu, Lijuan, and Nestor Gil. "Librarians as Co-Teachers and Curators: Integrating Information Literacy in a Studio Art Course at a Liberal Arts College." *Art Documentation: Journal of the Art Libraries Society of North America* 36 (Spring 2017): 122–36.

Yenawine, Philip. "Teaching to the (New) Tests: The Benefits of Discussion." *The Whole Child* (blog), September 12, 2013. https://www.philipyenawine.com/teaching/2020/8/23/teaching-to-the-new-tests-the-benefits-of-discussion.

———. *Visual Thinking Strategies: Using Art to Deepen Learning across School Disciplines.* Cambridge, MA: Harvard Education Press, 2014.

Yenawine, Philip, and Alexa Miller. "Visual Thinking, Images, and Learning in College." *About Campus* 19, no. 4 (September/October 2014): 2–8.

Zorich, Diane, Gunter Waibel, and Ricky Erway. *Beyond the Silos of the LAMs: Collaboration Among Libraries, Archives and Museums.* Dublin OH: OCLC Research, 2008. https://www.oclc.org/content/dam/research/publications/library/2008/2008-05.pdf ..

CHAPTER 4

Pieced Together:
Community Engagement Through Collaboration

Susan Dreher and Andrea Packard

Swarthmore College Libraries and Swarthmore College's List Gallery engaged in an innovative collaboration in 2018 that celebrated the quilts and quiltmakers of the remote and historically Black community of Gee's Bend, Alabama. Their close collaboration, along with strong support from academic departments and faculty, enabled the gallery and the libraries to extend their capabilities to present an ambitious program that promoted artwork, student scholarship, and community engagement. The successful completion of the project established a protocol for the libraries and gallery to maintain their transformed relationship as they consider and plan future projects.

Introduction

In 2018, Swarthmore College Libraries and the List Gallery, a fine arts exhibition space at the college, initiated an innovative collaboration that celebrated the quilts and quiltmakers of the remote and historically Black community of Gee's Bend, Alabama titled *Piece Together: The Quilts of Mary Lee Bendolph*. The exhibition emphasized the historic and communal aspects of Gee's Bend quilting. The partnership also allowed Swarthmore College to concurrently present an exhibition that was co-organized by the List Gallery and took place in Swarthmore's main library titled *Responses to Gee's Bend*. That companion exhibition featured works by seventeen quilters from throughout the United States who were inspired by the legacy of Gee's Bend. Many of those quilters participated in the programming related to both exhibitions and interacted with students,

53

faculty, and the community. The artists raised important questions about history, society, and identity. The historic significance of Gee's Bend and the variety of collaborative outreach projects related to the concurrent exhibitions enabled students to apply their course learning, meet diverse populations, and participate in community engagement.

Collaboration at Swarthmore

An ongoing goal at Swarthmore is to integrate art and library projects with student scholarship and engagement. This can be challenging at Swarthmore because although students are consistently excellent at academics, most class-work does not directly engage the community. The Gee's Bend project was well suited to accomplish this goal as it provided many different avenues of exposure. There were ongoing exhibitions with artwork on display, talks, panel discussions, and receptions that engaged Gee's Bend community members together with quilters, scholars, and artists from around the country. The project also involved a course co-taught by a history professor and local quilter. Finally, a grant-funded project sent two students to Gee's Bend, Alabama, to record oral histories and then to integrate these histories into the ultimate exhibition.

The gallery and the libraries had successfully collaborated on large grant-funded exhibitions and shared programming for over twenty years. The way for this level of collaboration began with joint exhibitions of sculptural works by book artists in the late 1990s and subsequently featured artists working in varied media such as photography, painting, ceramics, and sculpture. Through teamwork, List Gallery and McCabe Library staff organized concurrent exhibitions and related symposia that were increasingly complex, offering opportunities for interdisciplinary learning. One such collaboration was *Artist in Wartime*, an examination of artistic responses to the effects of war. When the List Gallery presented *Bearing Witness, Recent works by Daniel Heyman*, a solo exhibition that highlighted the torture conducted by US soldiers at Abu Grahib prison, McCabe Library presented a concurrent exhibition featuring artists from around the world: *Printmakers Go to War: Works by Daniel Heyman in collaboration with Nick Flynn, Damian Cote, Eric Avery, Ehren Tool, and Michael Reed.* In conjunction with these exhibitions, the List Gallery published an exhibition catalog with an essay by the noted sociologist Robin Wagner-Pacifici and organized a series of artists' lectures and workshops. In addition, McCabe Library hosted a well-attended poetry reading by Nick Flynn. Collectively, these events offered varied insights into the effects of institutionalized violence and they reasserted imaginative space for critical thinking, restorative justice, and transformative creativity.

The opportunity for such collaboration is encouraged on an institutional level. Collaborative engagement is integral to the job descriptions of key employees involved in mounting exhibitions on campus. Interdisciplinary projects are also facilitated by the close working relationship between List Gallery Director Andrea Packard and the libraries' Visual Initiatives and Exhibition Librarian Susan Dreher. Serving in a somewhat unusual position, the visual initiatives and exhibition librarian oversees the exhibition program at the libraries, which includes not only the main atrium exhibitions but also smaller exhibitions in other library spaces as well as faculty-generated or student-generated pop-up displays responding to current news or events. Because the number of staff at a small college is limited, the visual initiatives and exhibitions librarian position was created to handle diverse needs, including library-wide graphic design and curation of the artists' books collection, programming, and communication. The libraries' exhibition programming and successful collaborations with the List Gallery have been made possible through dedicated library exhibitions funding, grants from a college-based foundation, and dedicated staff time.

When considering the "collaboration continuum," as described in the OCLC report "Beyond the Silos of the LAMs: Collaboration Among Libraries, Archives and Museums,"[1] the relationship between the List Gallery and Swarthmore College Libraries had long been a combination of cooperation and coordination relying "on informal or formal agreements between groups to achieve a common end."[2] Through the collaborative dialogue between the library and the List Gallery, "information is not just exchanged; it is used to create something new."[3] With the year-long process of planning and implementing the Gee's Bend project, we reached a deeper level of collaboration described by the same OCLC report, as when participants "discover new ways in which to leverage their combined assets, and over time realize the transformational quality which is the hallmark of deep collaboration."[4] The difference between this collaboration and our earlier efforts was in the depth and breadth of the collaboration and the overall impact of the project. The interdisciplinary reach of the project across multiple programs was unprecedented in our previous endeavors. Furthermore, the opportunities that arose for student scholarship as a result of this new connection were transformative: through our program, students integrated their curricular studies and connected with faculty, staff, and external communities. With the successful completion of the project, we now have a roadmap and strengthened relationship that will improve planning for future projects.

The Gee's Bend Project

The *Piece Together* exhibition project and related collaborations began in January 2017, when the List Gallery Director Andrea Packard conceived of the List Gallery exhibition of quilts from Gee's Bend. She initially partnered with Mount Holyoke College Art Museum, South Hadley Massachusetts (MHCAM), which had already begun organizing the exhibition titled *Piece Together: The Quilts of Mary Lee Bendolph*. As Packard considered ways to adapt the larger exhibition to the List Gallery, she reached out to Susan Dreher to see if the library would showcase a number of works in its Upper Atrium space and explore complementary programming. By March 2017, the William J. Cooper Foundation had funded Packard's funding proposal to mount *Piece Together* in both the List Gallery and library Upper Atrium from September 6 through October 28, 2018.

Although the Gee's Bend quilts had garnered national and international acclaim through numerous touring museum exhibitions, MHCAM's concept for *Piece Together* and its initial inventory of approximately eighteen quilts (all by Mary Lee Bendolph, except for a lone surviving quilt by her mother, Aolar Mosely) was notable in that it would be the first exhibition to focus on the creative trajectory of a single quilter from Gee's Bend. Packard determined that she could install approximately nine quilts and four prints by Mary Lee Bendolph in the List Gallery and that the library's Upper Atrium space could comfortably feature six more quilts. She traveled to Gee's Bend in the summer of 2017 to connect with the community, further fostering the academic mission of the project. Researching the exhibition and accompanying catalog, she discovered several extraordinary quilts by Mary Lee Bendolph's daughter, Essie Bendolph Pettway. Packard proposed adding them to the library Atrium portion of *Piece Together* along with the surviving quilt by Aolar Mosely in order to emphasize the historic and communal aspects of Gee's Bend quilting. Hung side-by-side, the quilts represented three generations of women who responded to the legacy of slavery and Jim Crow with remarkable faith, resilience, and creativity.

As Andrea Packard then organized, edited, and wrote the introduction for an eighty-two-page exhibition catalog, *Piece Together: The Quilts of Mary Lee Bendolph*,[5] with interdisciplinary essays by faculty and staff from both Mount Holyoke College and Swarthmore College, she also began to coordinate with Susan Dreher to extend the scope of the exhibition, plan for community engagement, and create opportunities for student scholarship. In fall 2017, as Packard and Dreher began collaborating more closely, they met with Swarthmore College Professor of History Allison Dorsey, who introduced them to Alicia Ruley-Nock, an independent quilt maker and resident of the borough of Swarthmore. At that time, Professor Dorsey and Ms. Ruley-Nock were preparing for their 2017 spring semester course titled *Black Art: Quilting as History and Culture*,[6] a class that would incorporate quiltmaking with learning in the classroom. Packard and Dreher then invited Ms. Ruley-Nock to help them curate a companion exhibition that would hang in the Lower Atrium exhibition space, directly beneath the planned installation of Gee's Bend quilts in the Upper Atrium, connecting quilting communities nationwide with both Gee's Bend and the Swarthmore College community.

Together, Packard, Dreher, and Ruley-Nock envisioned and curated *Responses to Gee's Bend*. They sent out a call for proposals to artists and quilters who felt inspired by the aesthetic legacy of the quilts of Gee's Bend. The resulting selection of work by seventeen artists reflected a wide range of approaches and aesthetics, but all of them responded, not only to the quilts of Gee's Bend, but to the broader qualities and values associated with the quilters, including beauty, craftsmanship, resourcefulness, ingenuity, spiritual faith, empathy, and resilience. Such was the enthusiasm for this exhibition that one of the artists selected later designed and published a catalog, *Responses to Gee's Bend*,[7] of all the works included in the *Responses to Gee's Bend*. This exhibition was one more piece in the overall collaboration that allowed a broader connection among our students, Gee's Bend, and the larger quilting community.

Student Scholarship

An ongoing goal throughout the planning of both exhibitions was to use the opportunity to promote teaching and student scholarship. As previously mentioned, the History Department at Swarthmore College provided a valuable connection between the exhibition and the curriculum, promoting scholarship through the design of a one-time special projects course entitled Black Art: Quilting as History and Culture, taught in spring 2018 by Professor of History Allison Dorsey and Alicia Ruley-Nock, who became an artist in residence at Swarthmore College. With Professor Dorsey, the students examined the long, rich history of African American quilt making. The students were then introduced to basic quilting skills and terminology by Alicia Ruley-Nock. The students designed and sewed their own quilts while working together on two larger collective class quilts, which were eventually displayed as part of *Responses to Gee's Bend* exhibition.

Further student scholarship related to the exhibition was supported by the List Gallery and the Swarthmore College Department of Sociology and Anthropology. When Andrea Packard visited Gee's Bend, Alabama, in July 2017, Tinnie Pettway, an elderly resident and quilter, asked Packard if she could help document the stories and cultural values of Gee's Bend, especially those of older quilters, before they are lost. Many of the quilters of Gee's Bend are in their eighties while many younger residents have moved away in search of educational and employment opportunities. Now that most homes have electricity and quilting is no longer a basic necessity, many community members fear the distinct style of quilting that originated in Gee's Bend will diminish. In September 2017, Packard partnered with Professor of Sociology and Anthropology Sarah Willie LeBreton, who now serves as Swarthmore's Provost, to oversee student research. They drafted and sent out a call for proposals from rising juniors or seniors with experience working with human subjects. They selected two students, Yixuan Maisie Luo '19 and Catherine Williams '19, and guided their application for Swarthmore College Humanities Grants to fund their travel to Gee's Bend to conduct an oral history project in summer 2018. Packard established a network of Gee's Bend community members who would support the students during their travel and research. During the students' conversations with Gee's Bend quilters, they recorded numerous stories about growing up in the community, practicing their religious faith, farming, and participating in the Civil Rights Movement. The students' research resulted in a forty-four-page book designed by Yixuan Maisie Luo '19: *Gee's Bend: Oral Histories*. Overseen and edited by Packard and published by the List Gallery, *Gee's Bend: Oral Histories* is comprised of transcribed interviews as well as photographs taken during the students' visit. The book was shared with members of the Gee's Bend community, visitors to Swarthmore, and online to help preserve intangible and ephemeral aspects of Gee's Bend's cultural heritage.

Programming: Community Engagement

Varied public programming for the two exhibitions was designed to have broad appeal, with the goal of engaging both Swarthmore College and external communities through a variety of interactive experiences related to the theme of Gee's Bend. The enthusiastic participation of members of the Gee's Bend community provided the connection between their community and ours, built upon previous student classroom learning, and encouraged new forms of creative engagement. The following events took place:

Screening of *While I yet Live*—a short documentary about Gee's Bend directed by Maris Curran. The film was followed by a panel discussion including Maris Curran; Rubin Bendolph, Jr., curator of Bendolph family quilts; quilter Essie Bendolph Pettway; and Hannah W. Blunt, associate curator at the Mount Holyoke College Art Museum.

Personal Narratives and Artistic Legacies—a morning-long panel discussion featuring Gee's Bend residents and members of Mary Lee Bendolph's family; Yixuan Maisie Luo and Catherine Williams, the oral history students; Ellen M. Alvord, Weatherbie Curator of Education and Academic Programs at Mount Holyoke Art Museum.

Quilting and Conversation—an informal public gathering in the Library Atrium with quiltmakers from Gee's Bend, local quilt maker Alicia Ruley-Nock, and numerous artists who participated in *Responses to Gee's Bend*. Essie Bendolph Pettway had a prepared set of discussion points and brought one of her quilts, with which participants could interact. Ruley-Nock brought quilting materials and had participants make individual squares, which she then pieced into a single quilt.

Curators' Talk for the exhibition *Responses to Gee's Bend* —featuring prepared comments by curators Andrea Packard; Alicia Ruley-Nock; Susan

Dreher; *Responses* participant and Gee's Bend Oral History researcher, Yixuan Maisie Luo '19. *Responses* artists in attendance were also invited to address the large gathering of more than 40 visitors.

Publications:
Piece Together: The Quilts of Mary Lee Bendolph (82-page exhibition catalog)
Gee's Bend: Oral Histories by Yixuan Maisie Luo and Catherine Williams (44-page book)
Responses to Gee's Bend (40-page exhibition catalog published by William Johnson)

Lectures:
Andrea Packard distilled lessons learned from the above events and exhibition projects through public lectures in fall 2018 to the Swarthmore Rotary Club and the community of Kendal at Longwood, Kennett Square.

Community School Group Engagement:
More than 100 first-grade students from the Wallingford Elementary School toured both exhibitions, participated in discussions led by Andrea Packard and Alicia Ruley-Nock, and completed subsequent classroom projects based on their experience.

Assessment

The complementary exhibitions *Piece Together* and *Responses to Gee's Bend* received rave reviews in the major regional newspaper *The Philadelphia Inquirer,*[8] in *Artblog,*[9] an online publication focused on Philadelphia area art and culture, and in *The Swarthmorean,* the local Swarthmore newspaper. Both exhibitions and all events were extremely well attended, with some of the largest numbers of visitors ever seen for both the List Gallery and the library. There was a great diversity in the audiences for exhibitions and events, from six-year-old students to a multitude of visitors from outside the College community. For many participants, it was their first visit to Swarthmore College. Within the campus community, there was an enhanced awareness and appreciation of the exhibitions and related projects due to the high caliber of the art and interpretive programming, the large number and variety of events, the interdisciplinary character of programming, and the diversity of locations used throughout campus.

Conclusion

The List Gallery and Swarthmore College Libraries strive to create easily navigable paths to ideas, people, places, and things and to engage with centers of excellence on campus. The Gee's Bend project was uniquely suited to this due to its broad appeal, the enthusiasm of the participating quilters, and the varied possibilities for student involvement. The success of the Gee's Bend project and

60   Chapter 4

the interdisciplinary dialogue it fostered was underscored when the college purchased two of the quilts from the *Piece Together* exhibition for its Permanent Collection. Ken Soehner, chief librarian at the Metropolitan Museum of Art, has stated, "True collaboration that goes beyond cooperation towards partnership, may be able to give us the resources and generate the pressure to force us… into a new and more dazzling performance."[10] The close collaboration between the List Gallery and the library, along with the strong support from academic departments and faculty, did just that, enabling both the gallery and the library to extend their capabilities, achieving a new level of community engagement, connection to the curriculum, and promotion of student scholarship.

Endnotes

1. Diane Zorich, Diane, Gunter Waibel, and Ricky Erway, *Beyond the Silos of the LAMs: Collaboration Among Libraries, Archives and Museums* (Dublin OH: OCLC Research, 2008), https://www.oclc.org/content/dam/research/publications/library/2008/2008-05.pdf.
2. Zorich, Waibel, and Erway, *Beyond the Silos*, 11.
3. Ibid.
4. Ibid., 12.
5. Andrea Packard, *Piece Together: The Quilts of Mary Lee Bendolph*, Swarthmore, https://www.swarthmore.edu/cooper-series/piece-together-quilts-mary-lee-bendolph.
6. "College Bulletin—Course Catalog," Swarthmore, http://catalog.swarthmore.edu/preview_course_nopop.php?catoid=7&coid=63499.
7. *Responses to Gee's Bend*, Blurb, 2019, https://www.blurb.com/b/8985673-responses-to-gee-s-bend.
8. Edith Newhall, "What to see in Philly galleries: A Gee's Bend genius, a big group barn show, more," *The Philadelphia Inquirer* (October 10, 2008), http://www2.philly.com/philly/entertainment/arts/philadelphi-galleries-mary-lee-bendolph-david-brewster-art-at-kings-oaks-20181010.html.
9. Michael Lieberman, "Piece Together, The Quilts of Mary Lee Bendolph at Swarthmore's List Gallery," *Artblog* (blog), October 13, 2018, https://www.theartblog.org/2018/10/piece-together-the-quilts-of-mary-lee-bendolph-at-swarthmores-list-gallery/.
10. Kenneth Soehner, "Out of the ring and into the future: The power of collaboration" (paper presented at the RLG Members Forum: "Libraries, Archives and Museums–Three Ring Circus, One Big Show?," 2005, 3), http://worldcat.org/arcviewer/1/OCC/2007/08/08/0000070504/viewer/file1201.doc.

Bibliography

Blurb. *Responses to Gee's Bend*. Accessed December 6, 2019. https://www.blurb.com/b/8985673-responses-to-gee-s-bend.

Lieberman, Michael, A. Kirsh, D. Krieger, and W. López. "Piece Together, The Quilts of Mary Lee Bendolph at Swarthmore's List Gallery." *Artblog* (blog), October 13, 2018. Accessed December 6, 2019. https://www.theartblog.org/2018/10/piece-together-the-quilts-of-mary-lee-bendolph-at-swarthmores-list-gallery/.

Luo, Yixuan Maisie, and C. Williams. *Gee's Bend Oral Histories: Collected by Yixuan Maisie Luo and Catherine Williams*. Swarthmore College. 2018.

Newhall, Edith. "What to see in Philly galleries: A Gee's Bend genius, a big group barn show, more." *The Philadelphia Inquirer* (October 10, 2008). http://www2.philly.com/philly/entertainment/arts/philadelphi-galleries-mary-lee-bendolph-david-brewster-art-at-kings-oaks-20181010.html.

Packard, Andrea. *Piece Together: The Quilts of Mary Lee Bendolph*. List Gallery, Swarthmore College, and Mount Holyoke College. 2018. https://www.swarthmore.edu/cooper-series/piece-together-quilts-mary-lee-bendolph.

Soehner, Kenneth. "Out of the ring and into the future: The power of collaboration." Paper presented at the RLG Members Forum: "Libraries, Archives and Museums–Three Ring Circus, One Big Show?," 2005, 3. http://worldcat.org/arcviewer/1/OCC/2007/08/08/0000070504/viewer/file1201.doc.

Swarthmore.edu. *Libraries + Collections*. 2019. https://www.swarthmore.edu/libraries/libraries-collections.

———. *List Gallery*. 2019. https://www.swarthmore.edu/list-gallery.

Zorich, Diane, Gunter Waibel, and Ricky Erway. *Beyond the Silos of the LAMs: Collaboration Among Libraries, Archives and Museums*. Dublin OH: OCLC Research, 2008. https://www.oclc.org/content/dam/research/publications/library/2008/2008-05.pdf.

CHAPTER 5

The Cultural Heritage Collaborative:
Shared Mission, Expertise, and Spaces for Natural History and Library Collections

Patrick Kociolek, Robert H. McDonald, Leslie J. Reynolds, and Jennifer Knievel

> This chapter describes the broad set of collaborations that have existed for nearly a decade between the University Libraries and the Natural History Museum at the University of Colorado, Boulder. This collaborative partnership focuses on areas of collection management, access, user engagement, and programming as well as joint-use facility development. Continued program, accessibility, stewardship, and shared facility development will build on the sturdy foundations of shared opportunities and challenges that have defined current high levels of collaborations between these two CU-Boulder campus units.

Introduction

Founded in 1902, the University of Colorado Museum of Natural History,[1] with nearly five million objects, is the largest repository of natural history objects in the Rocky Mountain Region and one of the oldest. Eight scientific disciplines across biology, geology, and anthropology are represented in the museum, and tenure-track faculty in the museum have their tenure homes in one of these three departments. The museum also offers a master's degree in museum and field studies.

The Museum of Natural History finds itself, in the context of collections, deeply engaged in the activities of relatively new initiatives funded by the Advancing Digitization of Biodiversity Collections (ADBC) program of the National Science Foundation,[2] capturing high-resolution images of label data and specimens across nearly the entire diversity of our collections as well as documentation of other associated materials such as field notes and photographs. This democratization of the collections has created new awareness of the specimens, spawned new collaborations with a diversity of other collection institutions (small colleges, native communities), and led to increased demand for the real objects in the current climate of "alternative facts and truths." In part, the increased use of specimens has been realized by an explosion in the need for access to the DNA of objects for use in a wide range of scientific studies, from changes in distributional ranges of species over the Anthropocene to reconstruction of the phylogenetic relationships and evolutionary history of specific species to large-scale taxonomic lineages, local, regional continental, and worldwide.

Digitized images and data from the label information have then been leveraged for a wide range of exhibitions and other programming, within and outside the museum. The Museum of Natural History has produced collections-based exhibitions and offered programs in the traditional museum venue on the CU-Boulder campus as well as the main library and at least six other buildings on campus in addition to venues in Boulder, in libraries, museums, and community centers, and even elementary schools across Colorado, the Rocky Mountain region, and nationally. The collections also provide additional training opportunities for students aspiring to become collection professionals.

The Libraries of the University of Colorado Boulder[3] represent the largest research library collection in the Rocky Mountain region. From our start in 1877 in a single room, the University Libraries have grown to encompass six physical facilities at CU Boulder that maintain a vast collection of academic resources. In addition to serving as a repository of knowledge, the University Libraries provide engaging learning experiences and seamless services that empower people to discover and integrate reliable information in new ways. The collections that have the most overlap with the Natural History Museum are a majority of the primary source materials included in the Archives as well as the Special Collections of the University Libraries. These materials are all kindred to the wealth of scientific-related research and papers of professors at the university, many of whom were leaders in developing the Museum of Natural History into the organization that it has become today.

The Archives contain more than 1,500 distinct collections and 50,000 linear feet of materials, including manuscripts, correspondence, files, diaries, photographs, posters, newspapers, and published works. Established in 1917, the Archives hold internationally renowned manuscripts, photographs, records, and media collections relating to Colorado and the Rocky Mountain West. Special Collections houses rare works and contemporary artworks that support teaching and research in the arts, humanities, and sciences. The collections include rare books, medieval manuscripts, contemporary artists' books, and a signature photobook and photography collection. Signature collections associated with natural history include the Roger G. Barry Glaciology collection, the Walter Orr Roberts Papers (founding director of the National Center for Atmospheric Research), the papers of Theodore Dru Alison Cockerell, and Western Americana.

As the flagship university of a multi-campus system in the State of Colorado, the University of Colorado Boulder[4] is the only Association of American Universities (AAU) member in the Rocky Mountain region. CU Boulder hosts a student body of 34,500 in addition to 9,000 faculty and staff. CU Boulder is home to numerous award-winning faculty across the academic spectrum, including five Nobel Laureates in the sciences. CU Boulder is a public institution in a state with the fifth-lowest government funding for higher education[5] and a publicly elected (and therefore unusually political) governing board. As a result, the university functions in a particularly resource-limited environment for an institution of its size and scope. Perhaps not coincidentally, the university values collaboration, rewards interdisciplinary work, and encourages partnerships to reduce duplication of effort. For the libraries and museums, in environments where none of us has sufficient resources to gather all of the expertise we would like, we are motivated to work together and use the scaffolding of one another's excellence to build our own goals and programs. Our institutional culture of collaboration and commitment to excellence to the best of our abilities drives us to proactively connect with one another in ways that are mutually beneficial.

Programming and Advancement of Missions

Many of the collaborations between the University Libraries and Natural History Museum at the University of Colorado have revolved around digitization efforts related to archival documents, individual objects in the Special Collections of the University Libraries, joint programs and exhibitions, and emergency response issues for areas of preservation.[6]

Chapter 5

One illustrative example of these collaborations has focused on the archives and collections of Theodore Dru Alison Cockerell,[7] an entomologist and one of the founders of the natural history museum. Cockerell was an avid naturalist, scientist, and communicator/teacher, and he contributed many thousands of specimens to the collections and published more than 2,000 articles and species descriptions. Holdings related to Cockerell in both the museums and the libraries represented a meaningful opportunity to bring attention to his contributions to the university as well as to his early scientific work, which forms the foundations of the Natural History Museum as we know it today. Various of the fossil specimens that Cockerell collected are held in the museum, and the libraries hold many of his photographs, slides, correspondence, and research notes. Collaborative endeavors between the museum and libraries created rich opportunities to unify specimens and documentation held in our two collections for the purposes of both exhibition and study.

Cockerell's work in the study of bees is a particular use case that has helped shape a key opportunity for library/museum collaboration. At a time when scientists are observing worrisome trends in bee populations worldwide, this unique set of museum and library collections has provided the Natural History Museum and University Libraries the opportunity to bring together digitized versions of Cockerell's movies of bees, his extensive collection of the bees from around Colorado, digitized images of his entomological and fossil collections, as well as his educational materials. The result of this collaboration was a series of lectures on the topic, which drew attendance from both the campus community as well as the surrounding public community. In addition, the two organizations built an extensive project developing, implementing, and promoting a citizen science project on the diversity and distributions of bees in Boulder County. That project involved hundreds of families, community gardens, and local open space parks and recreational areas. This use case highlights the ways that libraries and museums can leverage public programs, educational outreach, management, and biodiversity societal issues that are critical to our future as cultural heritage organizations to expand the use, awareness, and engagement of their related collections.[8] Additional collaborative projects have focused on the importance of the Florissant fossil beds as well as mutation in sunflowers. In addition to his papers and collections, Cockerell was a promoter of science in Boulder schools and in the community, as well as nationally, and many of his educational resources have also been the focus of collaborative work between the libraries and Natural History Museum. In 2019, some of the first natural history films ever made in the 1930s and 1940s (by Cockerell) were digitized, a joint project among the University Libraries, Museum of Natural History, and Film Studies faculty.[9]

Collaborative Expertise for Collection Stewardship

Knowledge is shared among the experts in the University Libraries and the Museum in a number of practical ways. First, a graduate program of study in museum and field studies is offered at the University of Colorado Boulder. Within the program, students can pursue a wide variety of professional interests, identified by academic discipline, including anthropology, geology, and biology, as well as art and art history, all of which have formal ties with academic units on the Boulder campus as well as through the History and Geography Departments and the libraries, where academic ties have been through individual faculty members. In the case of the libraries, at least four library faculty have served as the primary advisor for museum and field studies students, and others have served formally on committees and informally as content advisors. Many student projects and theses have been, naturally, collection-focused, drawing on library faculty expertise in archives, digital organization of data, and data accessibility. Other theses and projects completed by museum and field studies students have found their way into the library as programming and exhibitions within the library spaces.

The University of Colorado campus holds a variety of collections beyond those in the libraries or natural history museum. Other collections organizations on campus include a vibrant Art Museum and the Heritage Center, where archives, news articles, and memorabilia related to the Boulder campus are housed and presented to the public. Staff from all of these areas come together regularly to discuss topics that affect cultural heritage collections of all kinds. Initially, these regular meetings began as informal group discussions for individuals in separate collections responsible for the physical environment. Slowly, the group grew to include collections managers from the cultural heritage institutions but also safety officers, insurance experts, and other campus organizations whose expertise is required in the event of emergencies involving collections. For example, the safety officer was added when a museum visitor took a sword out of a display and began threatening other museum guests with it, bringing into clearer focus the need for safety planning in exhibits. They discuss, review, and address best practices, challenges/opportunities related to existing, newly established, or prospective rules/regulations, as well as funding opportunities, collection security, emergency response, and care methodologies. The group found these connections so valuable that they formalized their membership and structure to ensure that the group continues regardless of the individuals in the different roles and departments.[10] These meetings have led to important shared understandings and campus-wide policies and procedures for emergency response, collaborative programming, and grant proposals. They have also provided an excellent opportunity for the individuals involved to share their expertise with other departments on campus, allowing everyone to better plan and prepare for collection emergencies.

These efforts came to helpful fruition when the group provided emergency teamwork and help after floods in two natural history museums on campus and when an antiquated heating system burst and forced hundreds of gallons of near-boiling propylene glycol-based solution into the herbarium of the museum. Policies and procedures developed by this active and engaged community of collections professionals were deployed, and a team of collections-based responders from across the campus, as well as Facilities Management, were able to address health and safety issues related to the heat and content of the propylene-glycol solution as well as clean-up and recovery in the collections affected. The ongoing collaboration of the collection stewards ahead of these emergencies led to a far more effective response to the emergency, and in particular, the response was much more sensitive to the nature of cultural heritage collections than it might have been without the collaborative planning across these groups.

Individual faculty, as well as collections staff, in the libraries and museum, have collaborated and become engaged in supporting and directing student activities. Through these extensive collaborations, it has become clear that many activities of the two units have a great deal of common ground. For example, the types and scales of digital projects (the museum has over 5 million natural history objects; the library holds over 7.5 million volumes and is the largest library collection in the Rocky Mountain region), and, increasingly, as advocates for "real, verifiable facts" as opposed to "alternative facts," as touchstones and resources for a wide range of on- and off-campus users (see below). These faculty, staff, and students are also exploring how the domains of natural science, archives, and computational methods can open up the tremendous resources stewarded by these two units to help answer pressing questions related to conservation biology and species discovery[11] as well as reveal these collections to new sets of users and help them be applied to new sets of questions being posed by today's and subsequent students, classes, teaching and research faculties, as well as off-campus users. It has been through the activities of individual faculty and staff, as well as more formalized, facilitated activities driven by an interest in shared facilities, that we have come to realize the broad and deep set of common purpose, interests, opportunities, and challenges.

Shared Facilities and Addressing the Accessibility-Stewardship Paradox

A common challenge for museums and libraries relating to communication and advocacy with university administrations is the notion that our institutions are warehouses for published or finished works that are read and perhaps commonly held in other institutions or objects (or species) for which we have, or could get, many duplicates. "Why do we have so many insects in our collections?" and "If we want them, can't we just go outside and get them?" are common questions. Libraries and museums are conceived of as serving the same purpose as warehouses for big box stores: a place to keep stuff until you need it, and when you need it, move it somewhere else; put simply—supply chain management. This perception and the issues around it are based on the need for large amounts of secure storage space that can preserve the museum and library collections. The issues faced by collections-based units do indeed relate to space and appropriate facilities for the storage of the objects which we steward for—in our cases, the citizens of Colorado in perpetuity. Cultural heritage institutions like ours have likely done ourselves a disservice by couching facilities needs stridently in terms of storage and not emphasizing enough the high levels of engagement, proximity, and activity that occur in the collections by students, faculty, staff, and community members in the pursuit of our common mission of education and intellectual discovery.

The fundamental value to society of preserving and conserving our collections is unserved if those collections are never accessed, studied, or used to contribute to the greater understanding of society, nature, and the world around us. And we are still working on strategies to introduce, provide access, and better facilitate the use of these collections for instruction and utilization in ways that provide access, encourage new views and uses of the collections, and maintain or elevate levels of stewardship for the collections. While the digitization of collections is sometimes seen as a panacea for addressing the stewardship-accessibility paradox, our own data, from both the libraries and museum, suggest that digital access to resources, rather than eliminating the need for holding and preservation of the physical object, in fact drives *increased* demand for access to the primary source materials.

The two institutions have undertaken comprehensive program reviews as part of a standard campus practice at CU Boulder. This led to one of our first detailed collaborative assessments of library and museum space requirements. Detailed follow-up work by both internal and external specialists suggests that the wide-ranging types of collections at the library and Museum of Natural History require new facilities to meet acceptable professional levels of stewardship and care. Joint staff meetings were organized to discuss challenges and needs, examine workflows, suggest shared resources, and define physical needs and attributes of a true shared museum/library facility. We envision a facility that would further extend and preserve the mission of both of these important Rocky Mountain cultural heritage institutions but also extend the missions of both units to serve our broad and diverse audiences and users. The next phase of planning will look more closely at workflows and possible adjacencies of spaces, allowing for preliminary design work to begin. Due to financial constraints, a joint facility may have to be phased, requiring other types of design considerations.

Gaining support for such a new facility within the realm of a state higher education institution for the CU Boulder urban campus, both from a sponsor standpoint as well as from a campus footprint standpoint, has been challenging, despite decades-old recognition and subsequent validation of pressing issues, whether they be from faculty, staff, and students from within the units or external reviewers or experts. The juxtaposition of viewpoints of creating "storage" for these units within precious campus real estate in both established and developing campus settings, along with evolving campus priorities (central good units such as libraries and museums versus units with renewable revenue streams) and needs (aging infrastructure with annual discoveries of concern), and/or donor-driven interests. These also occur in a financial context in which state funding for higher education is exceptionally low and has been on a continual decline since 1980 with expectations of zero funding by 2022.[12]

Conclusions and Future Expectations

In recent years, comprehensive surveys of library and museum collections have led to a vision for a new joint-use facility. This facility would further extend and preserve the mission of both of these important Rocky Mountain cultural heritage institutions. Such an endeavor will require deep collaboration between the museum and the libraries both from a collection standpoint as well as a service and delivery standpoint as we look to tie the facility and its preservation capabilities for collections to an immersive space that transcends both museums and libraries and offers a bridge to knowledge encompassing both of these unique collections.

The Cockerell collections held in the museum and library continue to uncover additional opportunities for collaboration on research and joint public programming highlighting nature films taken by Cockerell that have never been shown publicly. Future plans include deep-dive retreats among museum and library staff in order to uncover more of these joint programming opportunities that will continue to drive research visits to our physical and online facilities—all while both organizations continue to support research, scientific workflows, and educational missions of the two cultural heritage institutions.

Endnotes

1. University of Colorado Boulder, Museum of Natural History, https://www.colorado.edu/cumuseum/.
2. Advancing Digitization of Biodiversity Collections (ADBC) Program, National Science Foundation Directorate for Biological Sciences, https://www.nsf.gov/publications/pub_summ.jsp?WT.z_pims_id=503559&ods_key=nsf15576.
3. University of Colorado Boulder, University Libraries, https://www.colorado.edu/libraries/.
4. University of Colorado Boulder, https://www.colorado.edu/.

5. "State Support for Higher Education per Full-Time Equivalent Student," National Science Board, Science and Engineering Indicators 2018, State Indicators, Alexandria, VA: National Science Foundation (NSB-2018-1), 2018, https://www.nsf.gov/statistics/state-indicators/indicator/state-support-for-higher-education-per-fte-student/table.
6. Günter Waibel and Ricky Erway, "Think globally, act locally: library, archive, and museum collaboration," *Museum Management and Curatorship* 24:4, 323–35 (2009), https://doi.org/10.1080/09647770903314704.
7. Theodore Dru Alison Cockerell Papers Finding Aid, University of Colorado Boulder University Libraries, accessed on December 22, 2018, https://archives.colorado.edu/repositories/2/resources/752.
8. Leonard Krishtalka and Philip S. Humphrey, "Can Natural History Museums Capture the Future?," *BioScience* 50, issue 7 (July 1, 2000): 611–17, https://academic.oup.com/bioscience/article/50/7/611/354777.
9. T.D.A. Cockerell Collection, University of Colorado Boulder, University Libraries, Museum of Natural History, and Film Studies faculty, https://cudl.colorado.edu/luna/servlet/CUB~11~11.
10. CU Collections Management Group, University of Colorado Boulder, https://www.colorado.edu/group/cu-cmg/.
11. Andrew Hill et al., "The Notes from Nature tool for unlocking biodiversity records from museum records through citizen science," ZooKeys 209, The National Library of Medicine, 2012, https://doi.org/10.3897/zookeys.209.3472.
12. T. G. Mortensen, "State Funding: A Race to the Bottom," American Council on Education, Winter 2012, https://www.acenet.edu/the-presidency/columns-and-features/Pages/state-funding-a-race-to-the-bottom.aspxc (site discontinued).

Bibliography

Hill, Andrew W., Robert Guralnick, Arfon Smith, Andrew Sallans, Rosemary Gillespie, et al. "The Notes from Nature tool for unlocking biodiversity records from museum records through citizen science." ZooKeys 209. The National Library of Medicine. 2012. https://doi.org/10.3897/zookeys.209.3472.

Krishtalka, Leonard, Philip S. Humphrey. "Can Natural History Museums Capture the Future?" *BioScience* 50, issue 7 (July 1, 2000): 611–17. https://academic.oup.com/bioscience/article/50/7/611/354777.

Mortensen, T. G. "State Funding: A Race to the Bottom." American Council on Education. Winter 2012. https://www.acenet.edu/the-presidency/columns-and-features/Pages/state-funding-a-race-to-the-bottom.aspxc (site discontinued).

National Science Board. "State Support for Higher Education per Full-Time Equivalent Student." Science and Engineering Indicators 2018, State Indicators. Alexandria, VA: National Science Foundation (NSB-2018-1). 2018. https://www.nsf.gov/statistics/state-indicators/indicator/state-support-for-higher-education-per-fte-student/table.

National Science Foundation Directorate for Biological Sciences. Advancing Digitization of Biological Collections (ADBC) Program. https://www.nsf.gov/publications/pub_summ.jsp?WT.z_pims_id=503559&ods_key=nsf15576.

University of Colorado Boulder. CU Collections Management Group. https://www.colorado.edu/group/cu-cmg/.

———. Museum of Natural History. https://www.colorado.edu/cumuseum/.

———. University Libraries. Theodore Dru Alison Cockerell Papers Finding Aid. Accessed December 22, 2018. https://archives.colorado.edu/repositories/2/resources/752.

Waibel, Günter, and Ricky Erway. "Think globally, act locally: library, archive, and museum collaboration." *Museum Management and Curatorship* 24:4 (2009): 323–35. https://doi.org/10.1080/09647770903314704.

CHAPTER 6

Restoring Indigenous Heritage:
Building Community through Tribal Partnerships at the Glenn A. Black Laboratory of Archaeology

Jennifer A. St. Germain, Kelsey T. Grimm, and April K. Sievert

> The Glenn A. Black Laboratory of Archaeology (GBL) at Indiana University (IU) combines a research laboratory, museum, and library. Along with over five million artifacts representing the archaeology of Indiana and the Midwest, the GBL also houses extensive photographic collections and archival materials documenting the history of archaeological work in the region and the heritage of its indigenous peoples. Over the past few years, the GBL has been working to digitize, preserve, and disseminate these collections online and has built up a broad and diverse community around them in the process. This includes not only partners in IU Libraries Digital Collections Services (DCS) but also

students, tribal partners, and other cultural heritage institutions. Projects highlighted include digitization of the Great Lakes-Ohio Valley Ethnohistory collection and the GBL's historic archaeological image collection. Continued conversations with project collaborators will help the GBL and the broader academic community better understand how to manage digital heritage projects in an environment that increasingly embraces open access policies. This chapter discusses both the challenges and opportunities of such collaborations and their potential for lasting impact on institutional practices in higher education.

Introduction

Despite the name, the Glenn A. Black Laboratory of Archaeology (GBL)[1] at Indiana University is more than a laboratory, encompassing many of the features and activities of a larger museum institution. As a repository of archaeological material, the GBL houses over five million artifacts representing the archaeology of Indiana and the Midwest. It is also home to the James H. Kellar Research Library and the Erminie Wheeler-Voegelin Archives. Together, the GBL's extensive collections of artifacts, photographs, films, field records, maps, and archival materials document the history of archaeological work in the region and the heritage of its indigenous peoples. Despite the size and scope of these collections, and like many other cultural heritage institutions, the GBL functions with a relatively small staff and operating budget. Prior to 2018, the GBL had few full-time staff positions; library, archive, and other collections-focused positions were filled mainly by part-time professional staff, student workers, and volunteers. The GBL has worked to overcome labor shortfalls and supplement resources by pursuing grant funding and creative collaborations to help improve access to its collections.

Indiana University itself is home to vast collections of library, archive, and museum materials, and with over 200 research centers and institutions[2] produces and stewards invaluable resources for education, scholarship, and community engagement; yet most collections across the university are kept administratively and physically separate. While IU Libraries[3] administers most library centers as well as the University Archives,[4] many museum collections, including the Glenn Black Laboratory, operate under the Office of the Vice Provost for Research[5] (OVPR). Until recently, research collections were effectively siloed within these and other administrative units.[6] This separation hinders the potential for knowledge generation across repositories and impedes the development of a cohesive strategy for building infrastructure and sharing collections information. The emergence of digital technologies has helped break down the walls of these silos, with the IU Libraries pioneering efforts to digitize, publish, and aggregate collections online. Over the past few decades, they have developed the models and services that continue to be more broadly extended to other IU collections[7]. The wider sharing of professional knowledge and services across administrative boundaries has been instrumental in recent efforts to publish GBL collections online. This foundation has opened up new possibilities for collaborative projects extending beyond the university, especially to the indigenous communities seeking greater access to their cultural heritage resources.

The work of sharing greater access to GBL collections has involved a broad community, one that connects the expertise of university library professionals, museum collections and curation staff, tribal partners, students, and other scholarly researchers. With diverse knowledge and experiences, this community has also brought to the forefront key considerations in how digital ethnographic and archaeological collections are published. While much work remains to be done, this chapter describes initial and ongoing efforts at the GBL that have involved this community collaboration and focus particular attention on the digitization of a unique archival resource, the Great Lakes-Ohio Valley Ethnohistory Collection.

Building Digital Capacity

To digitize and describe collections with limited resources and staffing, the university has proved to be a critical environment for the GBL. Our parent institution provides skilled student labor, professional resources, and the technical infrastructure required for disseminating and preserving digital collections. The IU Libraries has a long history of developing and supporting digital projects across campus.[8] The Digital Library Program (DLP) was founded in the mid-nineties as a joint initiative of the IU Libraries and University Information Technology Services and was an early adopter of Fedora repository architecture. Early efforts were focused on the creation, maintenance, and dissemination of digital library projects, including building custom platforms and digitizing collections in support of digital humanities scholarship. The DLP eventually moved from a project-based to a more service-focused approach and was re-conceptualized as Digital Collections Services[9] (DCS). The DCS works with students, faculty, and staff across the IU campus, offering consultation, training, and support for new and continuing digital projects. Although DCS continues to manage and maintain the repository infrastructure and technical support for digital collections, the work of content selection, digitization, and overall project management have shifted more toward participating scholars and repositories. The DCS repository currently houses over 100 digital collections that cover a variety of formats, including images, manuscripts, and sheet music.[10] With massive amounts of these humanities and cultural heritage collections across university campuses, library units alone cannot be expected to meet the demand for building digital collections. A model of consultation and support for digital projects appears far more feasible, allowing digital library staff and collections staff to contribute their relevant expertise. These collaborations help bridge disciplinary boundaries, creating learning opportunities and professional development for all partners.

Despite the pioneering efforts of the IU Libraries in support of digital collections, the GBL began exploring and taking advantage of these services only a few years ago. From its founding in 1965 until 2013, the mission of the lab "remained stable" by focusing on providing an "excellent research environment for scholars" and devoting a "significant portion of Laboratory resources" to curation services for archaeological material.[11] Other significant collections held by the lab, including the ethnohistoric archives, photographic collections, maps, and other resources received far less attention. Although a few projects were directed toward cataloging, digitizing, and long-term preservation of these collections, most were not completed, did not use standard protocols for digitization, neglected to include crucial documentation and metadata, and largely remained undiscoverable to anyone beyond GBL staff. Starting in 2013, with administrative changes, an expanded mission that included improving visibility[12] and the hiring of at least part-time staff who were trained in library and information science, these collections started to gain much-needed attention. New projects were aimed at digitizing these collections, not just for long-term preservation but also to provide increased access for research and public programming. These efforts required reaching out beyond the GBL for assistance from the DCS and IU Technology Services, helped build new relationships with tribal partners, enlisted and trained IU graduate students, and helped establish a more open and receptive atmosphere for research both within and outside the campus community.

Opening Archives

One of the more significant sources held at the GBL, the Great Lakes-Ohio Valley Ethnohistory (GLOVE) collection,[13] was also one of the first to be reinvigorated through a digitization project. The GLOVE collection comprises a unique assemblage of records gathered by researchers at Indiana University under contract with the Department of Justice between 1953 and 1965. Erminie Wheeler-Voegelin directed a research staff that acquired, assembled, and organized a vast number of primary resources, including explorer accounts, letters, lists, histories, trade documents, and military orders. Series in the collection include microfilm, transcribed documents, maps, court dockets, and index materials. These 469 linear feet of resources, reaching back to the fifteenth century, document the movements of native peoples throughout the region, providing significant historic details, geographic information, and indigenous names of people and places. The most requested materials belong to the Tribal History Document series. Consisting of approximately 158,000 individual pages, this series is arranged into seventeen broad tribal groups that actually represent at least fifty-nine distinct federally recognized tribes in the US and up to twenty Canadian First Nations (figure 6.1). Originally aggregated as evidence in the Indian Claims Commission land suits, the GLOVE collection continues to be an invaluable resource for these descendent tribes and other scholars interested in the history and heritage of the region.[14] For example, researchers can access a wealth of information on seasonal migrations, original place names, traditional uses of plants and animals, as well as study the interactions of early explorers, settlers, and indigenous peoples. Writing for the *Indiana Magazine of History* in 2003, a group of historians and archivists said of the GLOVE, "This collection is unique in scope, spanning over three hundred years of Native-Euroamerican relations, and it is one of the most comprehensive collections of ethnohistoric data in existence for Indian groups" and "the depth and breadth of the information contained in it is staggering, and it is one of the single most important achievements of historical research on early America...."[15]

FIGURE 6.1. GLOVE Tribal History Document Series at the GBL.

Despite its vast potential for cultural heritage research, only a few items from the GLOVE had been transcribed and made available through the GBL website; wider access to the collection and to original documents was otherwise limited to in-person visits. In 2015, a newly established summer research fellowship brought Ben Barnes, second chief of the Shawnee Tribe of Oklahoma,[16] to the GBL to work with the GLOVE collection. Conversations with then GBL librarian, Wayne Huxhold, brought this issue to the forefront. Limited access not only impairs research in general but particularly impacts the core tribal communities whose heritage is documented in the collection and who were historically removed from the region. Many descendent tribes now reside at great distances, with prohibitive time and travel costs required to access the physical collection in Indiana. Digitizing these materials and making them freely accessible online would help restore these histories to the communities they most directly represent.[17] Consultations with DCS about options for digitizing and hosting the collection online shortly followed. Archives Online, an established and well-supported platform hosted at IU, was chosen as the most expedient and cost-effective solution for providing description and access to the GLOVE collection online.

Archives Online[18] is dedicated to describing archives and other special collection materials from units and repositories across the IU campus. Hosted collection guides function as digital finding aids, built using the XML Encoded Archival Description (EAD) standard. Online finding aids can be encoded with varying levels of description, including collection level, folder level, and item level. Individual files, including digitized pages from the GLOVE collection, can thus be directly linked to item-level descriptions. Uploaded master TIFF files are automatically saved to the Scholarly Data Archive[19] (SDA), a high-performance storage system at Indiana University designed for long-term digital preservation. Derivative JPEG files are also automatically created and used as access copies for online research and download. Technical infrastructure, including quality control for uploaded files, is managed by the DCS while the editing and encoding of finding aids are managed by individual repositories.

Despite having this existing platform in place for building digital access to the GLOVE, the GBL had little in the way of funding or staff to make any digitization project a reality. To at least describe and digitize the Tribal History Document series for the Potawatomi tribes, the Citizen Potawatomi Nation[20] (CPN) joined the GBL to create the first collaborative digitization project. The CPN agreed to pay a per-document fee for digitizing the material. The GBL then worked to recruit graduate students from the IU Department of Information and Library Science[21] (ILS), many of whom already had training and experience in handling archival materials and coding finding aids with EAD. Under this agreement, GBL staff would also research the original GLOVE collection sources, pulling together a complete bibliography and providing links to any full-text resources already available. This bibliographic work was compiled on Zotero citation software and shared fully with CPN researchers. This model for funding a digital finding aid, digitizing materials, and conducting bibliographic research was later adopted by the Eastern Shawnee Tribe of Oklahoma[22] for work on the Shawnee Tribal History Documents also contained in the GLOVE collection. Initial conversations with Ben Barnes about limited access to heritage research materials had finally been translated into a solution for the Eastern Shawnee. In reference to this project, Barnes wrote, "The digital age has brought our history to our door, and we must step through and re-contextualize the narratives of our Shawnee people."[23]

Image Collections Online

Our initial collaboration with the DCS and tribal partners to digitize the GLOVE collection opened the door to pursue other digital collections projects. The historic image collection[24] at the GBL is one that had seen inconsistent or inadequate preservation and digitization attempts over the years. The collection consists of at least 30,000 items covering a variety of formats, including slides, negatives, prints, and glass plates. The images cover almost a century of history, offering insight into early archaeological fieldwork, excavation techniques, artifact collections, and key figures in the development of the profession. The collection as a whole had never been fully inventoried, let alone appropriately described. Most efforts at digitizing items from this collection appeared to be ad hoc and with no comprehensive cataloging or organization scheme used to manage the digital files. Digital copies and other derivative files were scattered across multiple folders on an internal shared server, with no accompanying metadata or documentation to identify people, places, or objects represented. Fortunately, the images had been retained in their original formats and in their original protective sleeves. Although not of archival quality, most of these sleeves included detailed captions that could be used for more descriptive cataloging.

With the help of an NEH Preservation Assistance Grant[25] awarded in 2015, the GBL began rehousing, inventorying, and preparing to digitize the historic image collection. Besides preserving these items for the long term, a key goal of the project was to provide greater access to these images across and beyond the IU community. Image Collections Online[26] (ICO) was originally built by the IU Libraries' former Digital Library Program and continues to be managed and supported by the new DCS unit. ICO publishes a wide number of historic photograph collections across campus and mirrors the system architecture used for Archives Online with similar cataloging features, quality control, preservation of master files in the SDA, and automated creation of derivative access copies.

The historic image digitization project ended in 2019 after four years with over 10,000 images cataloged and uploaded to ICO, close to 3,000 of those openly accessible. The bulk of these images had never been widely available before, and the collection has since sparked interest for additional research, public exhibitions, and student projects. The collection captures not only significant artifact collections and excavation techniques of the past but also depicts decades of student involvement in archaeological field schools led by Glenn Black. The significant participation of women in this field over the past century is also revealed through these photographs (figure 6.2). This realization and the wealth of historical imagery inspired the staff of the GBL to develop an in-house exhibit focused on the contributions of women to archaeology and to further organize a poster session at the 2017 Midwest Archaeology Conference[27] themed around this topic.

FIGURE 6.2. 1954 excavations at Angel Mounds site (GBL.S1701).

The GBL has also expanded its image collections on ICO to include digitized maps. A survey of tribal partner needs conducted by the GBL in 2017 revealed that maps were one of the most sought-after resources for heritage research.[28] Ethnographic maps included in the GLOVE collection cover Native American and Euro-American settlements in the Indiana and Ohio Valley regions and can be particularly useful for studying early trail systems, land use, and migration patterns. The map digitization project was originally initiated as a digital companion to a GBL-hosted map exhibit, *Mapping Indiana Territory: Exploring Indigenous and Western Representations.* An IU library student was engaged to digitize and upload a collection of related ethnographic maps to ICO. To complete the project, the GBL reached out to the IU Libraries, which provided access to their large-scale map scanner and technical assistance by map librarian, Theresa Quill. When the IU Libraries upgraded their map scanner in 2018, the GBL acquired their previous equipment in order to continue the map digitization project as staffing and resources permit. Since beginning collaborations in 2013, the GBL has benefited greatly from the resources and support of the IU Libraries and the DCS unit in particular. They have provided technical assistance, helped develop new projects, participated in workshops designed for our tribal partners, and contributed valuable supporting documentation for grant applications.

Lessons Learned

Work on these digital collection projects at the GBL has relied on close collaboration from an extended community, one that continues to grow professionally and learn from each other. Digital projects involving archaeological and ethnographic materials come with a particular set of ethical considerations, ones that may conflict with contemporary open access models. For instance, the historic image collection held by the GBL covers a broad history of archaeological work, including the photographic documentation of human burials. The excavation and collection of indigenous remains have a long and contentious history. With the 1990 passage of the Native American Graves Protection and Repatriation Act (NAGPRA),[29] federally funded institutions were required to inventory their collections for human remains and certain cultural items and to consult with federally recognized Native American tribes for repatriation of these materials. Consultations with tribes initiated through the IU NAGPRA[30] unit promoted a deeper understanding of the cultural sensitivities of GBL staff. Ethical considerations have been extended to the documentation of human remains and associated funerary items, and the GBL now restricts the online publication of moving or still images that depict ancestors and their belongings.

With these considerations in mind, the GBL still needs to properly digitize and catalog sensitive images as part of our overall collections preservation plan. An ideal digital collections platform would allow for a public description of sensitive items and preservation of digitized files but keep the image content restricted from public view. Although the ICO platform had not been originally designed with this capability, the GBL and DCS developed a workaround that allowed the digitized images to be preserved but required that both the images and their descriptive catalog information be kept in an unpublished "pending completion" state. As mentioned before, over 10,000 images have been cataloged on ICO but only 3,000 have been made public. Although the conditions may be less than ideal, the architecture built and maintained by the DCS will preserve both the images and their metadata for the long term and will allow these records to be migrated to future platforms that may contain more nuanced functionality for culturally sensitive items.

Another barrier to complete open access to digitized materials relates to the nature of archaeological work itself. The GBL archives and library contain over 280 linear feet of research reports, archival materials, and other forms of "grey literature" that often precisely document the locations of archaeological sites. Publishing these locations online invites site looting, which not only endangers site integrity but also violates the 1979 Archaeological Resources Protection Act (ARPA).[31] This act deepened the previous protections for archaeological resources; expanded penalties for selling, purchasing, and trafficking illegally obtained archaeological materials; and required that managers of archaeological information keep precise site locations confidential. Although the IU Libraries hosts a digital institutional repository, IUScholarWorks,[32] for document collections, this ARPA requirement prevents the GBL from publishing reports and other historical documents there without first redacting information that reveals site locations. The publication of these reports remains another potential project between the GBL, libraries, and other members of our extended community aimed at unlocking another valuable resource on the history and heritage of the region.

The manuscript and image collections at the GBL conform to many well-established standards for library and archival description, resulting in a clear path for cataloging and dissemination through the digital platforms managed by DCS. However, the GBL artifact collections, which consist of five million items described in over 300,000 records, pose special challenges for description and digital repository access. These materials represent a long history of artifact collecting and description, from eighteenth- and nineteenth-century antiquarian acquisition to more professional methods of excavation and analysis developed in the twentieth century. The identity and value of these artifact collections are also multifaceted. They possess wide appeal as museum objects for public exhibition and education but also exist as crucial data for ongoing archaeological research. An ideal digital repository would be able to describe and represent these materials adequately for a range of audiences and uses online. Exploratory consultation between GBL staff and IU Libraries has revealed a number of ongoing concerns and issues with meeting these needs with existing library systems. Developing a new and more comprehensive repository platform, one that can handle not only the collections of the GBL but other artifact collections around campus is one possible solution. Until these collections can be more fully described and accessible online, they will remain largely invisible to the public, including the indigenous communities whose material culture these collections represent.

Going Forward

Digitization of the GLOVE collections remains ongoing. Work completed on the Shawnee Tribal History Document series in 2019 with the help of grant funding[33] through the Institute of Museum and Library Services (IMLS). The GBL is also actively pursuing other grant opportunities to fund a more comprehensive digitization project covering all fifty-nine tribes included in the GLOVE collection. Future directions for our collaborations may also include developing a more integrated platform for incorporating tribal perspectives. A number of recent studies and digital archive projects have brought greater attention to the inherent needs and sensitivities for indigenous heritage collections.[34] For instance, the GLOVE collection consists entirely of Euro-American source material, sharing a one-sided perspective on the history and heritage of the indigenous people it documents. Incorporating indigenous perspectives into the description of materials and even the openness of content is a key goal for the GBL and our partners. The Mukurtu[35] platform, a digital collections management system specifically designed for co-curating indigenous collections, is one such solution. This open-source software provides an environment in which tribal partners can further annotate and contextualize materials, enriching the collections with their own oral traditions and perspectives. Mukurtu also includes protocols for granting or restricting various levels of access to particular documents and information, allowing for traditional knowledge practices to be honored and culturally sensitive materials to be better managed.

Collaborative and co-curated collections built using Mukurtu, such as the Plateau Peoples' Web Portal based at Washington State University,[36] can at least serve as useful models for managing and sharing collections at the GBL and more broadly for other cultural heritage collections throughout the Indiana University system. We plan to continue our valuable partnerships with our tribal partners and the IU Libraries' DCS unit to pursue further grant funding, help inform the publication of heritage collections, and develop more digital collections platforms that reflect growing community involvement. For the GBL, the idea of restoring indigenous heritage suggested by the title of this chapter extends beyond creating greater digital access for descendent communities. Indiana means "Land of the Indians,"[37] reflecting the region's former status as the western frontier of America and its long history of Native occupancy. We hope that opening our collections through these digital collaborations will also help to restore a deeper understanding of the state's indigenous heritage to a broader public.

More recent developments at Indiana University will also help better integrate and connect disparate collections. Turning a greater focus on comprehensive management of collections, the university has now established an Office of the Executive Director of University Collections and completed construction of a centralized collections storage facility to mitigate overcrowding in repositories. Also, in the fall of 2019, IU announced the merger of the Glenn A. Black Laboratory of Archaeology with the Mathers Museum of World Culture. The newly formed IU Museum of Archaeology and Anthropology (IUMAA) aims to become "a world-class museum whose collections and research resources, dynamic exhibits, engaging and accessible programming, and other outreach efforts will make it a leading destination for scholars, students, and the public."[38] The use of emerging technologies to provide greater and more innovative access to collections is a key goal for this combined institution. Much like the GBL, the Mathers Museum has worked closely with IU digital collection services and related units to share collections online and develop other educational resources. The new IUMAA will have an even greater capacity to attract and develop these valuable community partnerships around collections, both within and beyond the university community.

Endnotes

1. Glenn A. Black Laboratory of Archaeology, Indiana University, https://gbl.indiana.edu/.
2. "Research at IUMAA," Indiana University, https://iumaa.iu.edu/research/index.html.
3. Indiana University Libraries, https://libraries.indiana.edu/.
4. University Archives, Indiana University, https://libraries.indiana.edu/university-archives.
5. "Learn about the offices that oversee research activities at IU," Research, Indiana University Bloomington, https://research.iu.edu/about/research-units/index.html.
6. Lisa M. Given and Lianne McTavish, "What's Old Is New Again: The Reconvergence of Libraries, Archives, and Museums in the Digital Age," *The Library Quarterly* 80, no. 1 (January 2010): 7–32.
7. "Indiana University Libraries Strategic Plan 2016–2020," Indiana University Bloomington, 2016, Objective 2.4.
8. David E. Fenske and Jon W. Dunn, "The VARIATIONS Project at Indiana University's Music Library," *D-Lib Magazine* (1996).
9. "Digital Collections Services," Indiana University Libraries, https://libraries.indiana.edu/digital-collections-services.
10. H. Zhang, M. Durbin, J. Dunn, W. Cowan, and B. Wheeler, "Faceted Search for Heterogeneous Digital Collections," *Proceedings of the ACM/IEEE Joint Conference on Digital Libraries* (2012), 425–26.
11. "Report of the Director: Summary of the years 1996 to 2007," Glenn A. Black Laboratory of Archaeology, Indiana University Bloomington, 2008, 1.
12. "Glenn A. Black Laboratory of Archaeology Strategic Plan, 2013–2016," Glenn A. Black Laboratory of Archaeology, Indiana University Bloomington, 2013, Objective 1.3.
13. "Great Lakes-Ohio Valley Ethnohistory Collection [finding aid]," Archives Online at Indiana University.
14. Benjamin Barnes, "Becoming Our Own Storytellers: Tribal Nations Engaging with Academia," in *Eastern Shawnee Tribe of Oklahoma: Resilience through Adversity*, ed. Stephen Warren (Norman, OK: University of Oklahoma Press, 2017), 223.
15. John M. Glen, Alan F. January, Suzanne K. Justice, Glenn L. McMullen, and Saundra Taylor, "Indiana Archives: Indiana Before Statehood," *Indiana Magazine of History* XCIX, no. 3 (2003): 263–79.
16. Shawnee Tribe, http://www.shawnee-tribe.com/.
17. Kimberly Christen, "Opening Archives: Respectful Repatriation," *The American Archivist* 74, no. 1 (2011).
18. Archives Online at Indiana University, http://webapp1.dlib.indiana.edu/findingaids/.
19. "About the Scholarly Data Archive (SDA) at Indiana University," Knowledge Base, Indiana University Bloomington, 2020.
20. Citizen Potawatomi Nation, https://www.potawatomi.org/.
21. Department of Information & Library Science (ILS), Luddy School of Informatics, Computing, and Engineering, Indiana University, https://ils.indiana.edu/.
22. Eastern Shawnee Tribe of Oklahoma, https://www.estoo-nsn.gov/.
23. Barnes, "Becoming Our Own Storytellers," 223.
24. "Image Collections," Glenn A. Black Laboratory of Archaeology, Indiana University Bloomington, https://gbl.indiana.edu/collections/image-collections.html.
25. Dru E. McGill and Melody K. Pope, "Planning, Supplies, and Training for the Rehousing and Storage of the GBL Photographic Collection (#PG-233564-16)," National Endowment for the Humanities, 2015.

26. Image Collections Online at Indiana University, http://webapp1.dlib.indiana.edu/images/public-index.htm.
27. Leslie Drane and Kelsey T. Grimm, "Women at Work: Acknowledging Women's Legacy in Archaeology" (2017 Midwest Archaeological conference).
28. April Sievert, Wayne Huxhold, and Jennifer St. Germain, "Experimenting with an American Indian Resources and Services Portal," Indiana University New Frontiers Experimentation Fellowship, 2016.
29. Native American Graves Protection and Repatriation Act (Public Law 101-601; 25 U.S.C. 3001-3013).
30. Office of the Native American Graves Protection & Repatriation Act website, Indiana University Bloomington, https://nagpra.indiana.edu/.
31. Archaeological Resources Protection Act of 1979, 16 U.S.C. §§ 470aa–470mm (1979).
32. IUScholarWorks: Indiana University's Institutional Repository, Indiana University Libraries, https://scholarworks.iu.edu/dspace/.
33. "MN-00-17-0009-17," Institute of Museum and Library Services, 2017.
34. See Kimberly Christen, "Gone Digital: Aboriginal Remix and the Cultural Commons," *International Journal of Cultural Property* 12, no. 3 (2005); Timothy Powell and Larry Aitken, "Encoding Culture: Building a Digital Archive Based on Traditional Ojibwe Teachings, in *The American Literature Scholar in the Digital Age* (Ann Arbor: University of Michigan Press, 2010); Yale Indian Papers Project, Native Northeast Portal, https://nativenortheastportal.com/.
35. Mukurtu CMS, Center for Digital Scholarship and Curation at Washington State University, https://mukurtu.org/.
36. Plateau Peoples' Web Portal. Washington State University's Center for Digital Scholarship and Curation, https://plateauportal.libraries.wsu.edu/.
37. "Indiana, n," OED Online, December 2019, Oxford University Press, derived etymologically from "Indian" used in reference to the Native peoples of the Americas.
38. Indiana University Museum of Archaeology and Anthropology, https://iumaa.iu.edu/.

Bibliography

Archaeological Resources Protection Act of 1979, 16 U.S.C. §§ 470aa–470mm (1979).

Archives Online at Indiana University. Indiana University. Accessed February 5, 2020. http://webapp1.dlib.indiana.edu/findingaids/.

Barnes, Benjamin. "Becoming Our Own Storytellers: Tribal Nations Engaging with Academia." In *Eastern Shawnee Tribe of Oklahoma: Resilience through Adversity*, edited by Stephen Warren, 217–27. Norman, OK: University of Oklahoma Press, 2017.

Christen, Kimberly. "Gone Digital: Aboriginal Remix and the Cultural Commons." *International Journal of Cultural Property* 12, no. 3 (2005): 315–45. https://doi.org/10.1017/S0940739105050186.

———. "Opening Archives: Respectful Repatriation." *The American Archivist* 74, no. 1, 185–210. Accessed February 5, 2020. https://doi.org/10.17723/aarc.74.1.4233nv6nv6428521.

Citizen Potawatomi Nation. Accessed February 5, 2020. https://www.potawatomi.org/.

Drane, Leslie, and Kelsey T. Grimm. "Women at Work: Acknowledging Women's Legacy in Archaeology." Session at the 2017 Midwest Archaeological Conference. Accessed February 6, 2020. https://www.midwestarchaeology.org/gallery/WomenAtWork.

Eastern Shawnee Tribe of Oklahoma. Accessed February 5, 2020. https://www.estoo-nsn.gov/.

Fenske, David E., and Jon W. Dunn. "The VARIATIONS Project at Indiana University's Music Library." *D-Lib Magazine* (June 1996). http://mirror.dlib.org/dlib/june96/variations/06fenske.html.

Given, Lisa M., and Lianne McTavish. "What's Old Is New Again: The Reconvergence of Libraries, Archives, and Museums in the Digital Age." *The Library Quarterly* 80, no. 1 (January 2010): 7–32. https://doi.org/10.1086/648461.

Glen, John M., Alan F. January, Suzanne K. Justice, Glenn L. McMullen, and Saundra Taylor. "Indiana Archives: Indiana Before Statehood." *Indiana Magazine of History* XCIX, no. 3 (2003): 263–79. Accessed February 5, 2020. https://scholarworks.iu.edu/journals/index.php/imh/article/view/12009.

Glenn A. Black Laboratory of Archaeology. "Glenn A. Black Laboratory of Archaeology Strategic Plan, 2013–2016." Indiana University Bloomington. Report maintained by the institution.

86   Chapter 6

———. Office of the Vice Provost for Research. "Great Lakes-Ohio Valley Ethnohistory Collection [finding aid]." n.d. Archives Online at Indiana University. Accessed February 6, 2020. http://purl.dlib.indiana.edu/iudl/findingaids/ewv/VAD1751.

———. Office of the Vice Provost for Research. "Image Collections." Indiana University Bloomington. Accessed February 5, 2020. https://gbl.indiana.edu/collections/image-collections.html.

———. "Report of the Director: Summary of the Years 1996 to 2007." Indiana University Bloomington. 2008. Report maintained by the institution.

Image Collections Online at Indiana University. Accessed February 6, 2020. http://webapp1.dlib.indiana.edu/images/public-index.htm/.

Indiana University. Luddy School of Informatics. Computing, and Engineering, Department of Information & Library Science (ILS). Accessed February 5, 2020. https://ils.indiana.edu/.

———. University Archives. Accessed February 5, 2020. https://libraries.indiana.edu/university-archives.

Indiana University Bloomington. "About the Scholarly Data Archive (SDA) at Indiana University." Knowledge Base. 2020. Accessed February 5, 2020. https://kb.iu.edu/d/aiyi.

———. "Glenn A. Black Laboratory of Archaeology." Accessed February 5, 2020. https://gbl.indiana.edu/.

———. "Learn about the offices that oversee research activities at IU." Research. n.d. Accessed February 6, 2020. https://research.iu.edu/about/research-units/index.html.

———. Office of the Native American Graves Protection & Repatriation Act. Accessed February 6, 2020. https://nagpra.indiana.edu/.

Indiana University Libraries. Accessed February 5, 2020. https://libraries.indiana.edu/.

———. "Digital Collections Services." Digital Collections Services. July 2, 2019. https://libraries.indiana.edu/digital-collections-services.

———. "Indiana University Libraries Strategic Plan 2016-2020." Indiana University Bloomington. 2016. Accessed February 6, 2020. https://libraries.indiana.edu/document/iub-libraries-strategic-plan-pdf.

Indiana University Museum of Archaeology and Anthropology. Accessed February 7, 2020. https://iumaa.iu.edu/.

Institute of Museum and Library Services. "MN-00-17-0009-17." July 13, 2017. https://www.imls.gov/grants/awarded/mn-00-17-0009-17.

IUScholarWorks: Indiana University's Institutional Repository. Indiana University Libraries. Accessed February 6, 2020. https://scholarworks.iu.edu/dspace/.

McGill, Dru E., and Melody K. Pope. "Planning, Supplies, and Training for the Rehousing and Storage of the GBL Photographic Collection (#PG-233564-16)." Funded Projects Query. National Endowment for the Humanities. 2015. Accessed February 6, 2020. https://securegrants.neh.gov/publicquery/main.aspx?f=1&gn=PG-233564-16.

Mukurtu CMS. Center for Digital Scholarship and Curation at Washington State University. Accessed February 6, 2020. https://mukurtu.org/.

Native American Graves Protection and Repatriation Act (Public Law 101-601; 25 U.S.C. 3001-3013) (1990).

OED Online. "Indiana, n." December 2019. Oxford University Press.

Plateau Peoples' Web Portal. Accessed February 5, 2020. https://plateauportal.libraries.wsu.edu/.

Powell, Timothy, and Larry Aitken. "Encoding Culture: Building a Digital Archive Based on Traditional Ojibwe Teachings." In *The American Literature Scholar in the   Digital Age*, edited by Amy E. Earhart and Andrew Jewell, 250–74. Ann Arbor: University of Michigan Press, 2010. http://dx.doi.org/10.3998/etlc.9362034.0001.001.

Shawnee Tribe. Accessed February 5, 2020. http://www.shawnee-tribe.com/.

Sievert, April, Wayne Huxhold, and Jennifer St. Germain. "Experimenting with an American Indian Resources and Services Portal." New Frontiers Experimentation Fellowship, Indiana University. 2016. Proposal maintained by Glenn A. Black Laboratory of Archaeology.

Yale Indian Papers Project, formerly, now Native Northeast Portal. Accessed February 7, 2020. https://nativenortheastportal.com/.

Zhang, H., M. Durbin, J. Dunn, W. Cowan, and B. Wheeler. "Faceted Search for Heterogeneous Digital Collections." *Proceedings of the ACM/IEEE Joint Conference on Digital Libraries* (2012), 425–26. Accessed February 6, 2020. https://doi.org/10.1145/2232817.2232924.

CHAPTER 7

Building Bridges:
A Case Study in Community Engagement Between the Art Museum and the Library System at West Virginia University

Sally Brown and Carroll Wetzel Wilkinson

> *Though sometimes seen as competitors in an era of continuously diminishing financial resources, galleries, libraries, archives, and museums (GLAM) all navigate into the future seeking innovative ways to engage with relevant issues of higher education while influencing learning and reaching new audiences. Since complications can arise over turf wars, questions of ownership, or access to adequate resources, causing rifts, the development of a collaborative project can provide a roadmap, a fresh start, and a relationship-building opportunity. This case study provides the steps taken to build a positive relationship between a campus library (West Virginia University Libraries) and a campus art museum (the Art Museum of West Virginia University) through a collaboration that benefits the larger campus and city community through the development of a public art guide. The chapter outlines a model for a collaboration between two cultural heritage organizations. This case study shows a way forward for two cultural heritage organizations to reach out to new audiences with a strong and collaborative partnership.*

Introduction

While campus libraries and campus art museums both share the mission of attending to cultural heritage on campuses, they do so in unique ways. Their common mission can lead to misunderstandings and turf wars, and their differences in approach can make collaboration challenging.

This case study provides the steps taken to overcome past tensions and build a positive relationship between a campus library (West Virginia University Libraries) and a campus art museum (the Art Museum of West Virginia University) through a collaboration that benefitted the larger campus and the city in which it is located. The chapter outlines an evolutionary process of programmatic development of the libraries alongside the long-anticipated opening of the campus art museum. This evolution required intention, proactivity, persistence, and the right staffing for change to happen. What resulted is an opportunity for the libraries and art museum to serve the people of West Virginia through the publication of a public art guide that enhances the tourism and sense of self for the city of Morgantown. This case study fully explains the implementation of this project in the hope that other interested library and art museum partnerships can replicate it.

West Virginia University, its Art Museum, and the University Libraries System in Context

West Virginia University is a public, land-grant institution, founded in 1867. It is located in Morgantown, West Virginia. It holds the R1 classification (highest research activity) as described by the Carnegie Classification of Institutions of Higher Education. WVU System enrollment is 29,933: Potomac State College in Keyser, 1,300; WVU Tech in Beckley, 1,794; and the Morgantown campus, 26,839. Students at the Morgantown campus come from 118 nations, all fifty US states (plus DC), and all fifty-five West Virginia counties; 12,811 are West Virginia residents. WVU's land grant status means that the spirit of public engagement infuses all its courses, programs, and out-of-classroom learning experiences.[1]

Within the city limits of Morgantown, the population is 30,549 plus the students, but in the surrounding areas, the population of the county is 105,612.[2,3] The arts offerings in the community have evolved with an arts council formerly certified in 2014 and the Art Museum opening in 2015. Local galleries have supported the area's talent, including the Monongalia Arts Center, Appalachian Gallery, Morgantown Art Association, and Morgantown Art Party. Downtown Morgantown offers a regular Arts Walk. Music and theatre offerings include The Metropolitan Theatre, Mainstage Morgantown, and the WVU Clay Performing

Arts Center.[4] The Greater Morgantown Convention and Visitor's Bureau website boasts, "Local love for the arts has grown into artisan markets, high-production theatre performances, social art projects, and city-beautification through painted murals and sculpture. Many residents wonder how they will leave their mark on Morgantown, without even realizing the mark that it will leave on them."[5] The art guide collaboratively produced represents a growing evolution of collectivity in this community as will be described.

WVU Libraries

The WVU Libraries encompassed seven libraries statewide in 2018. Library history began in 1902 in Stewart Hall, now the central administrative offices of the university. In the fall of 1931, the library moved to its own building on the Downtown Morgantown campus. Facilities in Morgantown now include the Downtown Campus Library, Evansdale Library, Health Sciences Library, Law Library, the West Virginia and Regional History Center, and the book depository. Onsite collections include more than 1.8 million books, more than 400,000 e-books, and 117,000 e-journals.[6] Offsite holdings include over one million volumes and a variety of archival boxes, films, and court records.[7]

FIGURE 7.1. Downtown Campus Library, Courtesy WVU Libraries

West Virginia and Regional History Center

Mission statements in various histories of the West Virginia and Regional History Center, which is the special collections arm of the West Virginia University Libraries, do not mention art collecting directly. But the phrase "other historical information resources regardless of their format" does appear in early drafts of the mission. Now the mission is: "The WVRHC collects, preserves, and provides public access to materials that show the history and culture of West Virginia and the central Appalachian region." In practice, beginning before the 1950s, the "all formats" notion was in use and art acquisition was underway if the subject or the artist was related to the state of West Virginia. This was in part because the university did not yet have an art museum of its own. But it happened as well because of the interests of archival curators and the generosity of donors who wished to advance the understanding of the cultural and social history of the state. So, over six decades, the libraries amassed a significant collection of paintings, sculptures, and other artistic creations.

College of Creative Arts

Beginning in the 1960s, the WVU College of Creative Arts established the WVU Permanent Art Collection, a separate collection with the mission of supporting the teaching of the college. In 1991, this collection was transferred to the WVU Libraries for administration, cataloging, and preservation and thus integrated the West Virginia and Regional History Center collection. In 1998, the collections separated again, with the WVRHC focusing on West Virginia art and a historical perspective and the WVU Permanent Art Collection focusing on collecting fine art to serve as the foundation of an art museum collection. A curator, hired in 2000, separated and cataloged the collection, which remained housed in the WVU Libraries facility. There were some complications, as cataloging for an archive differs from that for a fine art museum.[8] Overall, the administrative authority changed from art to libraries and back, creating a long-term challenge for collaborative programming and future cooperation.

Art Museum of West Virginia University

In 2009, the founding director of the Art Museum of West Virginia University was hired.[9] A collections agreement was created in 2013 between the two campus organizations to distinguish each other's missions and collecting practices.[10] The evident back-and-forth of the collection and location demonstrates an unavoidable tension over ownership that has lasted decades.

Some items in the art inventory held by the University Libraries were transferred to the Art Museum collection before it opened in 2014. However, some remained in the libraries in cases to support West Virginia Regional History Center user research. Tensions existed between the Libraries and the Art Museum during this period of transfer; and some disagreements about what should be where were not resolved.

The Art Museum of WVU (under the College of Creative Arts) was dedicated and opened its doors on August 25, 2015. The facility includes two art galleries totaling approximately 5,400 square feet of exhibition space built to environmental standards to safely display fine art, a collection research and study room for examination of fine art, a collection storage area to securely protect and preserve fine art, lobby space to orient museum visitors, and a university classroom with electronic technology for twenty-five students.[11]

A New Beginning
Early Efforts to Build Collaboration Between the Libraries and the Museum

In 2015, the new WVU dean of libraries engaged the new Art Museum director and the WVU Libraries strategic initiatives director in conversations about ways to build bridges between the two cultures of the museum and the libraries. He saw common needs between the two institutions, including an imperative to reach out to new audiences and a shared concern for educational programming.

This led to hiring a consultant. At first, the library and museum leaders decided to set up representative groups from both constituencies. They brought them together in the fall of 2015 for a facilitated day of exploration about possible collaborative crossover programs facilitated by the consultant. Many excellent ideas came forward, including a panel discussion with English faculty, who discuss how art has influenced their writing and art faculty who talk about how books have influenced their art, and a public conversation about the history of libraries and museums in different cultures, with a speaker to stimulate thinking around economics, power, inclusion, knowledge, and art.

For a variety of reasons, none of these ideas came to fruition. The consultant's final report recommended that the art museum and libraries' representatives take a year to experiment with modest innovations. He suggested emphasizing West Virginia treasures with special appeal to the non-university community. His ideas included an afternoon of storytelling or short story reading based on West Virginia themes and writings and using artworks to set contexts. He also suggested that the WVU faculty "can make compelling connections to the museum and libraries" through course assignments and discussions that would bring students to the libraries and museum. Perhaps the most successful of the ideas floated during all these exploratory years was "developing living engagements with regional arts and artists in the libraries."[12]

The WVU Art in the Libraries program was initiated in 2014 with a mission to fill the empty walls of the three main campus libraries.[13] Several exhibitions took place in the three main campus libraries, all coordinated by this committee of librarians. The committee set forth with great initiative for this cause, bringing in prominent photography exhibits and purchasing art for the buildings. New outdoor banners promoted "Art in the Libraries" during this year (which also happened to coincide with the Art Museum opening) and the first large exhibition housed in the libraries called *Fractured Spaces*.

As the program expanded, a need for a permanent position for the work of exhibits coordination became apparent and the dean created an exhibits coordinator position. This position was not conceived as a librarian position but instead as an exhibits coordinator bringing a strong arts background, a willingness to foster intra-library collaboration, and contributing an overall creative perspective to the work.

In 2017, the libraries hired its first arts and exhibits coordinator. Among many other programmatic initiatives, she has organized online and print exhibitions of the work of regional artists in the libraries, in-person and virtual panel discussions with connections to library exhibitions on globally important subjects, and screenings of documentary films by West Virginians followed by well-attended discussions to name just a few of the programs to date. While this programming has not directly intersected with the WVU Art Museum, it has energized the community's understanding of what a library can do through art to stimulate thought and expand the creative uses of library spaces.

Setting the Stage for the Case Study

What *has* intersected with the Art Museum and has come to complete fruition in a university/community context is the Public Art Guide. It represents an innovative and effective bridge between the libraries and the art museum.

While the WVU dean of libraries in 2014 established a sense of urgency for the Art in the Libraries program, those implementing his vision were responsible for the successful realization of the program.[14] Their use of guiding coalitions to lead important components of the Public Art Guide in 2017–18 was an essential ingredient of the effective collaboration that fostered the guide's development. Included were the members of the Art in the Libraries Committee, the director of the strategy and planning in the Dean's Office, critical staff in the library dean's business office, the new interim dean and dean, and, most importantly, the exhibits and program coordinator for WVU Libraries. Later, in the implementation phase of the project, representatives for the Greater Morgantown Convention and Visitor's Bureau, Arts Monongahela (the local arts council), the College of Creative Arts School of Art and Design, the WVU Community Engagement

Program, and an AmeriCorps employee working for Clio were all instrumental in bringing the project to fruition.

Exhibits Coordinator

The exhibits coordinator who was hired was an art history graduate who worked with the art museum in her graduate studies. She recognized this relationship was essential, necessary, and positive for both parties and their constituents. She was also unaware of the past complexities described earlier. She knew that the shared resources, potential audiences, and the possibility of real impact when working together on projects held great promise. Finally, her fresh—and perhaps naïve—perspective helped remedy the fractured relationship.

One of the first things the new exhibits coordinator did was to re-evaluate the Art in the Libraries mission to examine the libraries' resources and their differentiation from other cultural organizations on campus, such as the art museum, to avoid duplication of initiatives or unintentional competition. Purchasing art was removed from the mission. In collaboration with the members of the Art in Libraries Committee, membership in the committee was expanded to include art faculty.

The interim (now dean) of the libraries was fully supportive of proposing new initiatives to the Art Museum for collaboration.[15] The exhibits and program coordinator's guidance of these coalitions, such as leading important components of the Public Art Guide, was essential in the effectiveness of the collaborations that fostered the guide's development. This collaborative technique is useful in any results-oriented collaboration in the GLAM community.

Public Art Guide Collaboration Begins

To encourage positive relations, with the libraries' director of strategy and planning, the exhibits coordinator developed several project ideas to bring to the art museum director. These ideas included a modest bookshelf at the art museum using libraries' art books around art, artists, and exhibitions to achieve a deeper grasp of the art or artists' work on display; collaborative online/digital exhibitions using both organizations' collections and resources; similarly collaborative programming; cross-promotion; an art book club; and a community art guide.

These ideas were brought to the then-director of the art museum who took a keen interest in the community art guide project. It was agreed that this would benefit our organizations, help with camaraderie, and serve as an opportunity for statewide outreach. With no other online or print documentation of public art in the area, and no funding between us for such an endeavor, it was an ambitious first project to take on. Combining the status of the art museum as the only land-grant, university art museum in the state with the rich resources and culture of documenting and disseminating information of the libraries, it seemed an apt fit and direction despite its enormity.

The partnership expanded for outreach effectiveness to include Arts Monongahela (the city arts council) as well as the College of Creative Arts School of Art and Design to round out the perspectives. This multiplied the benefits both internally and externally. Also during this time, the director of the art museum retired and an interim director was appointed. All of these changes made the project more complex and demanded strong coordination.

In effect, this coordination then moved beyond literal agreements to shared creation. As authors Diane M. Zorich, Gunter Waibel, and Ricky Erway assert in their 2008 report, "Beyond the Silos of the LAMS: Collaboration Among Libraries, Archives and Museums," the collaboration continuum they outlined below moved literally from contact to cooperation to coordination to collaboration to convergence.[16] What happened in creating the public art guide was that information was shared with investment, risk, and benefit, ultimately creating something new that was not there before, a transformation of both institutions.

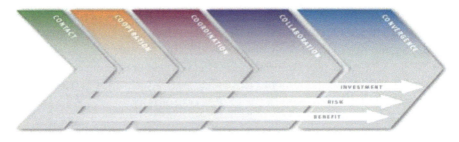

FIGURE 7.2. Collaboration Continuum, from Zorich, Diane; Waibel, Gunther and Erway, Ricky. "Beyond the Silos of the LAMS: Collaboration Among Libraries, Archives and Museums." OCLC Research, 2008. http://www.oclc.org/research/publications/library/2008/2008-05.pdf

The Nuts and Bolts of Creating the Public Art Guide

The partners discussed the parameters of defining public art. It was decided that going forward, public art would be defined as publicly accessible outdoor artwork or sites—no aesthetic valuing would be determined by this project. A preliminary list of public artworks in Morgantown was outlined by the exhibits coordinator while researching and pointing to various examples of aspirational art guides. Online versus print was also discussed, and the group decided both were necessary and important. For the online version, a connection was made with Clio, an educational website and mobile application that guides the public to thousands of historical and cultural sites throughout the United States.[17] A local AmeriCorps employee helps people research and add sites and tours to their interactive websites, so we decided to go that route to get us started.

A student intern of the exhibits coordinator started this process, and a group of volunteer students from a community service class helped with the preliminary research. Involving students multiplied the impact as well, as they were doing local research, visiting sites, and making observations and creative decisions.

As none of the partners had funding for such an endeavor, the libraries applied for grants to support the design, printing, and dispersal of this significant new project throughout the state. After a first unsuccessful attempt, WVU's Community Engagement Grant awarded the libraries funding for the printing and dispersal of the Public Art Guide.[18] However, the project still lacked funding for the design.

The exhibits coordinator, in attempting to utilize university resources, asked for a graphic design student to design the guide over the summer with the information gathered from the community service students in the spring semester. Unfortunately, though initial meetings proved hopeful, in the end, the student did not come through and the exhibits coordinator had to pull the project and go with a professional. The art museum and the libraries banded together with a little pool of funding, thought outside the box, and invited the Greater Morgantown Convention and Visitors Bureau (GMCVB) on board as a partner. Its new members were immediately thrilled and happy to help with this process.

The exhibits coordinator found a small local design firm that immediately took on this now complex and last-minute project. With the concept, ideas, and multi-layered and scattered information, the firm turned it around in one week with a stellar draft that was on the way to the finished product.

The exhibits coordinator and the interim director of the art museum worked closely on the edits, with help from the other partners. The process then turned to the dispersal through the community; certainly, it became clear that not just the museum and the library would hold these copies. The GMCVB offered to house and disperse several thousand at their site. WVU Libraries would disperse sets to each of the sites listed on the guide as well as email them about their inclusion with a link to the new page on the GMCVB website, where it would live (as the GMCVB counts its site visitors and likely gets the most tourist traffic).

Moreover, the director of Arts Monongahela had the idea to mail single copies to a few hundred local business and political and other community leaders to inform them personally about this truly collaborative and dynamic project. Arts Monongahela agreed to sponsor this mailing. WVU Libraries also sent similar letters to university deans, associate deans, and campus organizational directors to let them know about this outreach to the state. Again, in sharing information, something new was created—beyond the Guide, a transformation of institutions away from silo culture.

96   Chapter 7

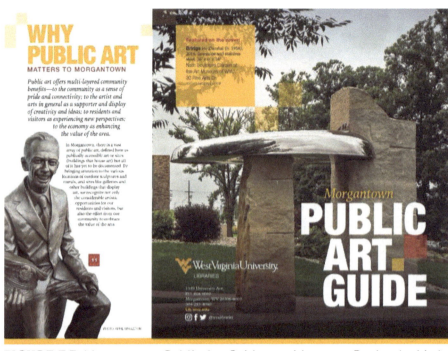

FIGURE 7.3. Morgantown Public Art Guide outside cover. Design by Little Fish Designs. Courtesy WVU Libraries.

FIGURE 7.4. Morgantown Public Art guide inside pocket. Design by Little Fish Designs. Courtesy WVU Libraries.

FIGURE 7.5. Morgantown Public Art Guide inside map. Design by Little Fish Designs. Courtesy WVU Libraries.

The GMCVB planned a winter annual celebratory event and invited WVU Libraries to partner and launch the guide officially at this event. There was a built-in launch and celebration, with dispersal and promotion that were done in-house. Also, Arts Monongahela agreed to manage and sustain the project by editing and maintaining future iterations, thereby turning the project over to the community.

Conclusion: Potential for Future Collaborations

While we tried very hard with various ideas to initiate collaboration, the only one that succeeded initially was the Public Art Guide. The aforementioned ideas are documented for future use. The art museum has since hired a new permanent director who is supportive of this project and continues open communication to build our momentum. In fact, since the project was completed, the museum's art educator has become part of the Art in the Libraries Committee, and the two organizations have collaborated on programming ideas, including the spearheading of a Campus Art Crawl.

Though different spaces with different specific missions, the museum and the libraries share foundational commonalities of vision. Officially, we share a common university administration and mission. We both celebrate and honor culture and heritage through the dissemination of information. We both have missions that support the teaching, research, and service missions of our university. We both want to enrich our community through our work, and with so many cuts for the arts and heritage organizations, collaboration can bring a greater impact both for our organizations and for our communities. Moreover, by collaborating we share each other's expertise and thus advance each other's fields. Lastly, we can have pride in working with other intelligent, competent colleagues in our university system.

Of course, there must be balance between goals and operational integrity as well as mutual knowledge of the roles for execution. In the best of collaborations, each organization must have the self-confidence and generosity to share the spotlight and credit. Both must be open to a two-way influence and sometimes even a lack of control. Each partner must be willing to exchange currencies, whether these are finances, inspiration, task, position, or relationship.

This case of the Public Art Guide has exemplified that one important thing worked in this collaborative effort. Reflecting on the tense history, the new position, and reaching out and moving forward with new ideas, we will continue initiatives so that great things, like the Public Art Guide, can happen.

Though Arts Monongahela took the responsibility of sustaining the Public Art Guide, we are involved in the process of updating the print and online editions over the next couple of years. In a similarly cooperative and transparent process—this time at the lead of a community organization in collaboration with the University Libraries—such a cohort could present a new case study. It is significant to point out that the libraries initiated a project that the community will build and that can build the community. With collaboration, resourcefulness, and grit, there are countless opportunities that can make impacts beyond spaces and entities.

Endnotes

1. "WVU Facts," West Virginia University, last updated 2019, https://www.wvu.edu/about-wvu/wvu-facts.
2. US Census Morgantown, 2019, https://www.census.gov/quickfacts/morgantowncitywestvirginia.
3. US Census Monongalia County, 2019, https://www.census.gov/quickfacts/monongaliacountywestvirginia.
4. "Visit Mountaineer Country: To Your Arts Content," Visit Mountaineer Country, https://www.visit-mountaineercountry.com/to-your-arts-content/.
5. "Visit Mountaineer Country," Greater Morgantown Convention and Visitor's Bureau, https://www.visitmountaineercountry.com/morgantown/.
6. "About," West Virginia and Regional History Center, last updated 2019, https://wvrhc.lib.wvu.edu/about.
7. Karen Diaz, email message to Sally Brown, October 5, 2020.
8. This history is based on the readings of a confidential business file in the Administrative Offices of WVU Libraries.
9. Bernadette Dombrowski, "Founding director of Art Museum of WVU to retire in July," College of Creative Arts News & Events, West Virginia University, May 14, 2018, https://arts.wvu.edu/news/2018/05/14/founding-director-of-art-museum-of-wvu-to-retire-in-july.
10. Unfortunately, this agreement was never formally implemented. From the authors' perspectives, it would be important to revisit this in the future.
11. "Facilities," Art Museum of West Virginia University, last updated 2018.
12. From David Carr, "The Libraries and the Art Museum at West Virginia University," consultant report, November 16, 2015, 4, on file in the office of the Dean of Libraries, West Virginia University.
13. The mission was written by the original committee chair, Alyssa Wright, with heavy input from the initial librarians on the Art in the Libraries committee.
14. The concepts of "sense of urgency" and "guiding coalitions" come from the work of John P. Kotter, *Leading Change* (Boston: Harvard Business Review Press, 2012).
15. The dean who instigated the Art in the Libraries committee left WVU in 2017, after which this project came about, under the leadership of the interim and now dean.
16. Diane Zorich, Günter Waibel, and Ricky Erway, *Beyond the Silos of the LAMs: Collaboration Among Libraries, Archives and Museums* (Dublin OH: OCLC Research, 2008), https://www.oclc.org/content/dam/research/publications/library/2008/2008-05.pdf.
17. To read more about The Clio App, see Chris Plattsmier, "Q&A: The Clio App," Humanities Ebook (article discontinued).
18. Community Engagement grants, formerly known as Public Service grants, are designed to stimulate and support community outreach and engagement projects that benefit the citizens of West Virginia and are available to faculty members. Funding from this program is intended to encourage development of additional support for these projects from other sources in the future as well as scholarly output. Funding is provided by the Provost's Office. The WVU Faculty Senate Service Committee recommended support for our proposal and it was administered by the WVU Provost's Office.

Bibliography

American Library Association. Committee on Archives, Libraries and Museums (CALM). American Library Association Institutional Repository. 2018. http://www.ala.org/.

Batykefer, Erin, Laura Damon-Moore, and Christina Jones. The Library as Incubator Project. 2007. http://www.libraryasincubatorproject.org/.

Deupi, Jill, and Charles Eckman. "Prospects and Strategies for Deep Collaboration in the Galleries, Libraries, Archives, and Museums Sector," *Academic Art Museum and Library Summit* no. 1 (January 2016).

Kotter, John P. *Leading Change*. Boston: Harvard Business Review Press, 2012.

OCLC Research. *Hanging Together* (blog), 2018. http://hangingtogether.org/.

Plattsmier, Chris. "Q&A: The Clio App." Humanities Ebook (article discontinued).

Society of American Archivists. 2018. https://www2.archivists.org/.

Waibel, Günter. "Collaboration Contexts: Framing Local, Group and Global Solutions." OCLC Research, 2010. https://www.oclc.org/content/dam/research/publications/library/2010/2010-09.pdf.

Zorich, Diane, Günter Waibel, and Ricky Erway. *Beyond the Silos of the LAMS: Collaboration Among Libraries, Archives and Museums*. Dublin, OH: OCLC Research, 2008. http://www.oclc.org/research/publications/library/2008/2008-05.pdf.

CHAPTER 8

Editing Wikipedia at Vanderbilt:
How Library-Art Gallery Collaboration Can Benefit Learning Beyond the Classroom

Mary Anne Caton and Joseph Mella

> Since its launch in 2001, Wikipedia has promoted itself as an encyclopedia of all knowledge for all users. As the project has grown, passing six million English-language articles in January 2020, it has come to occupy a unique place in the culture of teaching and learning. Vanderbilt University Libraries and the University Art Gallery collaborated to develop Wikipedia editing sessions, known as edit-a-thons, to teach students how their classroom learning can reach broader audiences and add measurable quality to an all-volunteer encyclopedia. Editing articles about objects and artists in the Gallery's collection allows students to hone their research and critical-thinking skills, creating the kind of autonomous, open-ended learning central to students-as-producers concepts in pedagogy. This collaboration between two parts of the university in this programming, as well as classroom Wikipedia instruction, have begun to connect curricular and co-curricular aspects of learning across many departments.

101

Introduction

Vanderbilt University Libraries (VUL) and the Vanderbilt University Fine Arts Gallery (UFAG) have developed a series of collaborative Wikipedia editing programs (edit-a-thons) that blend collection-centered learning and digital scholarship. This chapter addresses the collaboration among faculty, gallery staff, the libraries' Wikipedian-in-Residence, undergraduate student workers, and Wikipedians (as editors are called) from Vanderbilt's campus and in Nashville and Davidson County. This case study addresses two- and three-dimensional art objects in the collection of Vanderbilt University's Fine Arts Gallery, the growth of Wikipedia at Vanderbilt, and the potential for future programming.

Wikipedia Background

The encyclopedia founded in 2001 by Jimmie Wales aims to be the sum of all human knowledge.[1] Despite its acknowledged information gaps and controversies, the use of Wikipedia has become ubiquitous. Written by passionate volunteers, the English language encyclopedia now includes over six million articles as of January 2020 and gets over 200 million daily page views as the fifth most-used internet source globally.[2] The five pillars of Wikipedia noted here provide basic structure and clarification for editors: (1) it is an encyclopedia; (2) [it is written with a] neutral point of view; (3) its content is free for anyone can use, edit, and distribute; (4) editors should treat each other with civility and respect; and (5) there are no firm rules.[3]

Since its development in 2013, the Wiki Education Foundation has built tools and developed models for "connecting communities in the new form of knowledge synthesis that is Wikipedia."[4]

As Wikipedia Librarian Jake Orlowitz and OCLC Program Officer Merrillee Proffitt argue, libraries and Wikipedia are natural partners in collaboration.[5] Academic libraries are one pillar of the GLAM (galleries, libraries, archives, and museums) community preserving cultural heritage for interpretation by scholars, students, and other communities. GLAMs all manage and interpret their cultural resources to serve diverse audiences and connect communities.[6] Since 2011, The Wikipedia Library (TWL) promotes collaboration between Wikipedia and libraries with the goal of enlarging the community of practice around both groups.[7] The International Federation of Library Associations 2016 (IFLA) whitepaper proposed ways for academic libraries to strengthen collaboration between Wikipedia and GLAMs to support research across multiple frameworks.[8] Wikipedia editing skills offer librarians professional development for teaching digital information literary, collaborative knowledge production, and community-building through outreach highlighting their collections.[9] As more information is summarized and cited on Wikipedia, the role of libraries in managing the discovery and citation process becomes more important. Teaching collaborative content production between libraries and galleries helps students use materials and skills integral to their classroom learning to advance the encyclopedia's mission "to share knowledge with the world and all of its people."[10]

Wikipedia in the Classroom

While every undergraduate has Wikipedia stories in their past, they are often horror stories of high school teachers railing against the encyclopedia. At university, this perception lingers for many students, until they are surprised and empowered to learn the effect of their edits. Once students understand the process of editing, Wikipedia becomes not only the place where they can find resources but also a site where their knowledge can make a difference. Wikipedia relies on the verifiability of reliable sources to make articles transparent.

Writing for Wikipedia offers students clear ways to take action that matters in their world. Students have a greater role and responsibility in creating new knowledge and in understanding the contours and the changing dynamics of the world of information.[11]

Editing Wikipedia allows them to share their knowledge, battle fake news, correct underrepresentation of topics they care about, and flex their growing information literacy skills. As they edit, students learn that their writing process involves the evaluation of sources, inquiry, and response, all of which speak to the 2016 librarians' *Framework for Information Literacy for Higher Education.*[12]

Wikimedia Foundation, the independent, tax-exempt entity managing Wikipedia, Wikimedia Commons, and other wiki projects, created Wiki Education in 2013 to "connect higher education to Wikipedia, ensuring that the world's most-read source of information is more representative, accurate, and complete."[13] Wiki Education has supported instructors at more than 500 universities that have incorporated creating new content for Wikipedia into their curricula. Students gain twenty-first-century skills, including media literacy, writing and research development, and critical thinking, while content gaps on Wikipedia are filled as a result of students' contributions. These efforts have resulted in more new content than was contained in the last print edition of Encyclopædia Britannica. Work at Vanderbilt has included both single-session edit-a-thons and classroom work with an embedded instructor.

Wikipedia at Vanderbilt

While Vanderbilt has several faculty teaching with Wikipedia and participating on an administrator level, the Vanderbilt University Libraries' work developing a recurring program dates to 2013. Clifford Anderson piloted a Wikipedia project that year. The 2013–2014 Special Collections Topics in Wikipedia Fellow

104 Chapter 8

identified articles to improve using unique special collections materials and working with curators, faculty, and librarians. Two edit-a-thons held that year on global connections and on Vanderbilt's built environment resulted in uploads of Special Collections images of campus buildings and small improvements to pages.

Since joining the libraries in 2014, Mary Anne Caton has built a roster of repeating Wikipedia programs aimed at building a more active community of editors. Programs for librarians include 1Lib1Ref, and a Citation Hunt using

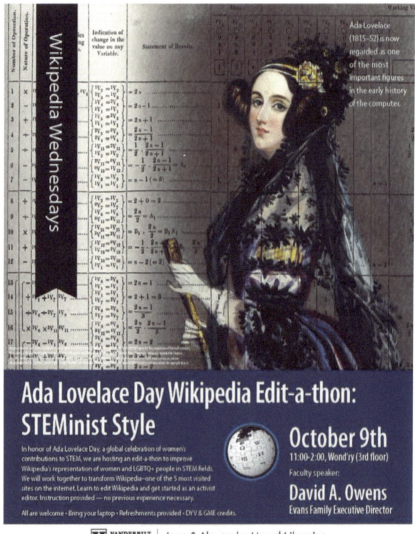

FIGURE 8.1. 2019 Ada Lovelace Day Edit-a-Thon Poster by Carla Beals

Wikimedia's Citation Hunter bot. In 2019–20, edit-a-thons included Asian Month in November, Open Access Week in October, Ada Lovelace Women in STEM in October, and Women of Peabody and ART+FEMINISM in March. (See figure 8.1, Ada Lovelace Women in STEM poster, Carla Beals.)

Caton's role as Wikipedian in Residence fits the libraries' work teaching information literacy. The libraries' mission to serve "the university's goal of advancing scholarship and learning… partnering with faculty and students to shape research, and [encouraging] the development of informed scholars and engaged citizens" aligns with the University's vision as a "center for scholarly research, informed and creative teaching and service to the community at large. Vanderbilt… [leads] in the quest for new knowledge through scholarship, dissemination of knowledge through teaching and outreach, and creative experimentation of ideas and concepts." Wikipedia outreach at the libraries grew from two works by the Digital Scholarship team led by Clifford Anderson and from Teaching and Learning work led by Melissa Mallon, director of Teaching and Learning. We want our students to succeed as productive global citizens, so our teaching and learning goals address the digital skills, real-world impact, and larger conversations that students have as Wikipedia editors. The writing and editing they do for courses and at events allow them to hone their critical-thinking skills and analyze the quality of sources and varied perspectives embedded in each article.

FIGURE 8.2. Architecture and Built Environment Edit-a-Thon at Special Collections, Vanderbilt Libraries, October 2017

Wikipedia events initially housed in Special Collections have branched out across campus. In 2014–15, DiSC staff and librarians partnered with faculty to host seven events: Edit-a-Thons for International Open Access Week, Women in Architecture, ART+FEMINISM, Citation Needed, Comédie Française Hackathon, Sites of African Memory at NPL, and an off-site event at TSU (figure 8.2). In all, these events resulted in over thirty-five usernames being created and over seventy articles edited. In 2016–2017, despite staff changes in DiSC, we collaborated on six events and presented our Nashville work with TSU and NPL's African American Collections at the National Public History Conference. In 2018, Open Access edit-a-thons moved to the Digital Humanities Center.

Edit-a-thons (or EaTs) revolve around editing for a specific theme or campaign. Vanderbilt Libraries joined the annual March ART+FEMINISM (A+F) campaign and has participated since 2015. We showcase recent scholarship about feminist art and artists and partner with the Department of History of Art to bring important feminist art historians to speak at A+F. Our edit-a-thons have two goals: to create new editor-activists and inspire them to continue editing about topics they value. We introduce topics with a faculty overview based on their work followed by training in how to edit and then hands-on editing.

Peabody College celebrated its 100th Anniversary in 2019–2020 with varied programming and events coinciding with Nashville's celebration of the centennial of the Nineteenth Amendment. The Women of Peabody Edit-a-Thon on March 18, 2020, aims to improve coverage of key women associated with the college. Faculty speaker Catherine Gavin Loss, associate dean for academic affairs and professional education at Peabody College, discussed Women, Education, and Politics on Southern women's political activism on suffrage, their access to education, and Peabody's activists.

University Fine Arts Gallery

The gallery's 8,000-object collection includes notable holdings in Old Master paintings, works of art on paper, Asian art, Meso-American art and artifacts, American paintings, and modern photography. The libraries' growing Wikipedia program, begun in 2013, hosts and develops five to six annual edit-a-thons about Wikipedia campaigns like ART+FEMINISM, Open Access, and Asian culture. Other edit-a-thons cover topics such as Nashville landscapes, African American history, and Public Domain Day in response to local interests, community suggestions, and university programming. Wikipedian-in-Residence Mary Anne Caton teaches edit-a-thons for individual classes, most recently for medicine, health and society, and historic Black Nashville, as well as providing tutorials by appointment and teaching boot camps and drop-in hours. Many faculty members incorporate Wikipedia editing into their coursework and assignments. Students feel empowered when they use their course learning and critical thinking to improve one of the world's most-used encyclopedias. Indeed, recent research has shown that editing Wikipedia helps students hone their analytical and critical-thinking skills by evaluating how to edit or improve a page by adding text, images, or recent resources.[14]

Vanderbilt students are not alone in their response to Wikipedia's goal of transparency, which is often expressed as "all knowledge for and by all." They see that their classroom learning, when added to the encyclopedia, brings deep and varied knowledge to bear on many academic subjects. By adding their understanding of topics, students can make real improvements to pages that are read and consulted by large numbers of users, in contrast to the few readers of an exam or team paper.

Wikipedia Project for Collections

The model for the gallery project blends students' work as students of art history with Wikipedia's goals of improving article quality. Caton designed a framework for students that helped them assess article quality and where the gallery's collections could be included on Wikipedia. This inversion of structure helped students evaluate their familiarity with art historical research. Working with student interns, gallery curator Margaret Walker and Mary Anne Caton helped the spring-summer intern edit content from the gallery's 2018 exhibitions on photography (Joyce Tenneson), contemporary portraiture (Everett Raymond Kunstler), as well as important collectors (Samuel H. Kress Collection) among others.

We asked students to pick artists from major collections that we preselected. Students considered the following questions about Wikipedia pages: Did artists' pages include recent exhibitions since 2000? Were key recent catalogs and books published since 2000 included in the resources section? Were open access resources used when possible? How comprehensive was coverage of major museum and gallery collections of the artist's work?

Preparing work to add to Wikipedia helped students understand how their research experience helps them make edits that improve Wikipedia. Searches for recent scholarly exhibitions, catalogs, and books published since 2000 revealed that additions of recent scholarship were easily added to relevant pages. By searching online museum and gallery catalogs, students were able to develop lists of major collections for each artist and genre. This was also repeated for regional museums and university galleries. The resulting data summaries and links were added to the relevant pages, allowing the students to write historiography of artists whose works in the gallery collection were mentioned in the context of similar institutions and recent scholarship.

Working with the UFAG collections, curator Margaret Walker and director Joseph Mella developed a series of key collections and objects to feature. Mary Anne Caton, library Wikipedian-in-residence, taught the gallery staff (including student interns) Wikipedia editing and developed templates based on art history research for article additions over a semester. Students developed a list of pages to improve that were vetted by Caton, Mella, and Walker. Improving the amount and level of detail on a Wikipedia page can improve its status in the overall structure and its frequency of use.

The first groups were Japanese woodblocks prints and modern artists. Intern Echo Sun[15] an art and psychology major, researched and developed a small exhibit installed in spring 2019 with works by Katsushika Hokusai, Utagawa Hiroshige, Tsukioka Yoshitoshi, Kiyoshi Saito, and Takahashi Hiroaki (Shotei) among others. Following this project, she will update Wikipedia articles related to her exhibit. Her work built on that of a prior intern, Tita Peterson,[16] who worked on articles about modern artists Everett Raymond Kinstler and Joyce Tenneson featured in the 2018 exhibits, and made the first updates to pages relating to Japanese woodblock prints. The initial template developed by Walker and Caton required students to use their research skills in several ways. They created a list of pages of artists and genres that would benefit from more resources and assessed the quality of the Wikipedia page using Wikipedia's internal article ranking system and their own art historical knowledge of source materials. They needed to compile a bibliography of exhibitions and new scholarly research on the subject since 2000, a list of collections with major holdings including university and college collections, and a list of any key digital history projects about the topic. By summarizing recent scholarship and key collections, students would include many useful resources for all users that made recent written and born-digital works part of articles. The gallery's collections would be included among its peers in Southern collections as well as in university collections. As many art-related pages are written around collections in large museums in New York and the Boston-Washington corridor, the relevant Wikipedia pages would show more museums and gallery collections. A future step will be adding categories to pages, which drives traffic to individual Wikipedia articles.

The trial run for this project was two-fold in the summer and during the fall semester of 2018. Edit-a-thons held at Tennessee State Library and Archives and at Tennessee Humanities were designed to teach basic editing and the Wikipedia backend to new editors at local cultural organizations. For the member groups of Humanities Tennessee, a basic editing session was held at Vanderbilt Central Library, so the staff of other libraries, museums, and departments could develop editing skills and plan how to improve Wikipedia pages related to their institutional content, whether that was graduate student fieldwork in architectural preservation or two- and three-dimensional objects in museum collections.

Our Asian Month Edit-a-Thon held in the Fine Arts Gallery on November 13, 2018, was designed to build on the basic structure Margaret Walker and I developed around Japanese woodblock prints. Edit-a-thons with broad topics like this are designed to bring new editors into Wikipedia. Wikipedia's parent, the Wikimedia Foundation, has developed the dashboard as an important tool for managing edit-a-thons and helping organizers track improvements and additions to articles. The dashboard lets organizers pre-select articles to be edited at the event, showing how an article is ranked in Wikipedia's own internal ranking system, which ranges from start-class or incomplete stub article to a fully developed and sourced article featured on Wikipedia's landing page. Importantly, the dashboard tracks sources added, a feature that makes tracking improvements easy.

For the Asian Month event, forty-eight pages related to Asian art, culture, and history were uploaded to the dashboard, including pages about Japanese woodblock, Japanese woodblock prints, and artists such as Kunisawa. The event attracted a fair turn-out of seven editors, including Asian History faculty, visual resources center staff, and four new student editors. To maximize faculty involvement, for 2019 Asian Month on Wikipedia, we are working with Asian History and Asian Language faculty as well as the Asianist art and architectural historians who were unavailable while on leave in fall 2018.

Working with new gallery director Amanda H. Hellman, Caton has developed Wikipedia as part of regular gallery programming. Since moving to the gallery in 2021, Caton continues to provide Wikipedia support for faculty and campus programs and new collaborations with the Peabody College Office of Student Engagement and Well-Being.

Students participate in Wikipedia events in two ways. All Vanderbilt students track their required immersion experiences with faculty via the campus Anchor Link system called Design Your Vanderbilt Experience (DYE) as well as their Greek member service experiences. Students swipe their IDs at events to compile a list of events they've attended over their four years. Wikipedia events are credited based on faculty involvement, which is often a short introduction to the topic of the edit-a-thon (ART+FEMINISM, Nashville preservation and landscapes, Asian history and visual culture, etc.). Several aspects of the trial succeeded while others require more sustained work as we build the program. The templates for adding recent scholarship to articles work well but require time for research and refinement.

Prior Collaboration

Library-gallery collaboration ties together both unit's exhibition programs, teaching, and outreach goals. The gallery staff collaborates with the history of art faculty for study collection visits and supports the annual Exhibiting Historic Art course in which undergraduates-as-curators interpret collections objects around a subject. The course appeals to art history majors but other arts and sciences majors in anthropology, classics, and others attend. Both units see community engagement as a core mission, whether through teaching, public programs, or other exhibitions interpreting collections.

Past collaborations between the two units included loans from each collection in support of exhibitions and shared curatorial expertise, particularly from the libraries' Bandy Center staff and doctoral student Daniel Ridge, lead curator for *The Dada Effect—An Anti-aesthetic and Its Influence*.[17] The gallery director and curator have taught in the gallery and, occasionally in Special Collections. A recent seminar on the history of printmaking was linked with the former director's exhibit surveying the gallery's woodcut collection.[18]

Staff changes at the gallery have affected its programming following curator Margaret Walker's departure in summer 2018 and director Joseph Mella's departure in spring 2019. Former curator Emily Weiner established a new schedule of exhibitions featuring more cross-campus exhibition programs from 2019 to–2021, prior to her departure. Most recently, Wikipedia components have been developed and are in process for the spring 2020 semester. The current exhibition, *Visionary Aponte: Art and Black Freedom* (2019–2020), combined twenty contemporary artists working in various media to interpret an important historical artifact now lost. Afro-Cuban revolutionary José Antonio Aponte created his "Book of Paintings" in Havana during his 1812 conspiracy trial; its maps and images of Black men as warriors, kings, and librarians formed important testimony at the trial. The exhibit programming included classroom Wikipedia teaching in organizer and historian Jane Landers's class, African Religions in the Americas. Her eight students wrote and edited articles based on the history of African religions transplanted to the Americas through the Atlantic slave trade, c. 1650–1815, emphasizing African regions of North and South America (including Aponte's Cuba, Brazil, Haiti, and the lower South of North America). Landers' course, Historic Black Nashville, co-taught with law faculty Daniel Sharfstein, enrolled eight students in a Wikipedia component centered on Black sites like Fort Negley during spring 2020. In spring 2021, we partnered with Peabody College of Education's Office of Equity, Diversity, and Inclusion and Peabody Library to start a month-long Edit-a-Thon built around *I'll Take You There: Exploring Nashville's Social Justice Sites*, co-edited by historians Learotha Williams, Jr. and Amie Thurber.[19] The event blended an authors' panel, editing, and public engagement over four weeks.

Margaret Walker's departure from the gallery in summer 2018 slowed down our work, but with the arrival of Emily Weiner in January 2019, the project was re-invigorated. Weiner's departure in June 2021 brought changes to the gallery, and for 2021-2022, Caton managed the gallery as the single full-time staff member. With Amanda Hellman's arrival as the new director in late spring 2022, we have focused greater attention on all programming including Wikipedia. Caton's new role as senior curator of campus and community engagement will allow for greater attention to Wikipedia. Our new weekly series, "Art for Lunch," includes a monthly Wikipedia event focused on Nashville public art. October

2022 featured a month-long LGBTQI Edit-a-Thon with Peabody College's Office of Equity, Diversity, and Inclusion, Peabody Library, and the K.C. Potter Center.

Intern Echo Sun's recent exhibit opened and will hopefully draw more students to the gallery. Faculty interest is high among Asian specialists (art history, history, and languages) in Wikipedia Asian Month as an annual event. These faculty members are also interested in editing materials connected to objects on campus. Students and the gallery's interns are interested in editing Wikipedia around their work for the gallery. Achieving student follow-through on articles about woodblocks proved challenging with a small group. One student editor added material to the page "Japanese pop culture" based on his experiences living in Japan as an exchange student. Another student edited the page "Americans in Japan." However, pages related to gallery collection objects: *Famous Views of the Sixty-odd Provinces, Kunisada, The Great Wave off Kanagawa, Thirty-Six Views of Mount Fuji*, and *Woodblock Printing in Japan* were not edited during the two-hour event. This has led to rethinking event length and the types of tasks for early-stage editors, whose interests in a topic may not dovetail with our goals for the gallery collection.

Creating long-term sustained editing patterns among student editors can be challenging. They are often drawn to editing familiar material as opposed to specifically chosen pages. Without academic credit attached, students are less motivated to edit topics chosen for them. The gallery's student interns and workers will hopefully build some Wikipedia editing into their work as we continue to develop portions of the collection to work on. As an aspect of navigating the digital world, we believe that Wikipedia literacy is part of the suite of digital literacy skills needed by our students. So, we are working to build Wikipedia into digital literacy discussions. Recent edit-a-thons for students in political science and Asian history have successfully added biographical material and other details to two dozen Wikipedia pages. For our GLAM colleagues who edit articles about Tennessee history and objects (Tennessee State Library and Archives, Tennessee Humanities members), our edit-a-thons have had good results training new editors who can then use the considerable knowledge of their own collections to improve the encyclopedia.

Planning future edit-a-thons will involve tailoring resources to add to Wikipedia articles as well as choosing articles related to the gallery collections. Greater faculty involvement is also important as we are promoting writing about objects, writing biography, and writing historiography. Sessions will also benefit from longer blocks of time. To attract more faculty participation, Caton is looking at graduate teaching assistants, post-docs, and other possible collaborators from our Center for Teaching and other campus hubs for writing.

Our 2019 ART+FEMINISM Edit-a-Thon focused on women artists represented in the gallery collection, including Carrie Mae Weems, Donna Ferrato, and Karen Finley. Caton reviewed and recommended articles to improve working with gallery staff and faculty. Faculty speaker Vivien Fryd discussed her book, *Against Our Will, Sexual Trauma in American Art since 1970* (2019). For 2020, ART+FEMINISM focused on the idea of activism and editing to women artists' lives and work visible. We invite participants to write about their favorite woman artist, curator, architect, photographer, or critic. Faculty Rebecca VanDiver spoke about *The Torture of Mothers: Black Reproductive Justice in Elizabeth Catlett's Prints.*

Article translation from other wikis into English Wikipedia also promotes students' expertise to improve Wikipedia. After Asian Month, Caton has been promoting translation editing with our Asian Studies faculty in hopes of building their awareness of how editing hones their students' skills. A larger project in development involves editing medical articles into needed languages, which in Nashville are Spanish and Arabic. The work we have begun with Wikipedia offers promise as we continue to build relationships with faculty across campus, in many disciplines, and in the community at large.

So how do students respond to writing for the online source most likely to have been disparaged by all their high school teachers? Once they understand the culture of the encyclopedia and their own ability to be activists writing women into the encyclopedia or improving coverage of historical figures, they dive into their work. Students in Danielle Picard's Medicine, Health and Society course, Eugenics and its Shadow, in fall 2019 "appreciated that their writing would have a longer lifespan than a traditional essay that was only read by the professor." The public writing had multiple benefits both pedagogically and personally for the students. Picard's students' articles currently have added 19,500 words and 256 references to twenty-six different articles after their semester project. Those edits have received over 297,000 views in just two months. Many students stated that they took the assignment more seriously because their work would continue to exist online for others to read. Another student added that he also liked that he could show others what he produced, including his parents. "My mom thinks it's cool," he stated in his final presentation.[20]

Wikipedia in the classroom also extends into graduate and professional schools at Vanderbilt. Dr. Jeremy Warner, before his 2022 move to Brown University, developed a month-long advanced Wikipedia elective for fourth-year medical students at Vanderbilt modeled on a similar course at UCSF (figure 8.3). October 2022 will be the fourth year of offering this elective at Vanderbilt, now co-taught by Caton, Vanderbilt Medical Center faculty Sheila V. Kusnoor, Ph.D. (Biomedical Informatics), and UCSF faculty Dr. Amin Azzam. Building this class combined Eskind Biomedical Library Director Philip Walker, Heard Library Wikipedian Mary Anne Caton, and UCSF medical faculty. Dr. Warner and his research assistant, fourth-year medical student Shervin Etemad, managed the

Editing Wikipedia at Vanderbilt 113

FIGURE 8.3. WikiMed Elective organized with Vanderbilt University Medical School, November 2019 with 4th year medical students; WikiMEd elective organizers Dr. Jeremy L. Warner, Associate Professor of Medicine and Biomedical Informatics and fourth-year medical student Shervin A. Etemad, Mary Anne Caton (Not Pictured: Philp Walker, Director, Eskind Biomedical Library)

course while Walker and Caton taught the students about medical sources and Wikipedia editing. The students' goals were to contribute high-quality content to Wikipedia to benefit patients. As Azzam has commented elsewhere, improving Wikipedia hones the students' skills evaluating and interpreting medical literature for themselves and their patients.[21] Etemad summarized the work of his seven peers like this: 24,300 words added to medicine-related pages, 209 references added, and 183,000 total views over the course of the month. Articles edited included "Bronchiectasis," "Coronary Artery Dissection," "Hypoalbuminemia," "Blue Baby Syndrome," "AV Block," "Alternative Cancer Treatments," and "Circulatory Shock." Fourth-year MD PhD student Nick Harris wrote:

> Whereas before I never fully understood what being hypoalbuminemic actually meant for my patients, now I feel like I could give a presentation on it to anyone at any time, including both patients and providers. Further, the page gets 300 visits a day, meaning that 300 readers are now getting deeper knowledge and more accessible information about the condition that is likely either affecting them or a family member. Now that I have the tools needed to edit Wikipedia, a presence in the

community of editors, and the drive to use this fantastic tool to its limit, I aim to continue to edit and engage with Wikipedia and other Medical Wikis throughout medical school and beyond.[22]

Endnotes

1. Jake Orlowitz, "The Wikipedia Library: The Largest Encyclopedia Needs a Digital Library and We're Building It," in *Leveraging Wikipedia: Connecting Communities of Knowledge*, ed. Merrilee Proffitt (Chicago: ALA Editions, the American Library Association, 2018), 69.
2. Merrilee Proffitt, *Leveraging Wikipedia: Connecting Communities of Knowledge* (Chicago: ALA Editions, the American Library Association, 2018), Introduction, 1.
3. Proffitt, *Leveraging Wikipedia*, 239; "Wikipedia: Five pillars," Wikipedia, https://en.wikipedia.org/wiki/Wikipedia:Five_pillars.
4. Proffitt, *Leveraging Wikipedia*, Introduction, 3.
5. Orlowitz, "The Wikipedia Library," 79.
6. Proffitt, *Leveraging Wikipedia*, 3.
7. Orlowitz, "The Wikipedia Library," 70.
8. Ibid., 71
9. Ibid.; Alex Stinson and Julia Brungs, "Engaging the world's libraries with Wikipedia—what are the opportunities?," International Federation of Library Associations and Institutions, September 20, 2016, accessed September 19, 2022, http://www.ifla.org/node/10871.
10. Proffitt, *Leveraging Wikipedia*.
11. *Framework for Information Literacy for Higher Education*, American Library Association, http://www.ala.org/acrl/standards/ilframework.
12. For greater detail, see Authority is Constructed and Contextual, Research as Inquiry, and Scholarship as Conversation in *Framework*, American Library Association.
13. WikiEdu, accessed February 13, 2020, https://wikiedu.org/.
14. "Wikipedia:Training/For educators/Improve research skills," Wikipedia, https://en.wikipedia.org/wiki/Wikipedia:Training/For_educators/Improve_research_skills.
15. Faith Rovenholt, "Teaching Innovation at Vanderbilt: Danielle Picard, Mary Anne Caton and Wikipedia Editing," *Center for Teaching* (blog), Vanderbilt University, accessed January 20, 2020, https://cft.vanderbilt.edu/2019/12/teaching-innovations-at-vanderbilt-danielle-picard-mary-anne-caton-and-wikipedia-editing/.
16. Vanderbilt, Class of 2022, Vanderbilt University.
17. *The Dada Effect—An Anti-aesthetic and Its Influence*, Vanderbilt University, Jean & Alexander Heard Libraries, Fine Arts Gallery, 2017.
18. Joseph Mella, Director and Curator, IUPUI, Herron School of Art and Design, Indiana University Purdue University in Indianapolis, email to the author, February 5, 2020.
19. Amie Thurber and Learotha Williams Jr., *I'll Take You There: Exploring Nashville's Social Justice Sites* (Nashville, TN: Vanderbilt University Press, 2021).
20. *Center for Teaching* (blog), Vanderbilt University.
21. Juliana Bunim, "UCSF First U.S. Medical School to Offer Credit for Wikipedia Articles," USFC.edu, September 26, 2013, accessed September 16, 2022, https://www.ucsf.edu/news/2013/09/109201/ucsf-first-us-medical-school-offer-credit-wikipedia-articles.
22. Shervin Etemad, email to author, December 9, 2019.

Bibliography

Alexa. "Top 500 Sites on the Web." Accessed February 15, 2020. https://www.alexa.com/siteinfo/wikipedia.org.

Association of College & Research Libraries. *ACRL Framework for Information Literacy for Higher Education*. American Library Association. February 2, 2015. http://www.ala.org/acrl/standards/ilframework.

Bunim, Juliana. "UCSF First U.S. Medical School to Offer Credit for Wikipedia Articles." September 26, 2013. https://www.ucsf.edu/news/2013/09/109201/ucsf-first-us-medical-school-offer-credit-wikipedia-articles.

Davis, LiAnna L. "Wikipedia and Education: A Natural Collaboration, Supported by Libraries." In *Leveraging Wikipedia: Connecting Communities of Knowledge*, edited by Merrilee Proffitt, 87–105. Chicago: ALA Editions, the American Library Association, 2018.

Doyle, Kelly. "Minding the Gaps: Engaging Academic Libraries to Address Content and User Imbalances on Wikipedia." In *Leveraging Wikipedia: Connecting Communities of Knowledge*, edited by Merrilee Proffitt, 55–69. Chicago: ALA Editions, the American Library Association, 2018.

Etemad, Shervin. Email to author. December 9, 2019.

Jean and Alexander Heard Libraries. "About the Libraries." Accessed February 13, 2020. https://www.library.vanderbilt.edu/about/.

Lih, Andrew. *The Wikipedia Revolution: How a Bunch of Nobodies Created the World's Greatest Encyclopedia*. 1ˢᵗ ed. Westport, CT: Hyperion Press, 2009.

Mallon, Melissa. Vanderbilt University Libraries, in discussion with the author. February 2020.

Mella, Joseph. Indiana University Purdue University in Indianapolis. Email to the author. February 5, 2020.

Orlowitz, Jake. "The Wikipedia Library: The Largest Encyclopedia Needs a Digital Library and We're Building It." In *Leveraging Wikipedia: Connecting Communities of Knowledge*, edited by Merrilee Proffitt, 69–86. Chicago: ALA Editions, the American Library Association, 2018.

Proffitt, Merrilee, ed. *Leveraging Wikipedia: Connecting Communities of Knowledge*. Chicago: ALA Editions, the American Library Association, 2018.

Rovenholt, Faith. "Teaching Innovation at Vanderbilt: Danielle Picard, Mary Anne Caton and Wikipedia Editing." *Center for Teaching* (blog), December 2019. Vanderbilt University. https://cft.vanderbilt.edu/2019/12/teaching-innovations-at-vanderbilt-danielle-picard-mary-anne-caton-and-wikipedia-editing/ accessed January 20, 2020.

Snyder, Sara. "Edit-a-Thons and Beyond." In *Leveraging Wikipedia: Connecting Communities of Knowledge*, edited by Merrilee Proffitt, 119–42. Chicago: ALA Editions, the American Library Association, 2018.

Stinson, Alex, and Jason Evans. "Bringing Wikipedians into the Conversation at Libraries." In *Leveraging Wikipedia: Connecting Communities of Knowledge*, edited by Merrilee Proffitt, 31–54. Chicago: ALA Editions, the American Library Association, 2018.

Stinson, Alex, and Julia Brungs. "Engaging the world's libraries with Wikipedia—what are the opportunities?" International Federation of Library Associations and Institutions. September 20, 2016. http://www.ifla.org/node/10871.

Thurber, Amie, and Learotha Williams Jr. *I'll Take You There: Exploring Nashville's Social Justice Sites*. Nashville, TN: Vanderbilt University Press, 2021.

Vanderbilt University. "Mission, Goals and Values." Accessed February 10, 2020. https://www.vanderbilt.edu/about/mission/.

Walker, Celia. Vanderbilt University Libraries in discussion with the author. February 2020.

Wikipedia. "Wikipedia:Five pillars." https://en.wikipedia.org/wiki/Wikipedia:Five_pillars.

———. "Pamela Hardt-English." https://en.wikipedia.org/wiki/Pamela_Hardt-English.

———. "Wikipedia Training For Educators." https://en.wikipedia.org/wiki/Wikipedia:Training/For_educators/Improve_research_skills.

Zorich, Diane, Gunter Waibel, and Ricky Erway. *Beyond the Silos of the LAMs: Collaboration Among Libraries, Archives and Museums*. Dublin OH: OCLC Research, 2008. https://www.oclc.org/content/dam/research/publications/library/2008/2008-05.pdf.

CHAPTER 9

Paths to Partnership:
New Models for Museum-Library Collaborations at Northwestern University

Corinne Granof

> Recent collaborations between The Block Museum of Art and Northwestern University Libraries have gone beyond the conventional borrower-lender relationship to foster partnerships and deeper dialogues between museum and library staff. This chapter considers in detail two case studies of recent extensive collaborations between The Block Museum and Northwestern University Libraries. The first case study is a research project that brought about innovative ways of understanding and presenting the work of Charlotte Moorman, a seminal but overlooked performance artist. The multi-year collaboration resulted in a major traveling art exhibition featuring archival materials, a smaller archive-focused exhibition, cross-departmental programming, and a companion publication. The second case study provided a library-based residency to Kader Attia, a contemporary French-Algerian artist based in Berlin, whose work focuses on individual and societal trauma. Attia was invited to undertake sustained research in the Melville J. Herskovits Library of African Studies and joined this with research across the Northwestern campus to create an installation and an artwork commissioned by The Block. Both projects were examples of innovative ways

to encourage new approaches to library collections and visual culture. Facilitating access to library collections through exhibitions, artist residencies, and archival-based projects, The Block Museum and University Library have aspired to work in partnership in order to bring new ways of thinking about specialized collections and to make them visible and accessible to broader audiences.

Background

The Block Museum of Art and Northwestern University Libraries are situated on the Evanston campus of Northwestern University on the shore of Lake Michigan, separated by a two-minute walk through the museum's sculpture garden. While the history of Northwestern's library extends back to 1856, five years after the founding of the university, and the Block Museum just approached its fortieth year in 2020, the two have shared a history of partnering in innovative and productive ways since the mid-1990s. Through thematic, collections-based projects, the museum and library have also created bridges between university departments and provided opportunities for museum audiences to learn about university collections.

Over the past five years, the museum and library have embarked on even more extensive collaborations that promote interdisciplinarity, which is central to Northwestern University's mission.[1] After providing background on the institution and historic connections between the library and museum, this chapter focuses on two recent partnerships. They suggest models and possibilities for further and deeper collaborations between museums and libraries as especially compatible allies and non-academic units within the university structure.[2] With its vast holdings, the library is committed to collecting and preserving materials for researchers and scholars. The museum is dedicated to teaching and learning as well as the display and interpretation of art and material culture. It also serves as a portal to university resources and a platform for bringing its collections to broader, intellectually curious external audiences. The shared ethos of providing access to, creating, and sharing knowledge provides the basis for a symbiotic relationship that serves the greater university mission.

The Block Museum of Art is primarily a space for temporary exhibitions. Originally founded as the Block Gallery in 1980, it functioned as a one-room *Kunsthalle* and did not collect artworks. It began accepting donations of art in the 1980s and 1990s, was renamed the Block Museum in 1998 by a resolution of Northwestern's Board of Trustees, and in 2008 was accredited by the American Association of Museums. The museum expanded with a second floor in 2000, but apart from the campus sculpture garden, the museum does not have galleries designated for the display of the permanent collection or long-term collection installations. Since many of the works in the collection are prints, drawings, and photographs, long-term display is not possible. The advantage is that the museum operates with open programmatic parameters, and exhibitions fluidly explore art across time, cultures, and media. Over the past few years, the museum has presented the work of contemporary artists, including Hank Willis Thomas and Wangechi Mutu, but has also explored medieval Africa and art of the 1960s in the United States. This dynamic mission and presentation of art across time and culture encourages flexible thinking and allows museum staff to work with diverse faculty in developing exhibitions and programs, and especially to work with library staff and resources.

Fundamental to The Block Museum's core mission is providing opportunities to see art and visual culture through myriad lenses. Its mission statement positions The Block as a "convener of interdisciplinary discussions in which art is a springboard for exploring issues and ideas." The Block Museum is as committed to displaying and identifying visual and material culture in the form of fragments, relics, documents, and ephemera as it is to showing historical or contemporary acclaimed artworks. The museum is dedicated to making space for and giving voice to multiple disciplines—from anthropology and African studies to psychology and materials science. Students from disciplines across the university have curated exhibitions, and such units as the School of Music and the School of Engineering have partnered with the museum in programming.

Like many major research universities, the Northwestern University Libraries have rich holdings. The Distinctive Collections division within the library encompasses the Charles Deering McCormick Library of Special Collections, the Melville J. Herskovits Library of African Studies, the Music Library, the Art Library, the Transportation Library, University Archives, and Preservation. These collections house special, archival, and other curated collections in specific subject areas, uniting rich primary, original, rare, and unique materials in traditional and digital formats—among them are text, manuscripts, photographs, film, sound, and images.

One early transformative collaborative project based on library collections took place in the mid-1990s. *William Hogarth and 18th Century Print Culture* was a faceted research endeavor, including an exhibition at The Block Museum curated by an art history graduate student seminar that featured objects from Special Collections along with a companion website that was an early model for digital interpretation.[3] The project connected faculty and students in art history with library collections and curators as well as experts in digital technology. The students also worked with faculty in art theory and practice to develop content for the website, including filmed demonstrations of printing techniques. It was one of the first extensive collaborations between the museum and the library and one of the first examples nationally of an exhibition that was extended through its presence as a website.

Since then, Special Collections has been a resource and lender. Its collections expand and complement exhibitions and flesh out narratives. The libraries' active collecting around print culture—posters, prints, books, and periodicals—make it an incredible resource for the museum and a like-minded advocate for visual culture. Several exhibitions that were organized by The Block, curated by graduate students, have drawn significantly from Special Collections. These include *Political Currents across the Channel* (2006, curated by Shalini Seshadri, with Professor Hollis Clayson) and *Philipon's* La Caricature *and the Street* (2006, curated by a class of Art History graduate students with Professor Hollis Clayson).[4] For other exhibitions organized by the Block, such as *From the Trenches to the Street: Art from Germany, 1910s–1920s* (2007), significant loans of periodicals were drawn from Special Collections to augment the artwork and provide meaningful contextual content.[5] More recently, C. C. McKee, the 2015–16 Block Museum Graduate Fellow, curated the exhibition *Keep the Shadow, Ere the Substance Fade* (2016). The exhibition used the library's recently acquired Michael McDowell Death Collection as a starting point to explore parallel mourning practices in the Victorian Era and during the AIDS crisis at the end of the twentieth century.

This chapter considers in detail two case studies of more recent extensive collaborations between The Block Museum and Northwestern University Libraries—partnerships that have inspired research, teaching, and learning. The first case study is a joint research and exhibition project that brought about innovative ways of understanding and presenting the work of a seminal but overlooked performance artist. The Charlotte Moorman project was a multi-year collaboration between the library and museum that resulted in a book and major traveling exhibition combining archival materials with artworks, film, and audio recordings. In the second case study, Kader Attia, a French-Algerian artist, who is currently based in Berlin, was invited to undertake research in the Melville J. Herskovits Library of African Studies to create an exhibition and an artwork commissioned by The Block.

These two projects expanded and synthesized the mission and strategic vision of the museum, the library, and the university. While the university mission is focused on student growth and experiences, the library and museum are similarly aligned to offer research and interpretive opportunities and innovative ways of using the collections, all of which enhance the university's academic reputation and global presence. Both projects reflected an approach to museum-library collaboration that was particular to the culture at Northwestern—examples of productive partnerships that by working across campus units contributed to the larger vision of the museum, the library, and Northwestern University.

A Feast of Astonishments—2016–2017

Northwestern University Libraries claim several areas of strength and interest, among them a commitment to the study of the "long 1960s." The library actively collects materials that bring unique perspectives to what is considered a heightened period of rebellion, experimentation, and social change in the United States and across the globe. With this focus, Northwestern is becoming a center for scholars researching countercultures, alternative art practices, and protest and identity movements from the mid-1950s into the 1980s. The Charlotte Moorman Archive, which came into the Charles Deering McCormick Library of Special Collections in 2001, was an important addition to this area. The acquisition complemented the archives of contemporaries Dick Higgins and John Cage, whose work was similarly based on experimental practices and grew out of a postwar mid-twentieth-century ethos.[6]

The acquisition also became the basis for *A Feast of Astonishments: Charlotte Moorman and the Avant-Garde, 1960s–1980s*, a project that comprised two traveling exhibitions, extensive cross-departmental programs, and a publication (figure 9.1). It was the most ambitious and extensive collaboration between the library and the museum to date and was a model for how we can work together on future projects, especially because of the complex questions that arose out of the objects themselves. Opening at The Block Museum in 2016, *A Feast of Astonishments* was the first large-scale exhibition of the work of Charlotte Moorman, a groundbreaking, rule-bending artist, musician, and advocate

FIGURE 9.1. *A Feast of Astonishments* title wall, The Block Museum of Art, 2016.

for the experimental art of her time. Trained as a classical cellist, she performed and championed the works of visual artists, composers, and choreographers who were redefining art, collapsing the boundaries between creative media, and renegotiating relationships between artists and audiences. After opening at The Block Museum, the exhibition traveled to the Grey Art Gallery at New York University (NYU) and Museum of Modern Art in Salzburg, Austria.

A companion exhibition in the museum's 500-square-foot gallery focused specifically on the archive *as archive* and Moorman's personal life. The exhibition, titled *Don't Throw Anything Out: Charlotte Moorman's Archive*, based on Moorman's last words to her husband before her death, included sentimental objects relating to Moorman's childhood, her courtship with her husband, gifts from artist friends, and items that demonstrated her obsessive record-keeping (figure 9.2). These included answering machine messages and Moorman's daybooks, which she kept meticulously for decades. They included details of travel and public performances as well as mundane notes recording when she washed her hair or that she ate fish sticks for dinner. The main gallery exhibition focused on the career and public life of Charlotte Moorman and her work as an artist, performer, and curator. It aimed to give shape, order, and interpretation to a

FIGURE 9.2. Installation of *Don't Throw Anything Out*, The Block Museum of Art, 2016.

career that was original and groundbreaking but also complicated and messy. *Don't Throw Anything Out* gave visitors a glimpse into the breadth of the materials in the Moorman archive. The archive exhibition allowed for a deeply personal view of the artist. It also conveyed how an archive provides materials through which curators and historians make sense of an artist's oeuvre.[7]

Both exhibitions drew extensively from the vast Charlotte Moorman Archives, although *A Feast* was augmented significantly with loans from other US and European institutions. The Moorman Archive includes such typical items as photographs, correspondence, music scores, performance scores, grant applications, newspaper clippings, legal documents, and ephemera. It also includes an array of unusual objects that became the basis for the exhibition, especially performance relics—torn dresses, masks, props, smashed violins, and an "electric bikini" made by Korean-born artist Nam June Paik for a performance by Moorman (figure 9.3).

FIGURE 9.3. *A Feast of Astonishments* installation with props and ephemera.

When the materials first came to Northwestern in 2001, they arrived in a cargo truck that contained 178 banker's boxes, thirty-one oversized boxes and flat files, and nearly fifty poster tubes.[8] Because of the range of materials, cataloging the contents brought particular challenges and took place over many years. Soon after Block Museum director Lisa Graziose Corrin first arrived at Northwestern in 2012, she had envisioned an exhibition and inquired about the feasibility of the Moorman materials to be the foundation of a major exhibition. After several months of discussion and weighing all factors, it was agreed that an exhibition would open at The Block Museum in 2016, an ambitious goal that required many hands (figure 9.4).

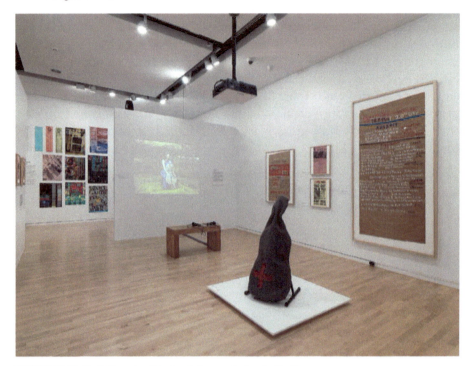

FIGURE 9.4. *A Feast of Astonishments* installation

The collection had not been fully processed, and work on the exhibition and the finding aid took place simultaneously. Because not all the objects in the archive had been cataloged, the curatorial process required extensive collaboration with Special Collections curator Scott Krafft. This was incredibly beneficial because Krafft was the first staff member to sort through the material and had deep knowledge of the contents.[9] He became a vital member of the curatorial team and agreed to curate the companion exhibition *Don't Throw Anything Out*, which was installed at the Block Museum and the Fales Library at NYU.

Beyond shaping the content of the exhibition, museum staff and library staff worked closely together to consider the logistics of conserving, displaying, and eventually traveling fragile and highly unstable objects. Museum staff worked with the library preservation team and curators to stabilize and prepare many unusual objects for display. An example of this was *Solo for Violin*, an important piece by Paik that Moorman included in her repertoire, performing it often during her engagements throughout the world between the late 1960s and mid-1980s. The riveting performance piece instructed the musician to lift a violin above her head in very slow motion and then bring it down quickly, smashing it on a table. In addition to photos, the archive held a number of smashed violins, debris that Moorman saved from a dozen or so performances. Needless to say, Moorman was able to use each violin only once.[10] As an obsessive saver, she kept a group of the destroyed violins, which came to Northwestern in plastic containers. Because they had already been degraded through the performances and poor storage, the violins were extremely fragile, and each time they were held or moved, there were losses. Ultimately part of the exhibition display was a group of six violins presented side-by-side in a case, along with photo documentation. In order to display the objects and prepare them for travel, each violin was mounted with all loose ends fixed with transparent fibers (figure 9.5). This near surgical stabilization process allowed the work to be shown consistently in three venues. More importantly, it allowed for the violin fragments to travel without further degradation. The resolution evolved through extensive discussions, communication, and coordination between the library and museum staff during the planning process

FIGURE 9.5. Conservators looking at violin shards.

Another major challenge was restoring the "Electric Bikini," an object Paik made especially for Moorman for the one and only performance of his *Opera*

Sextronique (1967). String and Christmas light bulbs form the two parts of a bikini, which are held together by packing tape and are connected to switches that were used during the performance to make the lights flash on and off. Composed of ordinary materials, items one would typically find in a hardware store, and in very poor shape, the object was nearly unrecognizable at first. The conservators eventually untangled and cleaned the various parts and brought new legibility to the object so that it made sense when displayed in proximity to a vintage photograph of Moorman wearing it. The invaluable work of the conservators made the inclusion of the piece in the exhibition possible.[11]

Such items as broken violins and makeshift costumes presented challenges in display and readability. Throughout the process of preparation, there was a constant negotiation between the needs of the fragile and time-worn objects and the narrative of the exhibition. These were addressed through sustained discussion about curatorial objectives, conservation requirements, and the mutually aligned goals of the museum and library to tell the story of Moorman through archival objects (figure 9.6).

FIGURE 9.6. Solo for Violin installation in *A Feast of Astonishments*.

Since the exhibition was one of the first major projects to look at the art practice of Charlotte Moorman in a serious and critical way, it was important to produce a publication as documentation of the project, to highlight objects in the archive, and to provide historical and critical context for the objects and themes of the exhibition.[12] We co-published the book, *A Feast of Astonishments,* with Northwestern University Press. The Press, a unit that is also under the auspices of the Northwestern University Libraries, was an ideal partner for the project. As the holder of many of the objects, the library was able to arrange scanning and photography well in advance of the exhibition. Since the exhibition included a great deal of ephemera, documentation, film, and relics, the book was more of a companion than a catalog, and since the exhibition only included a fraction of the objects in the archive, it was by no means comprehensive. Essays in the book were authored by the curators and scholars in the field, along with members of the curatorial team.

The exhibition and the book could not have been realized without extensive coordination and the various areas of expertise that each team member brought to the project. The Block spearheaded the organizing of the exhibit, which included grant writing for funding from the Terra Foundation for American Art, the Andy Warhol Foundation, and the National Endowment for the Arts. We received generous support for mounting the project, although much of the cost of labor for the exhibitions and book were covered by museum and staff salaries. The library supported the project, not only through critical loans but also financially. They also supported the project through the generous staff time in the contribution of knowledge and expertise, preparation of objects for the exhibition and travel, and the scanning of objects for the catalog. Such an ambitious project would not have been feasible without extensive cooperation and the use of staff time. From the first discussions in 2012 to the realization of the exhibition in 2016, it took four years to research and organize and eleven more months of travel.

Through the combined efforts, the museum and library achieved the goal of bringing the work of a well-known but little understood artist to a broad public. The project brought critical attention to an important archive at Northwestern and gave wider access to rare materials. The exhibition made it possible to reframe the archive in a way that brought it new value and importance, expanding the work from the province of scholars and academics to making it available to a broader public. The exhibition and book served as ways of making the archive visible and giving the viewers access to its contents while re-writing a history of art through it.

Reflecting Memory—2017

Reflecting Memory was conceived as a project that began in the Northwestern University Libraries and resulted in a new work of art by a contemporary artist shown at The Block Museum. The project reflected a shared aspiration on the part of the museum and the library to connect a living artist with the collections of the Melville J. Herskovits Library of African Studies at Northwestern University Libraries and to foster opportunities for innovative ways of thinking about the materials in the archive. There have been recent trends in projects involving contemporary artists who engage in unprecedented ways with library collections, making the collections relevant in new ways and thinking critically about historical documents and constructions. Inviting artists to work with library collections and facilitating communication across disciplines, these collaborations make meaningful intersections between artists and archives possible.[13]

In 2015, The Block Museum and Northwestern University Libraries invited French-Algerian artist Kader Attia (b. 1970) to work with the resources at the Herskovits Library of African Studies over several extended stays. The Herskovits Library is the largest in the world devoted to African studies. Founded in 1954, it collects a range of materials in diverse formats—colonial-era photographs, manuscripts, posters, newspapers, ephemera, maps, textiles, medical journals, and film, as well as some 400,000 books from and about Africa.

While Herskovits Library materials have been included in exhibitions at The Block, the idea of an artist engaging with them by conducting research in the library shed new light on the objects. An artist could provide new perspectives to approaching materials that may seem straightforward but actually have layered and complex histories. While the archives are a destination for scholars throughout the world, the nuanced and creative approach of an artist differs profoundly from the approach of a scholar or researcher.

For Attia, an artist whose work addresses issues around colonial and post-colonial Africa, the Herskovits collection was a rich resource that resonated with his previous work. In the past, his work has reflected on collective historical traumas—colonialism in Africa, World War I, the Armenian Genocide, and the Holocaust during World War II. He has used medical analogies, such as the "phantom limb" and "mirror neurons" to think through the impact of trauma on individual and societal levels.[14]

Attia's work with The Block Museum and the library originated from research and a proposal by a Northwestern art history graduate student, Antawan Byrd, who was the 2014–15 Block Museum Curatorial Graduate Fellow. Along with Byrd, the exhibition was co-curated by Kathleen Bickford Berzock, associate director of Curatorial Affairs, and curator Janet Dees, the Steven and Lisa Munster Tananbaum Curator of Modern and Contemporary Art. Byrd identified Kader Attia as an artist who would re-examine history through ordinary or unlikely objects and find residues of the past within them. His installation at Documenta 13 (2012), *The Repair from Occident to Extra-Occidental Cultures,* for example, explored culturally based ideas about healing and repair and how Western ideas of healing are grounded in beliefs about making the fragmented, the injured, and the wounded whole again. In contrast, the visibility of the wound, the missing limb, and the site of trauma is seen as an integral part of the person or a sign of change and growth in some non-Western cultures.

In an era when museums are working toward expanded ideas about history and visual culture, the archives provide means of accessing history through tactile objects, photographs, texts, and publications. The very materiality of objects within archives carries nuanced historical traces and is affective as a vehicle for contemplation.[15] For many contemporary artists, engagement with materials in an archive is a way of approaching historical questions and complexities. Attia is one among a number of contemporary artists whose work arises out of an engagement with archival resources as inspiration or as a catalyst for critical reflection.[16] His approach is one that acknowledges "the fallibility of the archive and the inscrutability of the discovered images" within it.[17]

Beginning in the spring of 2015, Attia made a series of visits to delve into the contents of the Herskovits Library. In addition to working with The Block Museum curatorial department, Attia was based in the library and worked closely with the staff there. Herskovits curator Esmeralda Kale and staff hosted Attia and responded to the unfolding of his research and sometimes unexpected trajectories and interests (figure 9.7). Over two one-month stays in Evanston, Attia consulted an abundance of materials in the Herskovits collection—photography, books, periodicals, and loose files. His research eventually led him to interview faculty at Northwestern across several campus disciplines, including

FIGURE 9.7. Kader Attia and Esmeralda Kale in the Herskovits Library of African Studies.

psychology, anthropology, and the Feinberg School of Medicine.[18] Beginning with the photography collections, Attia went on to conduct comprehensive surveys of a variety of objects, including materials on such topics as water, architecture, medicine, and prosthetics. While Kale and the team at the Herskovits Library aim to make the collections accessible to all, working directly with an artist in residence was a new experience. According to Kale, "We were all surprised by the quantity and the speed, the voraciousness at which [Attia] gets through thing."[19] While the library staff started with the goal of being supportive, they became collaborative in the sense that they began to think in new veins about what may potentially be useful for Attia's work and thinking. In that sense, the staff of the Herskovits Library were not only facilitators but also became true partners, part of the content development.

Attia's residency in the Herskovits Library inspired a campus program during the exhibition. In "The Artist in the Archive: Interdisciplinary Perspectives on Kader Attia in the Herskovits Library," which took place on Thursday, March 2, 2017, Esmeralda Kale shared objects in the collection that were springboards for Attia's installation and film. Members of AfriSem, a consortium of graduate students focused on African studies, also explored intertwined areas of Attia's research (figure 9.8).

FIGURE 9.8. Kader Attia presenting on his residency in the Herskovits Library of African Studies.

Attia became interested in particular themes and objects, as he described:

I had several moments in this research that I will never forget.... I was struck by some major photographs, old photographs... representing slaves in Tanzania. And what is absolutely fascinating with these documents is that... you just know that they are slaves because [of] the caption that is written [on the photographs], probably, if I remember, from [ca.] 1865. The caption says, "This is a slave market." I think this leads to... what I call the phantom limb, the thing that is still here but we don't see it.

Attia's exploration in the archive resulted in *Kader Attia: Reflecting Memory* (January 21–April 16, 2017), a tripartite installation that included a powerful forty-minute film essay, also called *Reflecting Memory*, which won the 2016 Marcel Duchamp Prize at the Centre Georges Pompidou in Paris (figure 9.9). These components of the exhibition all drew on Attia's practice and interest in themes of collective and individual trauma, psychological repair, physical repair, and dealt specifically with the phenomenon of phantom limbs from medical, psychological, and personal perspectives. All parts of the exhibition were inspired by and responses to materials Attia discovered in the archive and reconfigured in evocative ways. Attia's residency promoted new ways of thinking about the Herskovits archive and how to activate the collections imaginatively. Not only were they consulted as research resources and for content, but they were also interpreted in evocative ways as physical objects that speak to the past and present.

FIGURE 9.9. Still from Kader Attia's *Reflecting Memory*.

Conclusion

Recent partnerships between the museum and the library have promoted innovative approaches to using library collections in experiencing, interpreting, and presenting archival materials. Working together, The Block Museum of Art and Northwestern University Libraries have been partners in organizing exhibitions, publications, and commissioned artwork that are drawn from or inspired by library holdings. While the library's resources are generally seen or consulted by researchers and scholars often working in narrow fields and are generally only known to or viewed by limited audiences, the joint initiatives have opened tremendous new possibilities to bring these resources to broader audiences. Both examples represent a process of moving from cooperation and collaboration toward true convergence in the way we combine our approaches to collections to bring expertise from the library and the museum in the realization of complex exhibitions, publications, artist residencies, and commission of artworks.[20] Working with The Block on projects that evolve into public programs or exhibitions promotes the dissemination of scholarship and the fostering of community along with sustaining research and advancing learning through its collections.[21]

The examples cited are two of the recent, successful extended partnerships that fostered rich opportunities to work with objects from the past and think about the kinds of objects we value, what gets preserved, conserved, cataloged, and digitized, as well as what objects inform our constructions of history. While each endeavor has its unique shape and definition, these examples point the way toward future endeavors. Opening archive contents to a much broader public and audience, these recent practices embrace the changing positions of museums and libraries in the twenty-first century and challenge their traditional roles as authoritative keepers and shapers of knowledge.

Acknowledgments

Many thanks to colleagues Kathleen Bickford Berzock, Lindsay Bosch, Lisa Corrin, and Janet Dees for generously sharing their experiences and for their contributions. Thank you to editors Scott Walter, Julie Rodrigues Widholm, and Alexia Hudson-Ward for their helpful suggestions and insights.

Endnotes

1. The idea of interdisciplinarity is summed up in the recent communications, such as "Take a Northwestern Direction," featured in the short video, *Northwestern Global Anthem*, YouTube, accessed December 17, 2019, https://www.youtube.com/watch?time_continue=70&v=wOu2m3Vk11M&feature=emb_logo.
2. The broader goals discussed in this chapter and are addressed in Erica Pastore, *The Future of Museums and Libraries: A Discussion Guide* (Washington, DC: Institute of Museum and Library Services, 2009), accessed November 22, 2019, https://www.imls.gov/publications/

future-museums-and-libraries-discussion-guide; Ricky Erway, Günter Waibel, Diane M. Zorich, *Beyond the Silos of the LAMS. Collaboration Among Libraries, Archives, and Museums* (Dublin, OH: OCLC Research, 2008), accessed November 22, 2019, http://www.oclc.org/research/publications/library/2008/2008-05.pdf.

3. *William Hogarth and 18th century Print Culture*, Mary and Leigh Block Museum of Art, Northwestern University, accessed November 26, 2019, http://exhibits.library.northwestern.edu/spec/hogarth/. The website credits states that the project brought together many parts of the university community, including the Department of Art Theory and Practice at Northwestern, the Department of Theatre and Speech, the Block Gallery, as it was called in 1997, and the Multimedia Center, which created the website, and Special Collections of the Northwestern University. The exhibition was curated by Angela Rosenthal, Andrew W. Mellon Assistant Professor of Art History, Northwestern University, and a team of eight co-curators graduate students in the Department of Art History.

4. For exhibition descriptions: *Philipon's La Caricature and the Street*, The Block Museum of Art, Northwestern University, 2006, https://www.blockmuseum.northwestern.edu/view/exhibitions/past-exhibits/2006/philipons-la-caricature-and-the-street.html; *Political Currents across the Channel: James Gillray's Caricatures of France*, The Block Museum of Art, Northwestern University, 2006, https://www.blockmuseum.northwestern.edu/view/exhibitions/past-exhibits/2006/political-currents-across-the-channel.html.

5. *From the Trenches to the Street: Art from Germany, 1910s-1920s*, The Block Museum of Art, Northwestern University, 2007, https://www.blockmuseum.northwestern.edu/view/exhibitions/past-exhibits/2007/from-the-trenches.html.

6. The library collections have significant holdings in material culture of the 1960s, including documentation from Second Wave Feminism, hippie culture, and student activism. Within these, there are many specialized sub-collections that have potential for mining include the 1960s-focused collections, such as the John Cage archive, the archives of the Berkeley Folk Music Festival, graphic art of protest, such as posters from the student uprising in France in 1968 (the May–June strike), Fluxus artist Dick Higgins Archive, and counterculture ephemera of the 1960s, such as the *Chicago Seed* and *Outsider* magazine. See Drew Scott, "The Revolution Will Be Archived: The 1960s at Northwestern," Northwestern Libraries, November 30, 2017, https://sites.northwestern.edu/northwesternlibrary/2017/11/30/the-revolution-will-be-archived-the-1960s-at-northwestern/.

7. Both exhibitions traveled to New York, to the Grey Art Gallery and the Fales Library and Special Collections at New York University. *A Feast of Astonishments* also traveled to Museum der Moderne Salzburg.

8. Scott Krafft, "'Don't Throw Anything Out': Charlotte Moorman's Archive," in *A Feast of Astonishments: Charlotte Moorman and the Avant-Garde, 1960s-1980s* (Evanston, IL: Block Museum and Northwestern University Press, 2016), 190–91.

9. Krafft had also worked closely with Joan Rothfuss, author of the biography *Topless Cellist: The Improbable Life of Charlotte Moorman* (Cambridge, MA: MIT Press, 2015). Rothfuss and Krafft were the first to mine the archive soon after it arrived at Northwestern. Rothfuss was also part of the curatorial team for *A Feast of Astonishments* and contributed to the catalogue.

10. Moorman used other performance props multiple times. For example, the work *Infiltration Homogen for Cello*, which was written especially for Moorman by German artist Joseph Beuys, included a cello wrapped in thick felt with a Red Cross attached to it.

11. The conservation team included Tonia Grafakos, chief conservator; Susan Russick, special collections conservator; and Carlynne Robinson, registration and collections coordinator. Their work is documented in Susan Russick, "An Avant-Garde Approach to the Exhibit of Objects in the Charlotte Moorman Archive," *Beyond the Book* (blog), April 29, 2016, accessed December 17, 2019, https://web.archive.org/web/20180818004126/http://sites.northwestern.edu/preservation/2016/04/29/an-avant-garde-approach-to-the-exhibit-of-object-in-the-charlotte-moorman-archive/.

12. The only other serious study of Moorman's work is Rothfuss's *Topless Cellist*.

13. One recent project to focus on artists working with and within the archive took place at The Block Museum. *If You Remember, I'll Remember* (2017) looked at six artists who engage with historic documents, photographs, sound recordings, oral histories and objects of material culture drawn from institutional and informal archives.

14. He is also as interested in the hierarchies of information presented in archives, as he is in the forms of the objects and documents that live there, all the while questioning the authority of the archives as well as the structures and systems of archives that reveal or obscure information within them. Kader's remarks on his experience within the Herskovits Library can be seen at "Kader Attia Opening Day Conversation," Vimeo, https://vimeo.com/201487578.
15. See also Hal Foster, "An Archival Impulse," *October* 110 (Fall 2004): 3–22. Foster writes specifically about artists for whom the tangible and fragmentary materials of a physical archive are crucial, and that the faculties of human interpretation are central to the approach.
16. See Mark Godfrey, "The Artist as Historian," *October* 120 (Spring 2007), 140–72. Godfrey has written, "There are an increasing number of artists whose practice starts with research in archives, and others who deploy what has been termed an archival form of research…. These varied research processes lead to works that invite viewers to think about the past; to make connections between events, characters, and objects; to join together in memory; and to reconsider the ways in which the past is represented in the wider culture"; Godfrey, "The Artist as Historian," 142–143.
17. Ibid., 143.
18. While at Northwestern, Attia met with scientists, doctors, anthropologists, sociologists, and art historians to discuss and think critically and from different perspectives about the research and archival materials.
19. See the forthcoming publication Kader Attia project (available digitally 2019) at "Kader Attia: Reflecting Memory," The Block Museum of Art, Northwestern University, 2017, https://www.blockmuseum.northwestern.edu/view/exhibitions/past-exhibits/2017/kader-attia.html.
20. Erway, Waibel, and Zorich, *Beyond the Silos of the LAMS*, 10–12.
21. "Strategic Plan 2018 Update," Northwestern University Libraries (Evanston, IL: Northwestern University Libraries and University Press, 2018), accessed November 22, 2019, http://www.library.northwestern.edu/documents/about/2018-plan.pdf.

Bibliography

Block Museum of Art, The. *From the Trenches to the Street: Art from Germany, 1910s–1920s*. Northwestern University. 2007. https://www.blockmuseum.northwestern.edu/view/exhibitions/past-exhibits/2007/from-the-trenches.html.

———. *Philipon's La Caricature and the Street*. Northwestern University. 2006. https://www.blockmuseum.northwestern.edu/view/exhibitions/past-exhibits/2006/philipons-la-caricature-and-the-street.html.

———. *Political Currents across the Channel: James Gillray's Caricatures of France*. Northwestern University. 2006. https://www.blockmuseum.northwestern.edu/view/exhibitions/past-exhibits/2006/political-currents-across-the-channel.html.

———. "William Hogarth and 18th century Print Culture." Northwestern University. Accessed November 26, 2019. http://exhibits.library.northwestern.edu/spec/hogarth/.

Corrin, Lisa, and Corinne Granof, eds. *A Feast of Astonishments: Charlotte Moorman and the Avant-Garde, 1960s–1980s*. Evanston, IL: Block Museum and Northwestern University Press, 2016.

Erway, Ricky, Günter Waibel, Diane M. Zorich. *Beyond the Silos of the LAMS. Collaboration Among Libraries, Archives, and Museums*. Dublin, OH: OCLC Research, 2008. http://www.oclc.org/research/publications/library/2008/2008-05.pdf.

Foster, Hal. "An Archival Impulse." *October* 110 (Fall 2004): 3–22.

Godfrey, Mark. "The Artist as Historian." *October* 120 (Spring 2007): 140–172.

Pastore, Erica. *The Future of Museums and Libraries: A Discussion Guide*. Washington, DC: Institute of Museum and Library Services, 2009. https://www.imls.gov/publications/future-museums-and-libraries-discussion-guide.

Rothfuss, Joan. *Topless Cellist: The Improbable Life of Charlotte Moorman*. Cambridge, MA: MIT Press, 2015.

Russick, Susan. "An Avant-Garde Approach to the Exhibit of Objects in the Charlotte Moorman Archive." *Beyond the Book* (blog), April 29, 2016. Accessed December 17, 2019. https://web.archive.org/web/20180818004126/http://sites.northwestern.edu/preservation/2016/04/29/an-avant-garde-approach-to-the-exhibit-of-object-in-the-charlotte-moorman-archive/.

Vimeo. "Kader Attia Opening Day Conversation." https://vimeo.com/201487578.

CHAPTER 10

Across the Square:
Collaborative Paper and Photograph Conservation at the University of Washington Libraries and the Henry Art Gallery

Stephanie Lamson and Sylvia Wolf

> At the University of Washington, the Henry Art Gallery (the Henry) and Suzzallo and Allen Library sit on opposite ends of a large brick plaza known as "Red Square." Several days a week, Claire Kenny, associate conservator of paper and photographs, crosses Red Square to provide conservation services at both locations. The Henry and the University of Washington Libraries (UW Libraries) have a long history of collaboration, but the joint appointment of a shared staff member is a recent effort made possible by the support of The Andrew W. Mellon Foundation. This new endeavor significantly advances the development of shared conservation services on the UW campus. It also brings together staff expertise in both the libraries and the Henry to explore other substantive collaborations to support our diverse collections, exhibitions, and communities.

Institutional Background

The University of Washington (UW), founded in Seattle on November 4, 1861, is one of the oldest state-supported institutions of higher education on the Pacific coast with a longstanding commitment to the preservation, advancement, and dissemination of knowledge. It is the goal of the university to foster

an environment in which students can develop critical skills to appreciate the range and diversity of human experiences. As noted in its mission statement, UW preserves knowledge through its courses, its faculty, and its libraries and collections.[1]

UW's academic offerings are extensive, from degrees in arts, humanities, social sciences, law, engineering, and medicine to programs in oceanography, fisheries, aeronautics, library science, and museology. To increase access to higher education, the university opened campuses in Bothell and Tacoma in 1990. More than 59,000 students attend UW's three campuses, with 42,000 undergraduates and 16,000 graduate/professional students. Underrepresented minority students make up 21 percent of the 2019–20 domestic freshman class, and 32 percent of incoming freshmen are the first in their families to attain a bachelor's degree. In 2019–20, about 55 percent of UW undergraduates are receiving some form of financial aid.[2]

The City of Seattle—home of UW's main campus and named after Duwamish leader Chief Sealth—was established as a townsite in 1851.[3] UW currently acknowledges the history of the Coast Salish people, whose land touches the shared waters of all tribes and bands within the Suquamish, Tulalip, and Muckleshoot nations.[4] Today, Seattle is a city of over 745,000 people in a region of over two million that is home to Amazon, Boeing, Costco, Microsoft, Nordstrom, Starbucks, and the Bill and Melinda Gates Foundation. Over the past decade, Seattle has been the fastest-growing big city in the United States.[5] As a public university integral to a rapidly expanding metropolis, UW is committed to "maintaining an environment for objectivity and imaginative inquiry and for the original scholarship and research that ensure the production of new knowledge in the free exchange of facts, theories, and ideas."[6] The Henry and UW Libraries are repositories of art and information that have supported UW's mission to foster inquiry, dialogue, and debate for decades.

The Henry Art Gallery at the University of Washington is an internationally recognized museum of contemporary art—accredited by the American Alliance of Museums—that serves UW's students, faculty, and staff as well as a broader public audience.[7] The Henry is operated and governed by the Henry Gallery Association, Inc., a separate 501(c)(3) non-profit organization established in 1968. It is a unit of the College of Arts and Sciences, which provides 25 percent of the museum's annual operating budget. With a permanent collection of over 28,000 objects, the Henry is a key cultural resource and training ground in the visual arts for students, scholars, artists, and general audiences of all ages. Every year, the Henry welcomes over 60,000 visitors on-site and reaches over 100,000 visitors online. The museum's facilities and collections are used by forty UW departments and twenty-five regional partners. The Henry's Eleanor Henry Reed Collection Study Center is one of a kind in the region, where faculty, students, and the public can study works of art in the museum's collection free of charge. The collaboration with UW Libraries focuses on the museum's collection of more than 6,000 photographs and works on paper by global artists from across five centuries.

Ranked in the top ten of US public research universities, according to the Association of Research Libraries, the University of Washington Libraries is one library system serving all three UW campuses. It consists of sixteen libraries in Seattle, Bothell, and Tacoma, in addition to a library on San Juan Island. The UW Libraries is widely recognized for its unique and diverse collections that include more than nine million volumes, two million photographs and other graphic items, and 100,000 linear feet of archival and manuscript materials. Many UW faculty members work closely with librarians to use the libraries' irreplaceable holdings in teaching their courses. The libraries' special collections are available to faculty, students, and the public both in person and via the libraries' extensive digital collections. Overall, more than five million users visit the libraries annually. The collaboration with the Henry concentrates on a subset of the UW Libraries' photographs and works on paper of historical and scholarly importance.[8]

Early Collaborations

Over the past forty years, the UW Libraries and the Henry have developed a long history of collaboration and exchange, particularly in the form of collection acquisition, exhibition loans, exhibition curation, public lectures, and course support. In 1982, for example, when the costume and textile collections of the School of Drama and the School of Home Economics were consolidated and transferred to the Henry, the book, print, and photographic resources related to the collections were sent to UW Libraries' Special Collections. In 2010, the UW Libraries collaborated with the Henry to create the Blanche Payne Regional Costume Photograph and Drawing digital collection, which provides access to the Blanche Payne Regional Costume Photograph and Drawing Collection at the UW Libraries and its associated costume materials held at the Henry.[9] Such collaborations generally relied on informal and personal connections between staff members developed over time. Their success has rested on the sharing of knowledge, objects, and staff time, with each institution pursuing funding separately to support a particular project or activity.

Today, the Henry and UW Libraries routinely loan materials to each other to enhance their respective exhibition programs. In addition to sharing content knowledge, the loans involve the exchange of expertise in object handling, display and presentation methods, and interpretive material development. Most recently, *Jacob Lawrence: Eight Studies for the Book of Genesis*[10] (2017)—a centennial exhibition at the Henry of a suite of works by renowned artist and former UW faculty member Jacob Lawrence—featured a *Nuremberg Chronicle* on loan from the UW Libraries to provide historical context for Lawrence's non-traditional biblical depictions of human creation. *Out [o] Fashion Photography: Embracing Beauty*[11] (2013), another Henry exhibition, featured photographs from both the museum and UW Libraries and resulted in a companion book of the same title. *Shadows of a Fleeting World*[12] (2011) presented over 200 works by photographers from the Seattle Camera Club, including objects and archival materials from UW Libraries. While the exhibition was curated by the Henry, a companion book was co-authored by the visual materials curator of UW Libraries and a local expert on the art of the period.

UW Libraries' curatorial staff frequently present lectures related to Henry exhibitions, work with visiting artists in researching materials, and deliver joint presentations to classes. For example, the UW Libraries Book Arts and Rare Book curator presented the public program, "Conversations with the Past: Inspiration and History," at the Henry to complement the exhibition *Ann Hamilton: the common S E N S E*[13] (2014-2015), which featured materials from the Henry, UW Libraries, and the Burke Museum of Natural History. The Henry's and UW Libraries' curators and collections staff also regularly contribute their expertise to the School of Art + Art History + Design, the iSchool, and the Museology Graduate Program by participating in seminars, hosting classes, and mentoring students.

Collaborative Conservation

In July 2016, the Henry and UW Libraries, along with thirty-five other public and private academic institutions, were invited by The Andrew W. Mellon Foundation to submit a proposal for museums and libraries to collaborate and share resources in new and imaginative ways. This invitation grew out of the January 2016 convening, "The Academic Art Museum and Library Summit," hosted by the University of Miami and jointly sponsored by the Kress and Mellon Foundations.[14] In response to the invitation, staff and leadership at the Henry and UW Libraries decided to put together a proposal to build on the success of our previous collaborations. Since we had already developed an ongoing commitment to joint projects around access, we chose to center our proposal on the greatest area of need: the care and preservation of our collections.

UW Libraries and the Henry have strong collections of photographs, prints, and other works on paper that are used extensively and loaned frequently for exhibition. Since their delicate nature makes access to those materials challenging, collections care has focused primarily on protective storage and preventive maintenance. Both the Henry and UW Libraries have established policies and trained staff that are devoted to collections preservation. For complex treatment of photographs and works on paper, however, we have sought outside expertise. At the Henry, for example, approximately five to ten items per year were contracted out to paper and photograph conservators to meet the most urgent treatment needs, often in support of exhibitions and loans. At the UW Libraries, in-house treatment of photographs and works of art on paper were limited to stabilization such as humidification, flattening, and housing. Without a specialist in paper and photographs conservation on staff, both the Henry and UW Libraries have struggled to address the conservation needs of the more than two million architectural drawings, maps, photographs, prints, and other works of art on paper in our collections.

When envisioning the greatest impact a Mellon grant could have on our two institutions, we concluded that a jointly appointed associate conservator for paper and photographs was critical to developing our conservation capacity and improving the care of our collections. With the dedicated attention of a new conservator, we could dramatically expand our treatment options—from basic stabilization to more specialized treatment. To that end, we submitted the proposal, *Collaborative Paper and Photograph Conservation at the University of Washington Libraries and the Henry Art Gallery*. Ours was among five projects selected by Mellon to cultivate sustainable shared practices between academic art museums and libraries. In 2017, we received full funding for the project for use over four years.

Bridging Organizational Frameworks to Establish Shared Conservation Services

Because the Henry is housed in the College of Arts and Sciences and the UW Libraries is overseen by the provost and executive vice president, our collaborative conservation effort bridges our formal reporting structures to establish a new framework for shared conservation services. Upon receipt of the Mellon grant, we established a steering committee of staff and leadership at both the Henry and UW Libraries to enhance communication and to meet the grant's objectives. This was the first formal organizational structure between the two entities to share programs and services. The steering committee established a search committee made up of personnel from both organizations as well as an art conservator from a nearby collecting institution. After reviewing hiring and evaluation practices at the Henry and UW Libraries, we used UW's Staff Diversity Hiring Toolkit to develop a strong recruitment process that incorporated the best of our collective personnel protocols.[15]

Following an extensive nationwide search, we hired Claire Kenny, preservation services manager at the Center for Jewish History, as our first associate conservator of paper and photographs in October 2017.[16] Kenny had an impressive background in conservation treatment of paper-based archival materials, including

140 Chapter 10

professional and internship experience at New York University Division of Libraries, the Morgan Library and Museum, the Metropolitan Museum of Art, and the New-York Historical Society. She also brought significant supervisory experience in overseeing staff, interns, and volunteers. We felt that her breadth of experience would enhance our efforts to provide conservation services to both the UW Libraries and Henry collections and to engage with students and faculty.

Addressing Unmet Conservation Needs and Improving Collections Care

As a part of preparing our grant proposal to the Mellon Foundation, both the Henry and UW Libraries identified a long list of conservation needs. When prioritizing specific collections, we considered the degree to which the materials were at risk, if their current condition was a barrier to use, their anticipated or current use (exhibition and study), their academic and cultural value, and their range and diversity of subjects. Our initial assessment allowed the incoming conservator to make quick progress in evaluating and completing work on prioritized items and collections.

The associate conservator has assessed more than 1,000 photographs and works on paper to develop treatment priorities. For example, she surveyed two new gifts to the Henry: the Feldmann Collection of Fifteenth to Eighteenth Century European Master Prints (410 items) and the Washington Art Consortium Collection of American Photographs, 1970–1980 (185 items).[17] At the UW Libraries, she assessed a collection of 300 photographs by Frank Asakichi Kunishige, Japanese American Pictorialist photographer and co-founder of the Seattle Camera Club, whose photographs were previously loaned by the libraries for exhibition at the Henry.[18] In addition, she contributed to a treatment and storage proposal developed by UW Libraries conservation staff and interns for a collection of delicate and large Chinese stele rubbings. The associate conservator also participates in the Henry's Collection Committee meetings where works of art are considered for acquisition based on a stringent set of criteria, including physical condition.

In addition to assessing and improving our care of these collections, the associate conservator has dramatically increased our conservation treatment of photographs and works on paper. She has performed a range of complex treatments, including tape removal and stain reduction, backing or mount removal, and consolidation of flaking pigments and emulsion. Minor treatments may include removing and replacing hinges, mending small tears and losses, slight humidification and flattening, and limited surface cleaning. For example, the associate conservator treated a number of prints from the Feldmann Collection, including works by Francisco Goya, Albrecht Dürer, and Giovanni Battista

Piranesi, that required surface cleaning and removal of tape and adhesive for safe handling in the Henry's Collection Study Center. In total, the associate conservator has completed forty-five significant treatments and sixty-five minor treatments for collection materials at UW Libraries and the Henry.

In prioritizing materials for treatment, we are mindful of including objects that have historical significance or cultural relevance to the diverse communities of our region. For example, three drawings (ink and gouache on boards) created by graphic artist Eddie Sato while he was incarcerated at the Puyallup Assembly Center during World War II were treated and stabilized. These drawings had significant handling and water damage as well as deterioration of the support material when they were acquired by the UW Libraries and could not be made accessible. With the expertise of the associate conservator, the UW Libraries was able to stabilize and make these drawings available for further study.

The associate conservator offers guidance on public exhibitions and proposed loans, particularly at the Henry. She examines objects for both display and loan, prepares condition reports, and provides conservation treatment for items prior to going on view as needed. To date, she has completed conservation support for six exhibitions, including *Carrie Yamaoka: recto/verso* (2019)[19] and *MUSE: Mickalene Thomas Photographs and tête-à-tête* (2018).[20]

Continuing Outreach and Education

The UW Libraries and Henry recognize the need to promote diversity in the fields of museum and library conservation and preservation. As Sanchita Balachandran's presentation, *Race, Diversity and Politics in Conservation: Our 21st Century Crisis*, from the 44th American Institute of Conservation Annual Meeting (2016) argued, our professions require both "a more diverse set of conservation professionals and community stakeholders, but also a more diverse understanding of what is important to conserve."[21] Similarly, the Association of Art Museum Directors lists diversity as a top priority, noting the persistence of disparities in the profession. A survey of employee demographics in Association of Research Libraries found that employees in Preservation were 76 percent white non-Hispanic.[22] The *2017 ALA Demographic Study* indicates that gains in diversity among American Library Association members remain small as well.[23] Furthermore, one of the key findings of the *Art Museum Staff Demographic Survey 2018* found that intellectual leadership positions in "education and curatorial departments have grown more diverse in terms of race/ethnicity, while conservation and museum leadership have not changed."[24]

To contribute to diversifying our respective professions, the Henry and UW Libraries are increasing outreach to campus communities, student employees, and regional organizations representing a range of backgrounds. As one of the largest employers of students on campus, UW Libraries is in a position to develop students who might have an interest in the library profession. As a globally recognized museum of contemporary art with networks worldwide, the Henry has the opportunity to provide its student volunteers and work-study students with a pathway to careers in museum practice. Both institutions have existing outreach programs but are expanding these to include exposure to the field of conservation. For example, UW students are invited to an annual drop-in session at the UW Libraries Conservation Center to learn more about conservation as a career and about internship opportunities for underrepresented students. Our outreach expands beyond the UW student body to younger students as well. We engage the Henry Teen Collective, a group of high school students from across Seattle who spends Thursday afternoons throughout the school year learning from Henry collections, exhibitions, staff, and resident teaching artists. With a strong representation of youth of color and diverse identities, the collective is continually working toward building an inclusive community of young people through contemporary art.

Another goal of our collaboration is to increase engagement with campus departments and other libraries and cultural heritage institutions in the region. Both the Henry and UW Libraries have long worked with faculty and programs at UW. The associate conservator has helped to provide tours of the Conservation Center for students in the Graduate Museology Program, the iSchool, and others. She also provides mentoring and training to the museology students employed by the Henry Collection Study Center and preservation and conservation interns at the UW Libraries. Recently, the associate conservator hosted an undergraduate Bioresource Science and Engineering class with a focus on pulp and paper and worked with undergraduate archaeology students seeking advice about a paper artifact from an archeological dig. The dig was part of Field Methods in Indigenous Archeology (FMIA), a community-based field school that offers hands-on training in tribal historical preservation and archaeological field methods.

The Henry and UW Libraries continue to build a community of conservation in the region by hosting continuing education opportunities, including the Image Permanence Institute's Digital Print Preservation Workshop and, with the Seattle Art Museum, the Foundation of the American Institute for Conservation's (FAIC) Seattle Heritage Responders Workshop, and others. We also participated in conservation research with the Pacific Northwest Consortium for the Science of Cultural Heritage Conservation[25] and hosted the consortium's annual meeting in 2019. We anticipate hosting additional professional development opportunities in the future. As the associate conservator has furthered her own professional development in both paper and photograph conservation, she has shared what she has learned with current conservation and collections staff at the Henry and UW Libraries.

Sustainable Cooperative Conservation Services

In *Beyond the Silos of the LAMS: Collaboration Among Libraries, Archives, and Museums,* the authors note that "the concept of 'collaboration' has many disparate aspects and is used in inconsistent ways."[26] They propose instead a collaboration continuum that evolves from contact to convergence. In 2019, we were invited by The Andrew W. Mellon Foundation to submit a proposal that would build upon the catalytic impact of our initial grant. We submitted a request for support to move beyond our initial collaboration to "convergence." The proposed project, Sustainable Cooperative Conservation Services at the University of Washington, received full funding in December 2019 for use over five years. With this extraordinary support from the Mellon Foundation, we will embed shared conservation services at the UW, thereby advancing our conservation goals, strengthening our conservation capacity, and expanding our role in meeting the needs of our campus and community audiences.

In this next phase in our collaboration, we will develop a mature infrastructure for shared conservation services and engage the third major collecting organization at the UW, the Burke Museum of Natural History and Culture (the Burke). Over the past 130 years, as the Washington State Museum, the Burke has built a world-class collection of natural history and cultural heritage materials, creating an irreplaceable record of our region and how it has changed over time. The museum's holdings currently include more than sixteen million objects in multiple disciplines of zoology, geology, and anthropology, including extensive collections of photographs and works on paper that would benefit from the care and expertise of the conservator.[27] Collections are housed in a new facility, opened in October 2019, which is 60 percent larger than the previous facility and provides much-needed space for collections storage, public programs, education, and research. The Burke's collections are cared for by curators and collections managers with specific areas of expertise. To date, conservation services have been provided by contract conservators.

Through our joint effort, we will strive to reinforce what is most distinctive, valued, and unique about each of our organizations while creating efficiencies and the potential for future and expanded collaborations. Mellon grant funding will continue to support the associate conservator position. We will also recruit a conservation technician and project conservator(s) to provide additional support to the associate conservator as we extend our conservation services across the UW Libraries, Henry, and Burke collections. To ensure the sustainability of shared conservation services, we will secure permanent funding for the associate conservator position at the conclusion of the grant period.

We will also establish a Collections Care Collaborative consisting of conservators, registrars, collection managers, and preservation staff from across the UW to share experiences, training, tools, and tips to benefit our collections. The work of the collaborative will create and formalize new synergies between our organizations that do not currently exist on campus. Establishing the collaborative will also help embed shared conservation practices within our organizations and provide a broader framework for joint efforts in the future.

Finally, we will continue to engage in outreach, research, and education by participating in initiatives that further conservation capacity in the Pacific Northwest. We will work with colleagues to host professional development opportunities and support local preservation efforts. In addition, we will contribute to the national effort to support and diversify the conservation field by offering a pre-program conservation internship hosted by the UW Libraries Conservation Center and by expanding upon our current outreach efforts.

Challenges and Opportunities

Our collaboration in establishing a shared program for paper and photograph conservation at UW has generated challenges and opportunities. Although we were able to recruit a diverse and qualified pool of applicants for the joint conservator position, we found that most candidates had more experience in one institutional setting (library or museum) or one specialty (paper or photographs). We expected that to be the case to some degree, but others who may want to pursue a similar collaboration should recognize that additional training may be needed to expand the conservator's skills to meet the needs of the library and museum collections. To support that training, we requested an ample professional development budget for the associate conservator to attend American Institute for Conservation conferences or other continuing education opportunities, particularly related to the care and treatment of photographic materials.

Since the Henry has not had a conservator on staff before, it was necessary to clearly outline the role and responsibilities of the position within the museum's organizational structure. Moreover, some museum personnel had to become familiar with the breadth of work a conservator can provide. Because the UW Libraries has other conservators on staff, there was more existing structure for the new position. Spending time at both locations allowed the conservator to develop and evolve her role to benefit the unique needs of each institution over time. It also enabled her to engage in collaborative problem-solving with existing museum and library staff. The knowledge of collections and their use provided by staff is often critical to the effectiveness of the treatment and storage recommendations made by the conservator.

The associate conservator has conducted most of her conservation treatment at UW Libraries Conservation Center, where she has access to the lab's specialized equipment, devoted space, additional security, and other conservation staff. The newer lab space, which opened in 2016, was built explicitly with the goal of supporting expanded staffing in paper and photograph conservation in the future. This proved to be particularly helpful for our collaboration, as there is no dedicated conservation space at the Henry. The associate conservator performs less complicated treatments in the Henry's collections and exhibitions spaces with a traveling tool kit. Interacting with the Henry staff as she makes minor treatments has provided the conservator with increased opportunities for educating and collaborating with Henry staff on collection care. We have not yet encountered the need to conserve very large objects from the Henry's collections. Transporting them across Red Square from the Henry to the Conservation Center will require extra preparation, planning, and care.

Sometimes the seemingly simple things like creating a double-sided business card or enabling building access at both institutions required extra effort. The Henry's hybrid status as a separate, nonprofit institution and a university entity occasionally complicates our work. The museum has its own computer support, for example, which means the UW's shared calendar system is not used for scheduling meetings, and the conservator must maintain parallel calendars. At other times, we benefited from existing procedures. A slight modification to the Henry's temporary custody receipt form, for example, allowed us to transport and track materials safely from the Henry across Red Square to be worked on using the equipment and space available at the Libraries' Conservation Center. In addition, we easily amended our Conservation Center treatment reports to include more information on photographs and works on paper and to encompass items from the Henry. We also incorporated treatment reports into the Henry's collection management system.

In the realm of opportunities, we will continue to explore collaborations where we have found synergy in the past: loaning materials for exhibition and exchanging staff expertise when appropriate for exhibition curation, public programs, course support, and collections care. Among other ways that we look forward to building the relationship between our institutions are disaster planning and response. As members of the Seattle Heritage Emergency Response Network (SHERN), the staff at the Henry, UW Libraries, and Burke have extensive training in disaster response. Although we each have our own disaster plans and trained staff, we may work more collaboratively in the future to communicate with the UW Emergency Operations Center (EOC).

We welcome the opportunity to share what we are learning from the collaboration with colleagues beyond the Henry and UW Libraries. To that end, we participated in the Academic Art Museum and Library Summit at Oberlin College in June 2018[28] and presented our work at the American Library Association Midwinter Meeting in January 2019 and Western Association of Art

Conservator Annual Meeting in November 2019. We are also promoting the work of the associate conservator across campus, as evidenced by the article "The Paper Protector" in the College of Arts and Sciences newsletter.[29]

As we begin to embark on a deeper and expanded collaboration among the Henry, UW Libraries, and the Burke centered around shared conservation services, we will continue to introduce staff in related areas of our respective institutions and encourage the exchange of ideas and practices. We also hope to further identify and share common themes in our collecting areas that may lead to new opportunities to bring them to light to larger and more diverse audiences. As the Henry, UW Libraries, and Burke's staff deepen our understanding of one another's work, we believe other collaborative projects will emerge.

Conclusion

As we near the end of our current grant and simultaneously begin to launch a new initiative to engage the Burke, our collaboration has already significantly increased awareness and understanding between the Henry and UW Libraries of the complex nature—and vital need for—collection conservation. Both the grant and our associate conservator have fostered the development of shared conservation services between the Henry and UW Libraries; improved care and appreciation for the photographs, works on paper, and other objects in our collections; and expanded training and awareness of the value of our collective work in libraries and museums among UW students and our broader community.

In the coming years, we look forward to exploring other substantive collaborations between the Burke, Henry, and UW Libraries to support our diverse collections, exhibitions, and communities. The preservation and dissemination of knowledge lie at the heart of our joint enterprise. While UW faculty and students continuously expand the frontiers of knowledge through innovative research, scholarly interpretation, and creative production, the Henry, UW Libraries, and Burke ensure that future generations will learn from and be inspired by the human experiences expressed in the works under our care.

Endnotes

1. "Board of Regents Governance, Regent Policy No. 1: Role and Mission of the University," University of Washington, University Policy and Rules Office, last modified September 17, 2019, https://www.washington.edu/admin/rules/policies/BRG/RP1.html.
2. "Fast Facts: 2020," University of Washington, Office of Planning & Budgeting, accessed February 1, 2020, https://s3-us-west-2.amazonaws.com/uw-s3-cdn/wp-content/uploads/sites/162/2019/01/28161828/2020_Fast_Facts.pdf.
3. "Brief History of Seattle," Seattle Municipal Archives, accessed February 1, 2020, http://www.seattle.gov/cityarchives/seattle-facts/brief-history-of-seattle.
4. "Native and Tribal Relations," University of Washington, Diversity at the UW, accessed February 1, 2020, https://www.washington.edu/diversity/tribal-relations/.

5. Gene Balk, "114,000 more people: Seattle now decade's fastest-growing big city in all of U.S.," *Seattle Times* (May 24, 2018), https://www.seattletimes.com/seattle-news/data/114000-more-people-seattle-now-this-decades-fastest-growing-big-city-in-all-of-united-states/.
6. "Board of Regents Governance," University of Washington.
7. "About the Henry," Henry Art Gallery, accessed February 1, 2020, https://henryart.org/about/about-the-henry.
8. "Libraries Fact Sheet 2018," University of Washington Libraries, last modified March 2018, http://www.lib.washington.edu/assessment/statistics/facts.
9. "Blanche Payne Regional Costume Photograph and Drawing Collection," University of Washington Libraries, Digital Collections, accessed February 1, 2020, https://content.lib.washington.edu/payneweb/index.html.
10. *Jacob Lawrence: Eight Studies for the Book of Genesis*, Henry Art Gallery, accessed February 1, 2020, https://henryart.org/exhibitions/jacob-lawrence.
11. *Out [o] Fashion Photography: Embracing Beauty*, Henry Art Gallery, accessed February 1, 2020, https://henryart.org/exhibitions/out-o-fashion-photography-embracing-beauty.
12. *Shadows of a Fleeting World: Pictorial Photography and Seattle Camera Club*, Henry Art Gallery, accessed February 1, 2020, https://henryart.org/exhibitions/shadows-of-a-fleeting-world-pictorial-photography-and-seattle-camera-club.
13. *Ann Hamilton: the common S E N S E*, Henry Art Gallery, accessed February 1, 2020, https://henryart.org/exhibitions/ann-hamilton-the-common-sense.
14. Jill Deupi and Charles Eckman, "Prospects and Strategies for Deep Collaboration in the Galleries, Libraries, Archives, and Museums Sector," University of Miami, 2016, https://scholarlyrepository.miami.edu/con_events_aamls2016/1.
15. "Staff Diversity Hiring Toolkit," University of Washington, Diversity at the UW, accessed February 1, 2020, http://www.washington.edu/diversity/staffdiv/hiring-toolkit/.
16. "Claire Kenny is UW Libraries and Henry Art Gallery conservator for paper and photographs," University of Washington Libraries, *News & Announcements* (October 20, 2017), http://www.lib.washington.edu/about/news/announcements/claire-kenny-is-uw-libraries-and-henry-art-gallery-conservator-for-paper-and-photographs.
17. Peter Kelley, "Modern American photos, centuries-old European prints donated to Henry Art Gallery," *UW News* (September 27, 2017), https://www.washington.edu/news/2017/09/27/modern-american-photos-centuries-old-european-prints-donated-to-henry-art-gallery/.
18. *Shadows of a Fleeting World*, Henry Art Gallery.
19. *Carrie Yamaoka: recto/verso*, Henry Art Gallery, accessed February 1, 2020, https://henryart.org/exhibitions/carrie-yamaoka-recto-verso.
20. *MUSE: Mickalene Thomas Photographs and tête-à-tête*, Henry Art Gallery, accessed February 1, 2020, https://henryart.org/exhibitions/muse-mickalene-thomas-photographs-and-tête-à-tête.
21. Sanchita Balachandran, "Race, Diversity and Politics in Conservation: Our 21st Century Crisis," *AIC Blog*, last modified May 25, 2016, http://www.conservators-converse.org/2016/05/race-diversity-and-politics-in-conservation-our-21st-century-crisis-sanchita-balachandran/.
22. Roger Schonfeld and Liam Sweeney, "Inclusion, Diversity, and Equity: Members of the Association of Research Libraries: Employee Demographics and Director Perspectives," *Ithaka S+R*, August 30, 2017: 17, https://doi.org/10.18665/sr.304524.
23. "2017 ALA Demographic Study," ALA Office of Research and Statistics, accessed February 1, 2020, http://www.ala.org/tools/sites/ala.org.tools/files/content/Draft%20of%20Member%20Demographics%20Survey%2001-11-2017.pdf.
24. Mariët Westermann, Liam Sweeney, and Roger C. Schonfeld, "Art Museum Staff Demographic Survey 2018," Ithaka S+R, January 28, 2019: 6, https://doi.org/10.18665/sr.310935.
25. "Pacific Northwest Consortium for the Science of Cultural Heritage Conservation," Portland State University, The Regional Laboratory for the Science of Cultural Heritage Conservation, https://www.pdx.edu/chemistry/pacific-northwest-conservation-science-consortium.
26. Diane Zorich, Günter Waibel, and Ricky Erway. *Beyond the Silos of the LAMs: Collaboration Among Libraries, Archives and Museums* (Dublin OH: OCLC Research, 2008). https://www.oclc.org/content/dam/research/publications/library/2008/2008-05.pdf.

148 Chapter 10

27. "About," The Burke Museum, accessed February 1, 2020, https://www.burkemuseum.org/about.
28. Andria Derstine, Alexia Hudson-Ward, Elizabeth Edgar, and Pamela Snyder, "Academic Art Museum and Library Collaborations: Current Practices and Future Directions" (2019), 2018 Academic Art Museums and Libraries Summit (Oberlin, OH: June 2018), https://digitalcommons.oberlin.edu/ocl_works/66/.
29. Nancy Joseph, "The Paper Protector," *Perspectives Newsletter* (July 2018), https://artsci.washington.edu/news/2018-07/paper-protector.

Bibliography

ALA Office of Research and Statistics. "2017 ALA Demographic Study." Accessed February 1, 2020. http://www.ala.org/tools/sites/ala.org.tools/files/content/Draft%20of%20Member%20Demographics%20Survey%2001-11-2017.pdf.

Balachandran, Sanchita. "Race, Diversity and Politics in Conservation: Our 21st Century Crisis." *AIC Blog*, May 25, 2016. http://www.conservators-converse.org/2016/05/race-diversity-and-politics-in-conservation-our-21st-century-crisis-sanchita-balachandran/.

Balk, Gene. "114,000 more people: Seattle now decade's fastest-growing big city in all of U.S." *Seattle Times* (May 24, 2018). https://www.seattletimes.com/seattle-news/data/114000-more-people-seattle-now-this-decades-fastest-growing-big-city-in-all-of-united-states/.

Burke Museum. "About." Accessed February 1, 2020. https://www.burkemuseum.org/about.

Derstine, Andria, Alexia Hudson-Ward, Elizabeth Edgar, and Pamela Snyder. "Academic Art Museum and Library Collaborations: Current Practices and Future Directions" (2019). 2018 Academic Art Museums and Libraries Summit (Oberlin, OH: June 2018). https://digitalcommons.oberlin.edu/ocl_works/66/.

Deupi, Jill, and Charles Eckman. "Prospects and Strategies for Deep Collaboration in the Galleries, Libraries, Archives, and Museums Sector." University of Miami. 2016. https://scholarlyrepository.miami.edu/con_events_aamls2016/1/.

Henry Art Gallery. "About the Henry." Accessed February 1, 2020. https://henryart.org/about/about-the-henry.

———. *Ann Hamilton: the common S E N S E*. Accessed February 1, 2020. https://henryart.org/exhibitions/ann-hamilton-the-common-sense.

———. *Carrie Yamaoka: recto/verso*. Accessed February 1, 2020. https://henryart.org/exhibitions/carrie-yamaoka-recto-verso.

———. *Jacob Lawrence: Eight Studies for the Book of Genesis*. Accessed February 1, 2020. https://henryart.org/exhibitions/jacob-lawrence.

———. *MUSE: Mickalene Thomas Photographs and tête-à-tête*. Accessed February 1, 2020. https://henryart.org/exhibitions/muse-mickalene-thomas-photographs-and-tête-à-tête.

———. *Out [o] Fashion Photography: Embracing Beauty*. Accessed February 1, 2020. https://henryart.org/exhibitions/out-o-fashion-photography-embracing-beauty.

———. *Shadows of a Fleeting World: Pictorial Photography and Seattle Camera Club*. Accessed February 1, 2020. https://henryart.org/exhibitions/shadows-of-a-fleeting-world-pictorial-photography-and-seattle-camera-club.

Joseph, Nancy. "The Paper Protector." *Perspectives Newsletter* (July 2018). https://artsci.washington.edu/news/2018-07/paper-protector.

Kelley, Peter. "Modern American photos, centuries-old European prints donated to Henry Art Gallery." *UW News* (September 27, 2017). https://www.washington.edu/news/2017/09/27/modern-american-photos-centuries-old-european-prints-donated-to-henry-art-gallery/.

Portland State University. The Regional Laboratory for the Science of Cultural Heritage Conservation. "Pacific Northwest Consortium for the Science of Cultural Heritage Conservation." https://www.pdx.edu/chemistry/pacific-northwest-conservation-science-consortium.

Schonfeld, Roger, and Liam Sweeney. "Inclusion, Diversity, and Equity: Members of the Association of Research Libraries: Employee Demographics and Director Perspectives." Ithaka S+R. August 30, 2017. https://doi.org/10.18665/sr.304524.

Seattle Municipal Archives. "Brief History of Seattle." Accessed February 1, 2020. http://www.seattle.gov/cityarchives/seattle-facts/brief-history-of-seattle.

University of Washington. Diversity at the UW. "Native and Tribal Relations." Accessed February 1, 2020. https://www.washington.edu/diversity/tribal-relations/.

———. Diversity at the UW. "Staff Diversity Hiring Toolkit." Accessed February 1, 2020. http://www.washington.edu/diversity/staffdiv/hiring-toolkit/.

———. Office of Planning & Budgeting. "Fast Facts: 2020." Accessed February 1, 2020. https://s3-us-west-2.amazonaws.com/uw-s3-cdn/wp-content/uploads/sites/162/2019/01/28161828/2020_Fast_Facts.pdf.

———. University Policy and Rules Office. "Board of Regents Governance, Regent Policy No. 1: Role and Mission of the University." Last Modified September 17, 2019. https://www.washington.edu/admin/rules/policies/BRG/RP1.html.

University of Washington Libraries. "Libraries Fact Sheet 2018." March 2018. http://www.lib.washington.edu/assessment/statistics/facts.

———. Digital Collections. "Blanche Payne Regional Costume Photograph and Drawing Collection." Accessed February 1, 2020. https://content.lib.washington.edu/payneweb/index.html.

———. "Claire Kenny is UW Libraries and Henry Art Gallery conservator for paper and photographs." *News & Announcements* (October 20, 2017). http://www.lib.washington.edu/about/news/announcements/claire-kenny-is-uw-libraries-and-henry-art-gallery-conservator-for-paper-and-photographs.

Westermann, Mariët, Liam Sweeney, and Roger C. Schonfeld. "Art Museum Staff Demographic Survey 2018." Ithaka S+R. January 28, 2019. https://doi.org/10.18665/sr.310935.

Zorich, Diane, Günter Waibel, and Ricky Erway. *Beyond the Silos of the LAMS: Collaboration Among Libraries, Archives and Museums.* Dublin, OH: OCLC Research, 2008. https://www.oclc.org/content/dam/research/publications/library/2008/2008-05.pdf.

CHAPTER 11

Librarians and Curators as Co-teachers:
Using Collaborative, Object-Based Teaching to Motivate Student Research and Inquiry

Alexander Watkins and Hope Saska

At the University of Colorado Boulder (CU Boulder), the art museum and library are building a model of collaborative teaching across our two departments. Together, we teach research practices that reinforce our complementary learning objectives: hands-on experience, close looking, and original analysis based on contextual research. Higher education has struggled to teach students to move from reporting to analysis and to build critical-thinking skills. Picking up this call, librarians have focused on moving students through the threshold concept of Research as Inquiry. However, this thorny concept has often proved difficult to convey in a typical one-shot library session.

Curators and educators at the CU Art Museum are similarly striving to bring to the curriculum methods of close looking and object-based research as foundational tools for acquiring critical skills in analysis and

interpretation. By joining together, librarians and museum professionals are able to provide an object-based learning experience where students attempt original analyses. This approach has proved to be an effective means of motivating students in their inquiry. Moving beyond lecture-based teaching models, students use contextual research to interpret works of art, creating meaningful experiences and interactions with artworks housed in our museum collection as well as building critical-thinking skills. In so doing, we also demonstrate the importance of campus cultural heritage resources in addressing the teaching and learning goals of the institution. This chapter presents a case study that uses hands-on experiences with museum collections combined with information literacy instruction to teach inquiry and original argumentation.

Introduction

The University Libraries and the CU Art Museum are neighboring institutions on the University of Colorado's flagship campus in Boulder. The Art & Architecture Collection is housed in the main campus library but is separate from the general collections. It contains over 100,000 volumes across the entire span of art history, with approximately 70,000 volumes shelved on-site in Norlin Library. The CU Art Museum is housed in the Visual Arts Complex; the museum moved into its current home in 2010. The collection of visual arts was established in 1939 and originated as a resource for the instruction of art and art history. The museum's collection contains more than 9,500 objects encompassing over 10,000 years of human history.

Dedicated to their respective academic missions, the University Libraries and the CU Art Museum mobilize collections as well as faculty and staff expertise to advance learning and scholarship on campus. Student success is a campus-wide strategic priority, and both the libraries and the art museum have made enhancing student learning an organization goal. Reflecting campus priorities, the University Libraries has made information literacy instruction a major focus of its efforts. It has cultivated information literacy expertise and dedicated significant staff and faculty resources to teaching. This has included hiring an art and architecture librarian with a major focus on student learning, information literacy, and visual literacy. For the CU Art Museum, which presently operates with a staff of nine divided between curatorial, collections management, and visitor services—but without a dedicated educator—collaborating with the art and architecture librarian has been essential to enhancing teaching in large survey courses. By joining forces, we have created a model for sustainably growing our support of student learning.

In this case study, we describe our efforts to address the needs of students and instructors in History of World Art I and II. World Art is a large survey class introducing artistic traditions and movements. The course is taught over two semesters, with World Art I covering the Neolithic to the 1400s and World Art II picking up to cover the 1400s to today. Course instruction consists of bi-weekly lectures by art history faculty assisted by a team of graduate teaching assistants (TAs) who lead weekly recitations. The two-part course is offered every year in both fall and spring semesters. It meets general humanities requirements for CU students and is a required course for undergraduates in the art history program. Every semester, approximately 350 students are enrolled in the course.

Faculty make object-based study a core element of World Art and have incorporated museum and library instruction to help students complete the two basic phases of course assignments: a close-looking exercise with a formal analysis and a research paper based on the same work of art. Until recently, these two phases were completed independently, leading library and museum faculty and staff to seek ways to create a more cohesive learning experience.

The museum's goal was to integrate the collection into the fabric of the course, providing students with firsthand access to works of art while teaching transferable skills in critical thinking and close looking. CU Art Museum staff work with course faculty to preselect a short list of artworks that best meet the scope of the assignment. Artworks are displayed in the museum's public galleries, and students may conduct research during open hours. This has the benefit of increased use and visibility of collections materials that might normally remain in storage. The library's goal was to teach students Research as Inquiry, a threshold concept outlined in the ACRL *Framework for Information Literacy for Higher Education*. Understanding this concept facilitates original arguments around works of art, challenging students to explore artworks in depth instead of reporting basic information. Students additionally learn to use library resources to find the evidence they need to support their arguments. By teaming up, we enhance learning experiences and make our own previously independent efforts more effective. Critical to our success in these efforts was the support of art history faculty and graduate students who shared many of our concerns and invited us into the course. We discussed instructor goals for student learning and consulted on assignment design. As a result of this collaboration, our interactions with students had greater structure and were more meaningful overall.

The Library's Educational Goals and Challenges

The CU Boulder Libraries endeavor to support student success by teaching students how to find, use, and evaluate information. To this end, we seek to work with disciplinary faculty to integrate core information literacy concepts into classes. The ACRL Framework outlines key concepts that information literate students understand. One of these concepts, Research as Inquiry, encompasses the idea that research is a process of asking questions, which may lead to more refined questions and that answering these questions leads to the creation of new knowledge. This stands in contrast to the reporting of already established facts. Once mastered, this concept can transform how students understand the work they are being asked to do in college. The library focuses on teaching this concept in World Art. The move from reporting to original argumentation is a key one for college students to make, but one that is not always taught explicitly. World Art asks first-year students to begin to make this transition, and we endeavor to walk students through this threshold.

The ACRL Framework is rooted in threshold concept theory, developed by Meyer and Land.[1] Thresholds are concepts that are core to understanding a discipline and that are hard for learners to grasp. They are so essential to a discipline that they can seem obvious to experts and therefore often go unremarked upon in teaching. They are bottlenecks or chokepoints for learning, and they impede students' success unless explicitly taught. Passing through a threshold fundamentally changes how one views a subject, and this learning is therefore irreversible. It was our goal to explicitly introduce students to the idea that research is a type of inquiry, hopefully fundamentally changing how they understand the purpose of a research paper.

Threshold concepts for information literacy were proposed in a series of articles by Hofer, Townsend, and Brunetti. In the first article, published in 2011, Research as Inquiry as a concept did not appear.[2] The second article surveyed information literacy instructors; it was in this article that the concept appears to have surfaced in an early version called "Research Solves Problems." In this article, survey respondents identified that students often did not understand the purpose of their research. Their experience was that students viewed research as an "information compilation exercise" rather than a process that "should lead to some original thought."[3] The authors identified students' misunderstanding of the purpose of academic research as a "significant trouble spot" and one that radically affects how students use information.[4] The information literacy threshold concepts were then refined through a Delphi Study which identified the concept "Research Process."[5] The article outlines research as a process of inquiry, of articulating questions, and applying information as evidence in an argument. It discusses this concept's potential to transform student understanding, shifting from compiling facts to answering questions. It identifies asking good questions as deceivingly difficult. This concept reflects the trouble students were having in World Art, as they were often compiling and reporting information rather than asking questions and creating arguments about the artworks.

In a study by Rachel Scott, students identified Research as Inquiry as the most transformative of the six frames of the Framework, while considering it one of the less difficult concepts to understand.[6] Students' previous exposure to the ideas of this frame was highly divergent, with some students reporting familiarity and others saying the concept was brand new to them. This study suggests that Research as Inquiry is one of the more accessible frames of the Framework, not as hard to understand as some of the other frames but the one with the most impact. The split in previous experience also suggests the importance of teaching this frame explicitly in order to level the playing field between students who already have some understanding of this concept and those who were not exposed in high school. For these reasons, first-year classes, such as World Art, can be a key intervention point for teaching this concept and improving student success.

There are many tactics that librarians have used to teach research as inquiry. Smita Avasthi focuses on evaluating and revising research questions. She identifies that students often create unsuitable research questions that won't lead to an original argument: They are often too broad, narrow, or even phrased as a yes-or-no question. She works through revising one question with the entire class and then breaks the students into groups to revise questions and report out.[7] Kevin Klipfel created a lesson plan that addresses the difficulty for students in turning authentic interests into a research question as well as the non-intuitive nature of needing to do research before being able to ask relevant and interesting questions in an iterative manner.[8] Couture and Ladenson find parallels between Research as Inquiry and feminist pedagogy, specifically that both expect students to develop critical questions and become active creators of new knowledge. Both Ladenson and Couture have had success developing classes that require students to develop their own critical questions.[9] In World Art we have borrowed several of these techniques, especially focusing on developing and refining critical research questions.

Research as Inquiry is a key gateway to college success. However, it's a troublesome concept that can be difficult to teach to students, especially in a single one-hour library instruction session. What we have heard from the TAs in previous iterations of World Art is that students ran into several difficulties. First, they had trouble generating questions and contexts from close looking that would lead them to productive avenues of research. Students would frequently ask simple factual questions that would not lead to an original thesis. Second, students fell back on reporting, a more familiar style of writing, when it was a possibility. This would often take the form of a biography of the artist rather than an analysis of the artwork. Finally, students often didn't make connections between their contextual research and interpretations of the artworks. These difficulties were not a failure of the students but rather a lack of explicit, scaffolded instruction on academic research and writing. We found that the library alone wasn't equipped to get students past these roadblocks. The library couldn't teach the close looking skills needed to generate relevant questions about works of art. We could help students support their arguments with evidence from the literature, but they also needed evidence from visual analyses. We needed to collaborate with the museum to expand our teaching.

The Museum's Educational Goals and Challenges

Since the mid-twentieth century, the role of the university art museum as a campus teaching resource has evolved from serving primarily the art department to having a broader impact on academic curricula across disciplines.[10] One driving factor for reorienting the campus art museum toward greater interdisciplinarity has been the impact of grants from the Andrew W. Mellon Foundation for the support of programs at university museums that "strengthen[ed] the educational role of the museum and its collections in the teaching and training of undergraduate and graduate students."[11] In their summary report of the Mellon College and University Museum Program, authors Marion M. Goethals and Suzannah Fabing noted that the Mellon CUAM Program resulted in a general shift among academic museums toward increasing curricular links between museums and their campus constituencies.[12] This shift in pedagogical outlook has impacted the way museum professionals perceive their roles (and has also changed institutional expectations). With this shift came greater emphasis on conducting research that demonstrates the values of object-based learning for increasing critical-thinking skills.

Numerous studies on the connection between close looking and critical thinking have underscored the museum's role in teaching visual literacy. Abigail Housen's research supports the concept that learning close looking and visual analysis facilitates the transferable skill of critical thinking.[13] Visual Thinking Strategies (VTS), the curriculum Housen developed, is structurally parallel to Research as Inquiry. In VTS, viewers are asked a series of three questions designed to facilitate analysis of a work of art. With each question, viewers are asked to perform increasingly complex tasks requiring articulation of a visual experience.[14] The questions sequence through observation and description to visual analysis, which requires reasoning through evidence. While VTS is a discussion-based program, the core principles offer a tiered approach useful for scaffolding student engagement with museum artworks. In theory, the museum visits that World Art students make during the semester correspond to assignments with staged tasks that will ultimately lead to the research component instructed by the libraries. Moreover, providing training in VTS to course instructors enhances in-class conversation and enables the students to gain confidence by practicing visual analysis in conversation before preparing written assignments.

Close looking requires students to carefully observe a work of art for what at the outset can seem to them like a needlessly long period of time. In a reflection on teaching slow looking and techniques of immersive attention, Jennifer L. Roberts describes the educational value of "deceleration," the process of slowing down and resisting the assumed immediacy of vision.[15] By practicing slow looking, details and nuances in a work of art are revealed, and such revelations open avenues for research. Despite it's benefits, it is a challenge to introduce this type of behavior to students especially when the rewards aren't immediately apparent. Moreover, in a lecture-style course where works of art are projected in succession via PowerPoint slides, techniques for close looking are rarely modeled. The museum, then, provides an opportunity for deep and sustained engagement with an artwork. This practice is fundamental to the discipline of art history and may also be transferable to a number of disciplines in the humanities and sciences.

The library-museum collaboration aims to create a clear roadmap for students by demonstrating how strong visual analysis is essential to developing viable research questions. In our combined experiences, we have observed that many students have a limited understanding of what it means to produce a fully realized visual analysis. They similarly had difficulty with identifying research questions derived from close looking. This difficulty in working with art extends more broadly to conducting research on original materials, a mode of research that many undergraduates may not have previously encountered. To better understand student and faculty use of archival materials in teaching, Doris Malkmus surveyed faculty and undergraduates and noted that one barrier to student facility with document analysis was their limited experience with archival research and a lack of understanding of differences between primary and secondary sources.[16] Yet, her survey also revealed that firsthand experiences with primary sources were course highlights and created the most memorable assignments.

Educational Benefits of Collaboration

We found that by teaming up we could help each other with our respective goals and challenges. Artworks in the museum are an excellent way to teach Research as Inquiry. Students cannot simply report on the artwork, but instead need to do contextual research and then make original connections to each piece. The artworks selected for this course are often chosen to represent a movement or a general concept. As a result, they often aren't well-known works by famous artists and so have paltry to non-existent publication records. Students begin to reckon with this lack of specific resources when they do their initial search in the library and discover there is very limited published information on their chosen artwork. This form of educational engagement funnels students into practicing Research as Inquiry and removes reporting as an option. Teaching students that research is meant to create new knowledge and original interpretations is a key goal for information literacy teaching in libraries, one that partnership with museums can help achieve.

For the museum, following up with a library visit helps students engage more deeply with the artwork and reminds them that it is the primary text that drives inquiry. It can help them develop research hooks that they can identify in their selected object: What is interesting about this artwork? What would they like to know more about? Once they have done this research, they are responsible for telling us something new and adding to the available information. What new connections have they made? What can they hypothesize about this artwork? As a result, students are required to identify and provide visual evidence for their original interpretations. We can use this challenge to excite the students; they get to make their own interpretations rather than regurgitate others' analyses. This kind of deep engagement with the artworks—its visuality, materiality, context, and its potential meanings—is a key goal for museums, one that partnership with libraries can help achieve.

Crucially, teaming up can expand both organizations' reach without requiring additional personnel. Museum educators and librarians may not have enough personal bandwidth to extend learning to multiple class sessions on their own. Where many academic museums may have dedicated museum educators or academic liaison positions, CU Art Museum staff—primarily curatorial, collections, and visitor services—share teaching and liaising activities. To fulfill the teaching demands, staff have been forming strategic partnerships on campus. Museum collaboration with the libraries is a good example of how faculty and staff across departments can identify shared needs and amplify their teaching capabilities. Moreover, by working with faculty and training TAs in teaching skills, we are not only able to meaningfully connect students to university resources, we train them in new pedagogical skills.

World Art Collaboration Case Study

At CU Boulder, the art and architecture librarian and museum curator collaborate to provide integrated learning experiences for World Art classes. The library has had a longstanding relationship with the World Art classes dating from 2013. It has used a train the trainer model, where the art and architecture librarian prepares TAs to teach their recitation in the library on research techniques.[17]

More recently, the class began working with the Art Museum to use museum artworks as the basis for their research papers, creating the opportunity for collaboration between the library and the museum.

With the increased use of museum artworks, CUAM staff have become increasingly engaged in ensuring that students and faculty have access to appropriate artworks from the collection.

Before the beginning of the semester, museum staff consult with faculty teaching the World Art course. Within the parameters of the syllabus, they select works for student study. A limited number (eight to ten) artworks are selected and the works vary across time period and culture. In some cases, the selection is made from artworks in current exhibitions while other works are placed on view specifically for this course. Each student is responsible for choosing one of the works for analysis and research. The aim is to make artworks accessible to students visiting the museum during normal working hours and students are expected to return to the museum at multiple points during the preparation of their project.

Museum staff interact with course TAs in an introductory session where TAs receive training in teaching close looking skills and are provided a packet of pedagogical resources. The TAs also walk through the museum with staff and discuss artworks selected for the course. The TAs then teach the recitations in the museum on their own, using the provided techniques. Since many graduate students go on to pursue teaching positions or positions in museums that have an educational component, teaching close looking skills is an important training experience for graduate students.

FIGURE 11.1. Unidentified artist, Chinese, Liangzhu Culture, Bi (Perforated Disk), Neolithic Period (c. 10,000 – c. 2,100 BCE), jade, diameter: 8½ in. Gift of Warren and Shirley King, CU Art Museum, University of Colorado Boulder, 2012.12.158. Photo by Jeff Wells.

Together, the authors taught a fifty-minute session to the class. This session consisted of an initial lecture, where we modeled the processes of visual analysis, refining a research question, and considering possible lines of inquiry. We wanted to pattern the process of asking simple questions and moving on to increasingly sophisticated research questions. We used the example of a Neolithic Chinese Bi disc (figure 11.1) to show how we might move from questions like "What is this object made out of?" to a research question like "Why would this object have been made out of jade?" We demonstrated how to evaluate the research and evidence that would be necessary to answer this question. In this specific example, contextual research might include seeking information on the symbolism of jade or Chinese burial practices. We stressed that evidence must also come from the object itself—for example, the scale, finish, and sheen of the disc. This process is at the heart of the Research as Inquiry concept and VTS methods that underpinned our learning goals. By presenting together on building research questions and close looking, we could each speak to our strengths

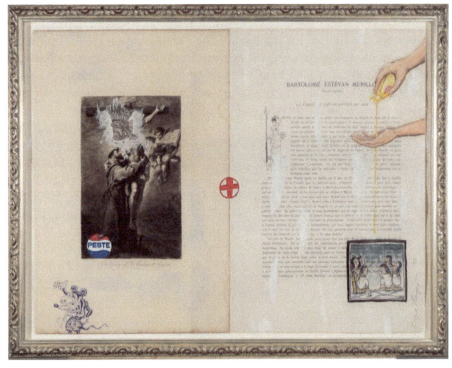

FIGURE 11.2. Enrique Chagoya, American, b. 1953, *The Vision of Saint Francis Assisi*, 1997, mixed media, 19¼ × 24 ¾ in. Gift of Polly and Mark Addison to the Polly and Mark Addison Collection, CU Art Museum, University of Colorado Boulder, 2014.07.11. Photo by Jeff Wells.

while demonstrating that these processes are critical and interconnected skills for art historical research. This short lecture portion provided scaffolding for asking students to form groups and to work through a second example on their own.

During the second half of the class, student groups submitted visual observations and initial questions on a second artwork, Enrique Chagoya's *The Vision of Saint Francis Assisi* (figure 11.2; 1997) via Padlet. We discussed their observations and answered some of their initial questions in order to mimic the process of doing initial background research. Then students submitted research questions, which we workshopped as a group to help create better questions that would lead to more successful inquiry. We found that students' ability to create strong research questions improved as they moved from closed "what" questions to more complex "how" or "why" questions. Students were able to build to strong questions such as "How might the combination of Mesoamerican and Spanish Catholic imagery comment on colonialism?" and "How does the artist use iconography and religious imagery to comment on the treatment of indigenous culture?" Students then broke down their questions into areas they would research and synthesize to answer their questions. This synthesis provides grounding for students to engage in more critical inquiry of their selected artworks during the library visit.

Following the lecture, recitation sections visited the library to work on refining a research question, considering necessary evidence, and finding information through the library's systems. These classes were led by TAs, following a lesson plan created by the library. The lesson plans were workshopped with the TAs, who provided feedback based on their experiences in previous semesters. When students came into the classroom, they wrote their research questions on whiteboards, with one board dedicated to each artwork. This collaborative activity brought together students working on the same artwork and facilitated peer-to-peer learning. The TAs then workshopped example questions and had students revise their questions. Special attention was paid to ensure that students' questions were of appropriate scope and focused on their chosen artwork. Students then brainstormed the evidence they would need to answer their questions, pairing with a neighboring student to discuss their ideas. We stressed that the evidence they identified could be both contextual information from their research as well as visual evidence found through close looking. This brainstorming helped students determine research avenues they would need to pursue. TAs modeled research in the library's systems, using their own example searches. Then students worked on finding the information they needed to create answers to their questions. During these sessions, it has been especially important to guide students toward contextual research and ask them to make their own connections to their artworks, as they will most likely not find information about their specific works outside of the museum collection database. Indeed, this necessitates that students synthesize visual and contextual research to make original claims about the works in the museum's collections.

The sequenced sessions, from museum to lecture hall to library, scaffolded student learning around close looking and Research as Inquiry. We could assess in real time students' mastery of creating strong research questions, as they were submitted and then revised in the lecture and at the library. The lead graduate TA noted that "collaboration with library and museum staff has improved understanding and the quality of student inquiry. In particular, collaboration with TAs on instruction has shown students how to use their observations and questions as a springboard for research in order to synthesize multivalent topics, not simply report back what previous scholars have written." We were also able to increase their use of library resources as they matched the evidence they needed to their questions and found that information through our databases. The art history faculty teaching the course said of our work, "The experiential learning of the close looking museum exercises gives students the opportunity to try a new way of seeing and learning, and the research tutorials are of critical importance, to guide students to expand their use of library resources."

Conclusion

By working together, library and museum educators can help one another achieve their goals, learn from each other's expertise, and create a more seamless educational experience for students. For teaching in museums, this provides opportunities to extend student interaction with artworks beyond in-gallery visual analysis. By working with the museum, librarians can help shape what students learn beforehand so that when students come to the library they are prepared to begin their research. Together, libraries and museums can extend our reach and provide coherent and meaningful educational experiences.

This collaboration provides a model for sustainable interdepartmental teaching. By leveraging collaboration and train-the-trainer models, we are able to scale our involvement to even very large courses and reduce the impact on library and museum faculty and staff. This ensures the museum and library will continue to be consistent partners for this course, irrespective of changes in faculty or staff. We additionally aim to introduce students to campus resources that will enhance their learning and academic careers at CU Boulder. For the undergraduates, this may take the shape of exposing them to materials and methods of research that will inspire and facilitate course work in other disciplines. And for the graduate TAs, who anticipate moving into professional teaching careers, the training they receive from the museum and library enables them to enhance and diversify their teaching portfolios. Finally, we collaborate to amplify our presence on campus. We wish to create ambassadors who feel a sense of ownership over their cultural experiences and understand the important role of libraries and museums on campus and in the cities and towns in which they live.

Endnotes

1. Jan Meyer and Ray Land, *Threshold Concepts and Troublesome Knowledge: Linkages to Ways of Thinking and Practising within the Disciplines*, ETL Project (Coventry and Durham: University of Edinburgh, 2003).
2. Lori Townsend, Korey Brunetti, and Amy R. Hofer, "Threshold Concepts and Information Literacy," *portal: Libraries and the Academy* 11, no. 3 (July 8, 2011): 853–69, https://doi.org/10.1353/pla.2011.0030.
3. Amy R. Hofer, Lori Townsend, and Korey Brunetti, "Troublesome Concepts and Information Literacy: Investigating Threshold Concepts for IL Instruction," *portal: Libraries and the Academy* 12, no. 4 (October 4, 2012): 387–405.
4. Hofer, Townsend, and Brunetti, "Troublesome Concepts," 402.
5. Lori Townsend et al., "Identifying Threshold Concepts for Information Literacy: A Delphi Study," *Communications in Information Literacy* 10, no. 1 (2016): 23–49.
6. Rachel E. Scott, "Transformative? Integrative? Troublesome? Undergraduate Honors Student Reflections on Information Literacy Threshold Concepts," *Communications in Information Literacy* 11, no. 2 (2017): 283–301.
7. Smita Avasthi, "Flawed Questions: Tools for Inquiry," in *Teaching Information Literacy Threshold Concepts: Lesson Plans for Librarians*, ed. Patricia Bravender, Hazel McClure, and Gayle Schaub (Chicago, IL: American Library Association, 2015), 40–42.
8. Kevin Michael Klipfel, "Developing a Research Questions: Topic Selection," in *Teaching Information Literacy Threshold Concepts: Lesson Plans for Librarians*, ed. Patricia Bravender, Hazel McClure, and Gayle Schaub (Chicago, IL: American Library Association, 2015).
9. Juliann Couture and Sharon Ladenson, "Empowering, Enlightening and Energizing: Research as Inquiry in Women's and Gender Studies," in *Disciplinary Applications of Information Literacy Threshold Concepts*, ed. Samantha Godbey, Susan Wainscott, and Xan Goodman (Chicago, IL: Association of College and Research Libraries, 2017).
10. Laurel Bradley, "Curricular Connections: The College/University Art Museum as Site for Teaching and Learning," caa.reviews, College Arts Association, August 12, 2009, https://doi.org/10.3202/caa.reviews.2009.80.
11. Marion M. Goethals and Suzannah Fabing, "College and University Art Museum Program: Summary Report Prepared for The Andrew W. Mellon Foundation," The Andrew W. Mellon Foundation, November 2007, http://mac.mellon.org/CUAM/cuam_report.pdf.
12. Goethals and Fabing, "College and University Art Museum Program," 3.
13. Abigail C. Housen, "Aesthetic Thought, Critical Thinking and Transfer," *Arts and Learning Research* 18, no. 1 (2002).
14. Housen, "Aesthetic Thought," 100. The three core questions of VTS curricula are: "What is going on here?" "What do you see that makes you say that?" and "What more can you find?"
15. Jennifer L. Roberts, "The Power of Patience," *Harvard Magazine* (October 15, 2013), https://harvard-magazine.com/2013/11/the-power-of-patience.
16. Doris J. Malkmus, "Teaching History to Undergraduates with Primary Sources: Survey of Current Practices," *Archival Issues* 31, no. 1 (2007): 25–82.\\uc0\\u8221{} {\\i{}Archival Issues} 31, no. 1 (2007
17. Alexander Watkins and Katherine Morrison, "Can Only Librarians Do Library Instruction? Collaborating with Graduate Students to Teach Discipline-Specific Information Literacy," *The Journal of Creative Library Practice* (February 2015), http://creativelibrarypractice.org/2015/02/27/can-only-librarians-do-library-instruction/.

Bibliography

Avasthi, Smita. "Flawed Questions: Tools for Inquiry." In *Teaching Information Literacy Threshold Concepts: Lesson Plans for Librarians*, edited by Patricia Bravender, Hazel McClure, and Gayle Schaub, 40–42. Chicago, IL: American Library Association, 2015.

Bradley, Laurel. "Curricular Connections: The College/University Art Museum as Site for Teaching and Learning." caa.reviews. College Arts Association. August 12, 2009. https://doi.org/10.3202/caa.reviews.2009.80.

Couture, Juliann, and Sharon Ladenson. "Empowering, Enlightening and Energizing: Research as Inquiry in Women's and Gender Studies." In *Disciplinary Applications of Information Literacy Threshold Concepts*, edited by Samantha Godbey, Susan Wainscott, and Xan Goodman. Chicago, IL: Association of College and Research Libraries, 2017.

Goethals, Marion M., and Suzannah Fabing. "College and University Art Museum Program: Summary Report Prepared for The Andrew W. Mellon Foundation." The Andrew W. Mellon Foundation. November 2007. http://mac.mellon.org/CUAM/cuam_report.pdf.

Hofer, Amy R., Lori Townsend, and Korey Brunetti. "Troublesome Concepts and Information Literacy: Investigating Threshold Concepts for IL Instruction." *portal: Libraries and the Academy* 12, no. 4 (October 4, 2012): 387–405.

Housen, Abigail C. "Aesthetic Thought, Critical Thinking and Transfer." *Arts and Learning Research* 18, no. 1 (2002).

Klipfel, Kevin Michael. "Developing a Research Questions: Topic Selection." In *Teaching Information Literacy Threshold Concepts: Lesson Plans for Librarians*, edited by Patricia Bravender, Hazel McClure, and Gayle Schaub. Chicago, IL: American Library Association, 2015.

Malkmus, Doris J. "Teaching History to Undergraduates with Primary Sources: Survey of Current Practices." *Archival Issues* 31, no. 1 (2007): 25–82.

Meyer, Jan, and Ray Land. *Threshold Concepts and Troublesome Knowledge: Linkages to Ways of Thinking and Practising within the Disciplines*. ETL Project. Coventry and Durham: University of Edinburgh, 2003.

Roberts, Jennifer L. "The Power of Patience." *Harvard Magazine* (October 15, 2013). https://harvardmagazine.com/2013/11/the-power-of-patience.

Scott, Rachel E. "Transformative? Integrative? Troublesome? Undergraduate Honors Student Reflections on Information Literacy Threshold Concepts." *Communications in Information Literacy* 11, no. 2 (2017): 283–301.

Townsend, Lori, Korey Brunetti, and Amy R. Hofer. "Threshold Concepts and Information Literacy." *portal: Libraries and the Academy* 11, no. 3 (July 8, 2011): 853–69. https://doi.org/10.1353/pla.2011.0030.

Townsend, Lori, Amy R. Hofer, Silvia Lin Hanick, and Korey Brunetti. "Identifying Threshold Concepts for Information Literacy: A Delphi Study." *Communications in Information Literacy* 10, no. 1 (2016): 23–49.

Watkins, Alexander, and Katherine Morrison. "Can Only Librarians Do Library Instruction? Collaborating with Graduate Students to Teach Discipline-Specific Information Literacy." *The Journal of Creative Library Practice* (February 2015). http://creativelibrarypractice.org/2015/02/27/can-only-librarians-do-library-instruction/.

CHAPTER 12

Of Primary Importance:
Connecting Social Studies Teachers to Library and Museum Resources

Adrienne Scott, Pamela Nett Kruger, and Irene Korber

> The California State University, Chico's Valene L. Smith Museum of Anthropology and Meriam Library developed a primary source document inquiry program for pre-service social studies teachers in the School of Education to address the 30 percent downturn in field trips to museums and libraries since the Great Recession. The program serves as a reminder that curators, archivists, and librarians have specialized research and interpretive skills that can support social studies education, which has increasingly been marginalized in the typical public school day. The museum exhibit space embraces constructivist learning theory. Nowhere is this more evident than when observing visitors work out new meanings and wrestle with the thought-provoking interpretations gained from primary sources. This program began by introducing the pre-service teachers to an exhibition on the internment of Japanese Americans coupled with primary source documents of the era. The sensitive topic of the internment chapter in American history was a powerful place to begin. Teachers often bypass this and other difficult

subjects, worried that they may not have enough information or they are concerned to address provocative issues. Additionally, high school textbooks often only contain a summary of this period. The pre-service teachers had two important "a-ha" moments from the primary source document activity associated with the exhibit. They realized that historical critical methods and new perspectives could be introduced without too much preparation. They also were able to imagine how other content in their teaching lexicon might be enhanced with this methodology. Our goal was to create a program that would be useful to future teachers as well as expose them to campus and community resources, including local historical materials, that might be overlooked or underutilized. This collaboration forged a connection with credential students' history and social studies curricula. The program has continued to include other exhibition themes and has proved to be a powerful experience for teachers in training. As the field of history grows and shifts, so do the voices who contribute to our knowledge of the past. Helping students and their teachers recognize that history still has tales to tell is the great reward of exposing learners to the power of primary source documents and the importance of designing collaborations between museums, archives, libraries, and schools.

Museums and libraries are recognized as community institutions with educational knowledge and value; however, they are still separated from classrooms and the formal learning process. John Dewey's original plans for the New School of Education at the University of Chicago situate classrooms in a two-story building with a library at the center of one floor and a museum at the center of another.[1] In Dewey's vision, libraries and museums would provide the primary sources to enhance student learning. Today, these institutions reach beyond mere tangible resources to embrace the inherent constructivist nature of learning. Museums are documenting their role in supporting critical thinking in school children, for example. In a study conducted at Chrystal Bridges Museum of American Art, researchers demonstrated a strong correlation between museum visits and a student's ability to make inferences about works of art never seen before.[2] Constructivism lies at the heart of most frameworks associated with museum education, beginning with George Hein, who first articulated that the museum experience encouraged active participation in visitors by muting the didactic voice of curators and other authorities.[3] This opens the space for inquiry and curiosity to bloom and supports the findings of museum researchers John Falk and Lynne Dierking that learning is both process and product.[4] Steven Conn, in his book, *Do Museums Still Need Objects,* recognizes museums as places that are shifting from didactic narratives to public places where new meanings are constructed.[5] Nowhere is this more evident than when observing visitors work out new meanings and wrestle with the thought-provoking interpretations gained from primary sources.

Regardless of the rich heritage and dedication to learning shared by museums, libraries, and schools, the traditional field trip is in decline. During the Great Recession, 30 percent of school administrators reported completely eliminating field trips in 2010–2011.[6] This was around the same time as the Common Core State Standards (CCSS) were being adopted across the country. These twin forces, coupled with increases in curricular content available online, seemed to justify K-12 principals pulling funding for field trips nationwide. Though the economy has revived and many CCSS clearly align with museum and library missions, only 12 percent of surveyed schools restored their field trips by 2016.[7] During that same period, similar parallels were happening in the library and archives worlds as they also experienced a downturn in visitors as more public funds dried up.[8] In response to these trends, and due to changing technologies, many libraries and archives began to more deeply engage users through increasing access to born-digital and digital surrogates of primary source materials. In support of these activities, guidelines for primary source instruction have been evolving for years. In 2018, the Association of College and Research Libraries' Rare Book and Manuscript Section and the Society of American Archivists published the final version of *Guidelines for Primary Source Literacy*. These standards were created to work not only in higher education but also applied to K-12 instruction.[9]

Further, the drop in numbers became the catalyst for changing the Valene L. Smith Museum of Anthropology's approach to school programs. Since fewer schools are making time for the traditional field trip, we wanted to reach teachers early in their careers to impart the message that curators, librarians, and archivists are partners in teaching history and social studies. Even if students can't come to us, we want teachers to be aware that museums, libraries, and their professional staff can assist with inquiry models and primary source instruction that align with CCSS. We began this program by introducing pre-service teachers who were earning their social studies credential to an exhibition on the internment of Japanese Americans coupled with primary source documents of the era. This was to demonstrate the accessible and important collaborative benefits classrooms can receive when including museums and libraries in their studies. The pre-service teachers had two important "a-ha" moments from the primary source document activity associated with the exhibit. They realized historical critical methods and new perspectives could be introduced through images without too much preparation. They also were able to imagine how other content in their teaching lexicon might be enhanced with this methodology. By meeting face-to-face with the next generation of social studies teachers and creating an activity for them to use during or after a museum visit, we also had the opportunity to introduce them to other resources available on regional history. Part of the combined objective on our parts was to plant a seed with these teachers for future collaboration and use of museum and library resources with their sixth- to twelfth-grade students.

On the California State University, Chico campus, the Meriam Library building houses both the Valene L. Smith Museum of Anthropology and the Special Collections & University Archives. Founded in 1887, Chico State began as a normal school with an enrollment of ninety students[10] and started educating teachers in 1889.[11] The university has grown into a mid-sized liberal arts university, with a fall 2019 enrollment of over 16,000 students.[12] The Liberal Studies Program, which offers "an interdisciplinary major for students who want to teach elementary school or want a broad education across a variety of disciplines,"[13] has the fourth-largest major enrollment on campus and is the fourth highest major for bachelor's degrees granted.[14]

The anthropology museum is much like a laboratory. The museum provides hands-on training to the next generation of museum professionals in all aspects of museum work. Exhibits change annually and provide a range of topics of regional interest. Museum studies students learn to write interpretive labels within a participatory museum framework, which helps provide historical context and local voices to the stories being told. The Meriam Library Special Collections & University Archives collect and make accessible materials documenting the campus, land, history, and peoples of Northeastern California. The museum, special collections, and the archives are all free and open to the public. This close proximity offers a natural partnership opportunity. We have often worked collaboratively as librarians and curators behind the scenes with librarian research for exhibitions or with curatorial assistance to set up displays in the library, but we had never combined all of our talents toward a mutual public endeavor. As institutions associated with the academic authority of a university, the perception can be that topics and programming might be inaccessible or highly specialized for middle and high school students. We wanted to break that perception with the community and model tearing down the silo walls that often build barriers between campus entities and academic disciplines. Our goal was to create a program that would be useful to middle and high school teachers as well as expose them to campus and community resources that might be overlooked or underutilized.

We developed this project with a constructivist approach. Constructivism, simply defined, recognizes that knowledge is created inside each learner based on the unique constellation of prior experiences and learning situations each student has encountered and the connections made between those and new experiences.[15,16] Museums are an example of constructivist theory in action,[17] as are active learning approaches employed in library instruction sessions.[18,19] It was essential that we adopt a method and design an activity that was accessible and interactive without being predicated on knowledge of the subject matter or historical critical experience. We realized that this might be a teacher's or a student's first experience with primary source documents and their interpretation, so we struck out to model a primary source activity that could be replicated easily. This approach, using two sources, would also model our aim as facilitators to provide the experience and let the students interact. Constructivist learning models work best when the teachers let go of being the perceived omniscient *sage on the stage* and instead serve as a *guide on the side*.[20]

With all of these goals in mind, we reached out to the School of Education to form a partnership. In the 2016–2017 academic year, 219 students completed credential programs through the School of Education, with thirty-six educators earning a master's of arts in education during the same academic year.[21] The School of Education offers a variety of credential pathways, including Single Subject Credential programs, Multiple Subject Credential programs, and Education Specialist Credential programs.[22] We presented our multilayered plans for a class session with social studies credential students, emphasizing how museums and libraries can be a resource for lesson planning and classroom curriculum development. This collaboration forged a connection with credential students' history and social studies curricula, providing a powerful experience for teachers in training.

Common Core State Standards creators and leaders acknowledge the curriculum-narrowing phenomenon that has been the legacy of *No Child Left Behind* and excessive standardized testing. The narrowing of the curriculum has taken its heaviest toll on social studies.[23,24] Particularly troubling to us is the virtual disregard for social studies topics that has happened over the course of the last decade in American schools. Elliot Eisner recognizes this as part of the null curriculum.[25] While CCSS focuses on math and language arts, it acknowledges that the reading content should be in science and social studies. Jeffery D. Nokes is part of the national CCSS team and an assistant professor in the history department at Brigham Young University. In his book, *Building Students' Historical Literacies: Learning to Read and Reason with Historical Texts and Evidence,* Nokes states, "The Common Core State Standards are a significant step in the right direction in terms of expecting students to engage in more historian-like activities in history classrooms."[26]

In our roles as librarians and curators, we saw an opportunity to impart these historian-like methods through the engagement with a museum exhibition using primary sources and methods of inquiry. Our guiding principle for this work comes from social studies researcher Walter Parker, who writes that primary source documents and artifacts are essential teaching tools. Textbooks, he explains, are only one resource that should not dictate the teacher's process or trajectory in deciding what to teach. He describes a "rich stew of primary documents"[27] as an essential teaching methodology. Parker elaborates on the limitations of traditional textbook programs when he states that too many topics are covered superficially. He concludes that "not only is this not powerful learning, it's boring!"[28] It was our hope that these newly minted teachers would seek to create powerful learning experiences with primary sources and that they might see the value of assembling this stew with curators and librarians.

The student teachers came to the Valene L. Smith Museum of Anthropology's exhibit, *Imprisoned at Home: Reflections on Civil Liberties*, which explores the incarceration of Japanese American citizens at Tule Lake during WWII.[29] The sensitive topic of the internment chapter in American history is an excellent case in point for a number of reasons. Teachers often bypass this and other difficult topics, worried that they may not have enough information, or they are concerned to address provocative topics for which they feel ill-prepared. Second, high school textbooks often only contain a summary of this period or spotlight a particular person or episode in the conflict. This is an improvement over past omissions but sends a message that this subject is not important enough for more in-depth examination or, at worst, glosses over the unpleasant facts to a softened resolution.

Another intention of our project is to expose teachers and their students to what Bruce VanSledright termed the "interpretive paradox."[30] Basically, this means what classes read in textbooks seem like settled facts when in truth they are derived from primary sources that have been interpreted and retold from a certain perspective. As the field of history grows and shifts, so do the voices who contribute to our knowledge of the past. Helping students and their teachers confront the interpretive paradox and recognize that history still has tales to tell is the great reward of working with primary sources. This interpretive power is placed in students' hands and they begin to appreciate the awesome power historians and all citizens truly have. The *Imprisoned at Home* exhibit tells the story of Japanese American internment by immersing visitors in the voices of prisoners, telling how they were forcibly removed from their homes, farms, businesses, and normal lives to be imprisoned in barracks behind barbed wire because they looked like the enemy who bombed Pearl Harbor.[31] Additional documents reveal that the Washington and California legislators of the 1920s, some twenty years before the bombing of Pearl Harbor, were attempting to limit migration from Japan. These letters include shocking phrases such as "unassimilable race" in the official documents.[32] Exposure to these documents offers insights that are absent when textbooks remain silent on these painful truths.

We selected primary source documents to allow participants to dive right into the topic. We did not focus on what they did or didn't already know about the subject. We felt confident that the primary sources would reveal a story to first-time researchers. In our initial preparations, we identified nine primary sources for teachers to work with: three letters, three photographs, and three cartoons. This early iteration of our ideas was informally tested with a group of retired teachers at the museum and with current California social studies teachers in a presentation given at the 2018 California Council of Social Studies.[33] Both sessions advised lowering the primary source document number to a more manageable number. We took their advice and selected two that seemed to prompt the most discussion without too much advanced preparation.

The first image was taken by War Relocation Authority government photographer Francis L. Stewart and portrays smiling prisoners on their knees in a shed surrounded by a great mound of turnips. The prisoners look cheerful and happy as they trim and load the produce into crates.[34]

FIGURE 12.1. Tule Lake Relocation Center, Newell, California. Evacuee workers in the packing shed, sorting and packing turnips that have been grown on the farm near this relocation center. Photo by Francis L. Stewart.

A second image comes from *Citizen 13660* by Minè Okubo, a camp prisoner.[35]

172   Chapter 12

FIGURE 12.2. Minè Okubo (1946). *Citizen 13660.* Seattle, WA: University of Washington Press.

Okubo created her own graphic diary of life in the camps. In one illustration, two women are swatting off a vicious fog of flies or other biting insect with the camp barracks in the background. After asking students to describe the documents, we ask students three simple questions:
1. Who do you think took the photo/created the illustration?
2. Who is the intended audience?
3. What else do you wonder about?

By asking these questions, we modeled for teachers and students how to ask questions of primary source material. In *Teaching with Primary Sources*, T. Mills Kelly, a history professor at George Mason University, is quoted as saying that his students are "good at answering questions, but not necessarily good at asking questions."[36] By exposing students to many primary sources, the practice of asking questions should become more routine over time. The inquiry-based method applied to the images from *Imprisoned at Home* underscores the stark contrast between forced incarceration on the one hand and the idyllic portrayal of the work camp on the other.

Even with such carefully selected examples of primary sources, we recognize it can be hard to engage with such materials through inquiry-based learning. We have observed that students and teachers often don't know where to start in the inquiry-based method. Also, an inquiry-based method can come in many forms from simple to complex, so our aim was to give teachers and students an easy place to start. Primary source literacy involves many factors. The Association of College and Research Libraries' Rare Book and Manuscript Section Joint Task Force on the Development of Guidelines for Primary Source Literacy created a helpful guiding document, *Guidelines for Primary Source Literacy*.[37] This identifies five components of primary source literacy:

1. Conceptualize
2. Find and access
3. Read, understand, and summarize
4. Interpret, analyze, and evaluate
5. Use and incorporate

This method builds on an observer's prior knowledge and slowly reveals that history and our understanding of it are not ever fully finished. These guidelines also align with concepts and learning objectives associated with the well-documented methods of historical empathy, cultural understanding, mediation, and the iterative process of research. These approaches can guide and inform our understanding of alternate perspectives and bring learners closer to the examination and evaluation of the silences and gaps often present in primary source research.

Paying attention to what is hidden or absent can be tricky when working with historical documents. One of the goals of the exercise is to make participants aware of these silences. When they are asked to examine the source's creator and intended audience, they may recognize that some voices have been left out. Was this on purpose, hidden bias, or dominant cultural privilege? For example, by comparing the government commissioned photos of the internment camps with the cartoon-like drawings of Minè Okubo, students can get a feel for the different perspectives. On one side, there is the government photograph that shows smiling, clean people at work. Okubo's drawing, however, shows a crowded, fly-infested space with tired people.

We asked the credential students to wear two hats while engaging with the lesson we had prepared. On the one hand, we wanted them to think about what their students might say or experience while doing this activity. On the other, we wanted them to contribute their thoughts as first-time participants as well. Many similar responses surfaced between this group and others we had worked with. Right away, participants identified and responded to aspects of the images we had not considered. For example, in the Okubo drawing, there is a lone electric power/telephone pole that seems not to have any wires attached. This brought up extensive concerns and conversations among students about the prisoners' ability to communicate with the outside world. It shouldn't be surprising that students who carry communication devices with them everywhere they go would be worried about this lifeline being forcibly removed. Of course, they were aware that cell phones didn't exist during WWII, but fully imagining such an isolated life sparked conversations about what life was like with only one landline per household. While the pole may have been an electric power pole and not a telephone pole, pointing this out was unnecessary as it sparked an interesting analysis among students.

In general, it was not always predictable where the students might head in their questions or comments about the images. This age group often paid close attention to gender-related observations. The clothes men and women wore, including details of fabric print, for example. The printed fabric was interpreted to mean that they had had nice lives before camp. Others interpreted this detail as the person wanting to look good for the photo shoot. Other gender-related observations came in the form of discussing the divisions of labor at the camp and speculation that men and women were separated during work.

Okubo's drawing was seen as reflecting the perspective of an insider. Some discussion of her intended audience took place, revealing that her audience might have been the Japanese Americans at camp. Some thought she could have also hoped that white Americans might see the camps as they really were. These discussions also led to comparisons between the two images. Questions arose regarding the reasons the government might want to control the message and portrayal of the camp to the wider American audience.

In one of the groups, we heard from a Hmong American student who added a nuanced understanding to the photo of the smiling farm worker. As of 2010, California accounted for the largest Hmong population in the nation,[38] for a total of 36 percent of the Hmong-American population in 2016,[39] many of whom fled Southeast Asia after the Vietnam War and have experienced displacement, relocation, and persecution.[40] This student shared that her grandmother says smiling is a good tool to make a bad situation better and that it is wise to never show outwardly what you truly feel inside. As group leaders, we had formed our own opinion that this prisoner was putting on a compliant face for the camera, and this subtle shift in thinking alerted us to our own cultural biases. It was also an opportunity for this student to share her cultural perspective with fellow students. Our deepening insight could only take place by listening to student perspectives and allowing them time to wrestle with thoughts and ideas evoked by primary source documents. Another overlooked element in the drawing was the insects. Rather than only seeing them as a motif to suggest the dirty conditions at the camp as we presenters did, the students' empathy could be seen when the flies caused them to wonder what kinds of medical facilities might be at the camps.

Within the art museum community, the concept of Visual Thinking Strategies (VTS) and the Museum Effect have taken hold. Some of the conclusions Jeffery Smith offers in his book *The Museum Effect* hold up when working with primary source documents as well. VTS espouses that we all have something to offer when we look at art. Patrons need not be steeped in the art history canon to understand what they see. "We vary. The work is constant," writes Smith.[41] This implies that our experiences and knowledge base inform our preferences and meaning-making abilities when we regard art and is true when approaching primary source documents. The first-time viewer needs encouragement that their impressions are valid. With further encounters, one's repertoire improves and grows. Along those lines, an anthropology museum brings a non-western perspective to the fore, which also requires practice and repeat exposures to realize the importance of broadening the human story. Primary sources from the Japanese American internment chapter of history add muted voices to the classroom conversation for teachers and students to explore.

We witnessed impromptu sidebars of student teachers thinking out loud with each other about how incorporating a museum visit could be a way for their students to see real-world outcomes associated with their learning—something the pre-service teachers ascribed to CCSS. Still others saw the museum set-up as a template for teaching. Their students could mount an in-class exhibit on topics explored with primary source document research. Many were also eager to share ways to use this method with other topics. The credential students also inquired about how they could utilize local materials available online for local history units. Further, while their professor toured the museum, she was reinforcing pedagogical reminders and tips that intersected with the exhibition displays. For example, the information about how an executive order becomes policy was displayed with a series of flip panels. The professor suggested the social studies credential students could replicate this idea for any number of facts pertaining to US laws or government in their own classroom settings. These observations underscored for us how these collaborative ventures provide more than the prescribed content. Truly, museums and libraries offer spaces to build on ideas and create meaning.

To conclude the session, credential students were encouraged to share their thoughts with the group and facilitators. We prompted students with questions on what they learned, how museum exhibits could be incorporated into their curriculum, and how primary source materials could supplement and inform class assignments and discussions. This provided us with an opportunity to solicit informal feedback from pre-service teachers, offering a method of formative assessment.

While most of the students expressed great interest in incorporating primary source materials and museum visits in their lesson plans, some students expressed apprehension and uncertainty regarding administrative support for field trips. This ranged from budgetary support to concern about museum content. One student brought up misgivings about administrator support of a class visit to the Japanese American internment exhibit in particular, due to the perceived political nature of the exhibit and the historical parallels to the migrant detention camps that were, at the time, being established on the southern border of the United States. This should not deter curators, archivists, and librarians from encouraging K-12 field trips, but exhibit content may well play into feasibility for class visits.

Students were excited about the possibility of incorporating museum visits into their curriculum, and this experience in the museum brought up many questions about the types of resources available in Meriam Library Special Collections & University Archives. Many credential students teach in the surrounding rural areas and were very pleased to hear that resources were available that documented local history. Nearly all of the students were previously unaware that they would have access to these resources and the museum once they graduated, erroneously believing that these resources were available only for current Chico State students and employees. They were also excited about the opportunity to continue their connection to the university through the library post-graduation with these publicly available resources. These pre-service teachers expressed that after this visit and activity they were highly likely to include primary source materials in their teaching and were more likely to request support for museum field trips.

The Valene L. Smith Museum of Anthropology's exhibitions change annually and the museum and our collaboration have continued through several exhibit cycles, including Mountain Maidu California basketry, avian and human connections, archeology of Chico neighborhoods, and ecological impacts of fire and water on the landscape. These have also been popular exhibitions for several pre-service teacher education courses. School of Education professors are linking their credential candidates to valuable teaching resources through this collaboration. They continue to express enthusiasm for exposing their pre-service teachers to ideas and history that happened in the region but for various reasons may not be included in their textbooks. After her pre-service student teachers visited the museum, Dr. Erica Colmenares commented, "Credential candidates discovered the power that museums can add to their future students' educational experiences."[42] Dr. Elizabeth Stevens, who teaches social studies credential candidates, recently said, "This year, I am hoping to have students notice the diversity of the artifacts on display and how different themes could be pulled from the exhibits to be used in cross-curricular, multidisciplinary units to engage their students."[43] These comments confirm that our program and attempts to reach pre-service teachers are making an impact. New teachers in our area have been introduced to the ways in which museums and libraries can assist their teaching. Feedback from one pre-service teacher particularly highlighted this connection: "CCSS try to get students to interact with primary source documents... and the textbooks try to help. I enjoy seeing artifacts from our area because I always like to incorporate local history into bigger ideas... [the] local level makes it more palatable and digestible."[44] The growing use and awareness of the program demonstrate the power of primary documents as a critical teaching tool.

Conclusion

Primary source documents are the front row seat to history. They allow students to interact with resources. For the Special Collections & University Archives department, this collaboration makes sense because our local history collections are a natural fit for teachers eager to make connections to local places, events, and historical figures. Many of these resources are available online and allow teachers to access them without the expense of a field trip. A basic rubric to measure the success of this primary document inquiry-based method was observation. Noticing whether insights could lead to further research and discovery proved a valuable tool. Though similar ideas came forward each time, every participant brought fresh perspectives and taught us the value of integrating primary documents in our teaching moments, whether they occur in a library, a museum, or a classroom. Inquiry-based methods, constructivist approaches, and VTS all focus on putting educational agency back in the learner's hands.

While society may be moving more institutional information to online formats and substituting artifacts for 3D replicas, learning still requires discourse and spaces to construct and deconstruct knowledge. With growing disrespect for news agencies, science, historical critical thinking, and academia, in general, the need to equip young people with the tools to interrogate and discern the world around them couldn't be more essential. Teachers too need to feel more confident to bring in resources they may not have encountered. Partnering with curators and librarians offers pathways to these resources.

New voices, previously excluded, are being restored to the historical record. From Monticello to historical societies across America, curators, librarians, and everyday custodians of history are rediscovering and including forgotten documents and overlooked stories of our collective past. Recognizing that different narrators offer divergent stories is the first step in introducing students to new perspectives. Students discover what they read in a textbook has been distilled from an original set of sources. This activity equips them to ask more questions about their learning and become ready to steer their own educations. We also remind future teachers that they can call on museums and libraries to provide primary sources from which to build more inquiry-based experiences.

While some school administrators seem to be closed to the new and challenging perspectives the exhibits and primary source documents can provide, we take solace in knowing that these experiences are being offered. We are hopeful that the muted voices of history are speaking to a new generation of Northern California teachers and remain committed to this work of building collaborative partnerships between schools, museums, libraries, and archives.

Endnotes

1. George E. Hein, *Progressive Museum Practice: John Dewey and Democracy* (Walnut Creek: Left Coast Press, Inc., 2012).
2. Jay P. Greene, Brian Kisida, and Daniel H. Bowen, "Why Field Trips Matter: A New Study Shows Visiting an Art Museum Improves Critical Thinking Skills and More," *Museum* 93, no. 1 (2014): 78–87.
3. George E. Hein, "Museum Education," in *A Companion to Museum Studies*, ed. Sharon Macdonald (Malden: Blackwell Publishing, 2006), 340–52.
4. John H. Falk and Lynne D. Dierking, *Learning from Museums: Visitor Experiences and the Making of Meaning* (Lanham: AltaMira Press, 2000).
5. Steven Conn, *Do Museums Still Need Objects?* (Philadelphia: University of Pennsylvania Press, 2010).
6. Noelle M. Ellerson and Daniel A. Domenech, "Weathering the Storm: How the Economic Recession Continues to Impact School Districts," American Association of School Administrators, last modified March 2012, http://aasa.org/uploadedFiles/Policy_and_Advocacy/files/Weathering_the_Storm_Mar_2012_FINAL.pdf.
7. Richard V. Reeves and Edward Rodrigue, "Fewer Field Trips Mean Some Students Miss More Than a Day at the Museum," The Brookings Institute, last modified June 8, 2016, https://www.brookings.edu/blog/social-mobility-memos/2016/06/08/fewer-field-trips-mean-some-students-miss-more-than-a-day-at-the-museum/.
8. Robinson Meyer, "Fewer Americans are Visiting Local Libraries—And Technology Isn't to Blame," *The Atlantic* (April 14, 2016), https://www.theatlantic.com/technology/archive/2016/04/americans-like-their-libraries-but-they-use-them-less-and-less-pew/477336/.
9. *Guidelines for Primary Source Literacy*, Association of College and Research Libraries' Rare Book and Manuscript Section and Society of American Archivists Joint Task Force on the Development of Guidelines for Primary Source Literacy, 2018, accessed January 11, 2019, http://www.ala.org/acrl/sites/ala.org.acrl/files/content/standards/Primary%20Source%20Literacy2018.pdf.
10. "Our History," California State University, Chico, accessed January 11, 2019, https://www.csuchico.edu/traditions/history/index.shtml.
11. "Accreditation and Performance Data," School of Education, California State University, Chico, accessed January 30, 2020, https://www.csuchico.edu/soe/credential/soe-numbers-text.shtml.
12. "Chico Facts," California State University, Chico, accessed January 29, 2020, https://www.csuchico.edu/about/chico-facts.shtml.
13. "Frequently Asked Questions," Liberal Studies, California State University, Chico, accessed January 30, 2020, https://www.csuchico.edu/lbst/about-us/frequently-asked-questions.shtml.
14. "Chico Facts," California State University.
15. Steve Olusegun Bada, "Constructivism Learning Theory: A Paradigm for Teaching and Learning," *IOSR Journal of Research and Method in Education* 5, no. 6 (2015): 66–70.
16. Paulo Freire, *Pedagogy of the Oppressed* (New York: Bloomsbury, 1970).
17. George E. Hein, *Learning in the Museum* (New York: Routledge, 1998).
18. Brian Detlor, et al., "Student Perceptions of Information Literacy Instruction: The Importance of Active Learning," *Education for Information* 29, no. 2 (2012): 147–61.
19. Susan E. Cooperstein and Elizabeth Kocevar-Weidinger, "Beyond Active Learning: A Constructivist Approach to Learning," *Reference Services Review* 32, no. 2 (2004): 141–48.
20. Alison King, "From Sage on the Stage to Guide on the Side," *College Teaching* 41, no. 1 (1993): 30–35.
21. "Accreditation and Performance Data," California State University.

22. "Pathways to a Credential," School of Education, California State University, Chico, accessed January 30, 2020, https://www.csuchico.edu/soe/credential/index.shtml.
23. Jere Brophy and Janet Alleman, "Early Elementary Social Studies," in *Handbook of Research in Social Studies Education*, eds. Linda S. Levstik and Cynthia A. Tyson (New York: Routledge, 2008), 33–49.
24. Beverly Milner and Lee Bisland, "The Marginalization of Social Studies in the Elementary Grades: An Overview," in *Contemporary Social Studies: An Essential Reader*, ed. William Benedict Russell III (Charlotte: Information Age, 2012), 173–91.
25. Elliot W. Eisner, *The Educational Imagination: On the Design and Evaluation of School Programs* (New York: Macmillan, 1994).
26. Jeffrey D. Nokes, *Building Students' Historical Literacies: Learning to Read and Reason with Historical Texts and Evidence* (New York: Routledge, 2013), 10.
27. Walter Parker, *Social Studies in Elementary Education 13/e* (Boston: Allyn & Bacon/Pearson, 2009), 345.
28. Parker, *Social Studies in Elementary Education*, 13.
29. "Past Exhibits," Valene L. Smith Museum of Anthropology, California State University, Chico, accessed January 30, 2020, https://www.csuchico.edu/anthmuseum/exhibitions/past.shtml.
30. Bruce VanSledright, "Confronting History's Interpretive Paradox While Teaching Fifth Graders to Investigate the Past," *American Educational Research Journal* 39, no. 4 (2002): 1089–115.
31. "Past Exhibits," Valene L. Smith Museum of Anthropology.
32. William Stephens, "Correspondence From William Stephens to Louis F. Hart, April 15, 1921," The Seattle Civil Rights and Labor History Project, University of Washington, accessed February 6, 2020, https://depts.washington.edu/civilr/images/alienlandlaw/alienlandlawWAstate_images/GovCA-toGovWa4-15-21.jpg.
33. California Council for the Social Studies, accessed January 31, 2020, https://ccss.org.
34. Francis L. Stewart, "Tule Lake Relocation Center, Newell, California. Evacuee workers in the packing shed, sorting and packing turnips which have been grown on the farm near this relocation center," National Archives Catalog, accessed January 29, 2020, https://catalog.archives.gov/id/538369.
35. Miné Okubo, *Citizen 13660* (Seattle: University of Washington Press, 2014), 189.
36. Tamar Chute, Ellen Swain, and Sammie L. Morris, "Connecting Students and Primary Sources: Cases and Examples," in *Teaching with Primary Sources*, eds. Lisa J. Hinchliffe and Christopher J. Prom (Chicago: Society of American Archivists, 2016), 145.
37. *Guidelines for Primary Source Literacy*, Association of College and Research Libraries.
38. Mark E. Pfeifer and Kou Yang, "Hmong Population and Demographic Trends in the 2010 Census and 2010 American Community Survey," in *State of the Hmong American Community*, eds. Mark E. Pfeifer and Bruce K. Thao (Washington: Hmong National Development, 2013), 9, accessed January 30, 2020, http://aapidata.com/wp-content/uploads/2017/04/State-of-the-Hmong-American-Community-2013.pdf.
39. "Selected Population Profile in the United States: Hmong," U.S. Census Bureau, 2016 American Community Survey 1-Year Estimates, accessed January 30, 2020, https://libguides.csuchico.edu/ld.php?content_id=40653961.
40. Serge Lee and Jenny Change, "The Need to Estimate Mental Health Status of Hmong Americans 37 Years Later," in *State of the Hmong American Community*, eds. Mark E. Pfeifer and Bruce K. Thao (Washington: Hmong National Development, 2013), 27, accessed January 30, 2020, http://aapidata.com/wp-content/uploads/2017/04/State-of-the-Hmong-American-Community-2013.pdf.
41. Jeffrey K. Smith, *The Museum Effect: How Museums, Libraries, and Cultural Institutions Education and Civilize Society* (Lanham: Rowman and Littlefield, 2014), 67.
42. Dr. Erica Eva Colmenares, email message to Adrienne Scott, January 17, 2020.
43. Dr. Elizabeth Stevens, email message to Adrienne Scott, January 27, 2020.
44. Cameron Scott, in discussion with Pamela Nett Kruger, January 2020.

Bibliography

Association of College and Research Libraries' Rare Book and Manuscript Section and Society of American Archivists Joint Task Force on the Development of Guidelines for Primary Source Literacy. *Guidelines for Primary Source Literacy*. American Library Association. Accessed January 30, 2020. http://www.ala.org/acrl/sites/ala.org.acrl/files/content/standards/Primary%20Source%20Literacy2018.pdf.

Bada, Steve Olusegun. "Constructivism Learning Theory: A Paradigm for Teaching and Learning." *IOSR Journal of Research and Method in Education* 5, no. 6 (2015): 66–70.

Brophy, Jere, and Janet Alleman. "Early Elementary Social Studies." In *Handbook of Research in Social Studies Education*, edited by Linda S. Levstik and Cynthia A. Tyson, 33–49. New York: Routledge, 2008.

California Council for the Social Studies. Accessed January 31, 2020. https://ccss.org.

California State University, Chico. "Accreditation and Performance Data." School of Education. Accessed January 30, 2020. https://www.csuchico.edu/soe/credential/soe-numbers-text.shtml.

———. "Chico Facts." Accessed January 29, 2020. https://www.csuchico.edu/about/chico-facts.shtml.

———. "Frequently Asked Questions." Liberal Studies. Accessed January 30, 2020. https://www.csuchico.edu/lbst/about-us/frequently-asked-questions.shtml.

———. "Our History." Traditions. Accessed January 11, 2019. https://www.csuchico.edu/traditions/history/index.shtml.

———. "Past Exhibits." Valene L. Smith Museum of Anthropology. Accessed January 30, 2020. https://www.csuchico.edu/anthmuseum/exhibitions/past.shtml.

———. "Pathways to a Credential." School of Education. Accessed January 30, 2020. https://www.csuchico.edu/soe/credential/index.shtml.

Chute, Tamar, Ellen Swain, and Sammie L. Morris. "Connecting Students and Primary Sources: Cases and Examples." In *Teaching with Primary Sources*, edited by Lisa J. Hinchliffe and Christopher J. Prom, 145. Chicago: Society of American Archivists, 2016.

Conn, Steven. *Do Museums Still Need Objects?* Philadelphia: University of Pennsylvania Press, 2010.

Cooperstein, Sarah E., and Elizabeth Kocevar-Weidinger. "Beyond Active Learning: A Constructivist Approach to Learning." *Reference Services Review* 32, no. 2 (2004): 141–48.

Detlor, Brian, Lorne Booker, Alexander Serenko, and Heidi Julien. "Student Perceptions of Information Literacy Instruction: The Importance of Active Learning." *Education for Information* 29, no. 2 (2012): 147–61.

Eisner, Elliot W. *The Educational Imagination: On the Design and Evaluation of School Programs*. New York: Macmillan, 1994.

Ellerson, Noelle M., and Daniel A. Domenech. "Weathering the Storm: How the Economic Recession Continues to Impact School Districts." American Association of School Administrators. Last modified March 2012. http://aasa.org/uploadedFiles/Policy_and_Advocacy/files/Weathering_the_Storm_Mar_2012_FINAL.pdf.

Falk, John H., and Lynne D. Dierking. *Learning from Museums: Visitor Experiences and the Making of Meaning*. Lanham: AltaMira Press, 2000.

Freire, Paulo. *Pedagogy of the Oppressed*. New York: Bloomsbury, 1970.

Greene, Jay P., Brian Kisida, and Daniel H. Bowen. "Why Field Trips Matter: A New Study Shows Visiting an Art Museum Improves Critical Thinking Skills and More." *Museum* 93, no. 1 (2014): 78–87.

Hein, George E. *Learning in the Museum*. New York: Routledge, 1998.

———. "Museum Education." In *A Companion to Museum Studies*, edited by Sharon Macdonald, 340–52. Malden: Blackwell Publishing, 2006.

———. *Progressive Museum Practice: John Dewey and Democracy*. Walnut Creek: Left Coast Press, Inc., 2012.

King, Alison. "From Sage on the Stage to Guide on the Side." *College Teaching* 41, no. 1 (1993): 30–35.

Lee, Serge, and Jenny Change. "The Need to Estimate Mental Health Status of Hmong Americans 37 Years Later." In *State of the Hmong American Community*, edited by Mark E. Pfeifer and Bruce K. Thao, 27. Washington: Hmong National Development, 2013. Accessed January 30, 2020. http://aapidata.com/wp-content/uploads/2017/04/State-of-the-Hmong-American-Community-2013.pdf.

Meyer, Robinson. "Fewer Americans are Visiting Local Libraries—And Technology Isn't to Blame." *The Atlantic* (April 14, 2016). https://www.theatlantic.com/technology/archive/2016/04/americans-like-their-libraries-but-they-use-them-less-and-less-pew/477336/.

Milner, Beverly, and Lee Bisland. "The Marginalization of Social Studies in the Elementary Grades: An Overview." In *Contemporary Social Studies: An Essential Reader*, edited by William Benedict Russell III, 173–91. Charlotte: Information Age, 2012.

Nokes, Jeffrey D. *Building Students' Historical Literacies: Learning to Read and Reason with Historical Texts and Evidence*. New York: Routledge, 2013.

Okubo, Miné. *Citizen 13660*. Seattle: University of Washington Press, 2014.

Parker, Walter. *Social Studies in Elementary Education 13/e*. Boston: Allyn & Bacon/Pearson, 2009.

Pfeifer, Mark E., and Kou Yang. "Hmong Population and Demographic Trends in the 2010 Census and 2010 American Community Survey." In *State of the Hmong American Community*, edited by Mark E. Pfeifer and Bruce K. Thao, 9. Washington: Hmong National Development, 2013. Accessed January 30, 2020. http://aapidata.com/wp-content/uploads/2017/04/State-of-the-Hmong-American-Community-2013.pdf.

Reeves, Richard V., and Edward Rodrigue. "Fewer Field Trips Mean Some Students Miss More Than a Day at the Museum." The Brookings Institute. Last modified June 8, 2016. https://www.brookings.edu/blog/social-mobility-memos/2016/06/08/fewer-field-trips-mean-some-students-miss-more-than-a-day-at-the-museum/.

Smith, Jeffrey K. *The Museum Effect: How Museums, Libraries, and Cultural Institutions Education and Civilize Society*. Lanham: Rowman and Littlefield, 2014.

Stephens, William. "Correspondence From William Stephens to Louis F. Hart, April 15, 1921." The Seattle Civil Rights and Labor History Project. University of Washington. Accessed February 6, 2020. https://depts.washington.edu/civilr/images/alienlandlaw/alienlandlawWAstate_images/GovCA-toGovWa4-15-21.jpg.

Stewart, Francis L. "Tule Lake Relocation Center, Newell, California. Evacuee workers in the packing shed, sorting and packing turnips which have been grown on the farm near this relocation center." September 8, 1942. National Archives Catalog. Accessed January 29, 2020. https://catalog.archives.gov/id/538369.

U.S. Census Bureau. "Selected Population Profile in the United States: Hmong." American Community Survey 1-Year Estimates. Accessed January 30, 2020. https://libguides.csuchico.edu/ld.php?content_id=40653961.

VanSledright, Bruce. "Confronting History's Interpretive Paradox While Teaching Fifth Graders to Investigate the Past." *American Educational Research Journal* 39, no. 4 (2002): 1089–115.

CHAPTER 13

Using Exhibitions for Teaching and Learning:
Collaboration Between a University Library and Museum

Alex Regan

> *The academic library and museum at the University of California, Santa Barbara, have engaged in collaborative activities to meet broader university goals of student learning in an interdisciplinary environment. Initial success of the collaboration shows the potential for both institutions to extend their impact on student learning beyond the classroom.*

Introduction

In this chapter, I discuss current collaborative activities the academic library and museum on the campus of the University of California at Santa Barbara undertake to meet broader university goals of teaching and learning. I discuss the use of "teaching exhibitions" and other approaches to building complementary exhibition programming between library and museum and discuss ways in which the library has worked with museum interns to provide experiential learning opportunities. I share challenges we faced in building the collaboration in hopes our experiences will provide a model that readers may be able to replicate locally. Finally, I describe the potential for deepening our collaboration.

Background

The University of California, Santa Barbara (UCSB), has an enrollment of approximately 25,000 students and is one of ten campuses that make up the University of California. UCSB's mission statement emphasizes student participation "in an educational journey of discovery that stimulates independent thought, critical reasoning, and creativity."[1] The library[2] and museum[3] share this vision of student engagement in the learning process and recognize that through collaboration we can better meet these goals. Additionally, both the museum and the library are cultural institutions for our campus community of faculty, students, and staff, and collaboration allows us to extend the reach and impact of our distinct event and exhibitions programming.

The library recently demonstrated its commitment to teaching with the establishment of a new Teaching & Learning Department. Teaching is central to the librarians in this department, but all librarians are involved in instruction. Librarians teach classes on conducting effective research, tailor instruction sessions to a faculty member's specific course or assignment, provide drop-in workshops to teach programming languages such as Python and R for students working with geospatial data, and develop online research guides to enable students to become more adept at identifying, locating, and using information resources. As the events and exhibitions librarian in the Division of Research, Learning & Engagement, I plan public events and rotating exhibitions designed to make the library a cultural hub of the campus and a place of extended learning that supports the teaching and research mission of the university. Library exhibitions showcase library holdings and collections as well as highlight faculty and student research and creative activity. Examples include *Art of Science*, which displays the winners of the annual Art of Science competition,[4] *Helmets of the First World War: Battle, Technology & Culture*,[5] and *Garimpeiros: The Wildcat Gold Miners of the Amazon Rainforest*.[6] In particular, I look for opportunities to connect to campus initiatives and courses. For example, in conjunction with the Environmental Studies Department's yearlong fiftieth-anniversary celebration, I worked to develop two environmentally themed library exhibitions. One of these showcased research by a visiting scholar in physics revealing the historical contributions to climate change by Eunice Foote, a nineteenth-century scientist, in *From Eunice Foote to UCSB: A Story of Women, Science & Climate Change*.[7] A second exhibition displayed student creative work incorporating environmental themes. With other exhibitions, I have reached out to faculty during the planning stage to see if they would consider integrating the exhibition into relevant courses and provide ideas and specific examples of how other faculty have done this. Student visitors frequently express their appreciation for what they have learned. Representative examples from visitor comment books include the following:

I really enjoyed learning about this. I love when women in STEM get the recognition they deserve, and this topic is especially important for us today. I hope to see more exhibits like this in the library that highlight women's contributions to STEM. Thank you. — Emily R.

The realism in the expressions of the black and white photos astounds me. I walk by them every day and see the raw emotion, the severity, and, in some ways, the raw beauty of these people and their lives. I find this exhibit both a tribute to the otherwise unknown legacies of these workers and a stark call to reality. I will research the Garimpeiros further thanks to you—please do more exhibits like this. Thanks! — Anonymous

Great exhibit! These photos were powerful and this exhibit achieved its purpose of conveying life in those gold mining towns. I had only heard of such operations abstractly and these photos made these places real. — James G.

In its beautiful setting alongside the campus lagoon, the AD&A Museum at the University of California, Santa Barbara, provides intimate access to art. Through rotating installations of its permanent collections along with special exhibitions and programs, the AD&A Museum is a teaching museum committed to the development of critical thinking and visual literacy in support of the university's goals of education, research, and service. The museum serves the university population as well as a growing community beyond our campus, serving as a resource for the wider Santa Barbara community.

UCSB has just one library, which is, not incidentally, the most-visited building on campus: more than 300,000 people enter the building each month. It is located in the geographic center of campus and consequently acts as both a physical and virtual hub of the university; many students and visitors use the library as a pass-through on their way to separate sides of the campus. In addition, in January 2016, the library completed an extensive addition and renovation project with abundant natural light, many green features, and attractive and functional furniture. The new design included several wall spaces dedicated for exhibitions, some of which are within view of visitors who are merely passing through, giving us an extra opportunity to showcase our exhibitions. By contrast, the museum, which is less centrally located, receives an impressive but much lower number of visitors. For these and other reasons, the library is the most ideally situated venue for promoting and stimulating cross-disciplinary exhibitions and learning opportunities on campus.

Teaching Exhibitions

The library's Art & Architecture Collection (A&A Collection) includes publications on architecture, sculpture, drawing, painting, prints, decorative arts, artistic photography, and interdisciplinary works on the arts covering all cultures and time periods. Collection strengths include medieval illumination, Northern and Italian Renaissance art, American art and architecture, and Chinese painting and calligraphy. In addition to circulating publications, the A&A Collection includes a special non-circulating collection of art exhibition catalogs.

In 2016, the museum and library embarked on a trial series of five temporary teaching exhibitions that were designed for close viewing of the objects within the semi-secure space of the library's A&A Collection. Museums have recently adopted object-based learning (OBL) as a teaching strategy,[8] and research undertaken by University College London found that it is effective across a range of disciplines.[9] Although libraries, especially special collections, are familiar with OBL, our own library increasingly displays digital surrogates, so the museum's willingness to display original objects from their permanent collection is especially appealing. In our trial, museum staff and faculty members jointly curated exhibitions related to an art history course, using a combination of display cases and vitrines owned by the museum and the library. For example, the teaching exhibition *Historical Arts and Cultures of the African Continent* was developed in conjunction with a course in the Department of History of Art & Architecture and was designed to increase students' direct contact with African artworks. The class studied the materials and methods of the production of specific African artworks and considered the implications for the economic, cultural, political, religious, and ritual functions of the artworks. Students used what they learned about these selected artworks to evaluate how to best display and interpret African artworks for a social media audience of their peers. Students in another art history survey course used a different teaching exhibition, *Revising the Archive: Arts of Africa, Oceania, and Native North America*, to study the ways in which the objects on display have been used by varying communities—from their original social function to their current place in the museum. The students gained an understanding of the importance of context for objects and applied this knowledge to rewrite the museum labels on display. For another course, Art and Archeology of the Ancient Andes, the specific learning outcome of the teaching exhibition was for students to go from close observation of the shape, form, and decoration of the unusually shaped vessels on display to developing a research agenda and hypotheses inspired by those vessels. In other words, the students used the artifacts to connect to larger questions about ancient Andean societies.

These mini-exhibitions were designed for close and multiple viewings by students, and the library's central position on campus and extended hours facilitated these repeat visits. The art and architecture librarian's office is nearby, and she is able to provide instruction sessions in which she can point students to additional library resources for their research papers. Having an adjacent subject librarian is one strength the library brings to this collaboration and one we hope to develop further. Another is its dynamic publicity and promotion program, which includes an image-central social media presence, website, a monthly e-newsletter, and quarterly emails to faculty. These various channels help the library reach new audiences for its exhibitions and can generate interest from faculty who may not have considered using exhibitions as a teaching tool. The library's own collections were not used in this initial experiment, but we would like to incorporate them into future teaching exhibitions in the space.

Our experience with the teaching exhibitions has not been without challenges arising in part from different attitudes toward exhibition spaces. For example, library spaces are multifunctional: with the exception of the Special Research Collections gallery, library exhibition spaces are in busy, twenty-four-hour student spaces. The museum, on the other hand, is accustomed to fully controlling its spaces and can place displays where the objects can be seen at their best advantage. Furthermore, it expects a high level of security within its walls. Although the A&A Collection has a staffed service desk that offers a measure of security, students frequently move the modular furniture to suit their need for individual and group study. There is also a risk that students might attempt to move and therefore damage the cases, although this has not happened. The A&A Collection is a popular quiet study area, and with demand for student study space growing each year as UCSB's enrollment increases, library administration is understandably reluctant to remove furniture to accommodate exhibition cases. Library exhibitions must therefore share student areas without reducing overall study space. The space issue was made more complicated by the fact that the library began this collaboration while we were still learning how best to use our brand-new spaces and furniture. A further challenge was determining how to make these displays accessible, interesting, and a learning opportunity for all library visitors. Although they were designed around a particular art history course assignment, the library worked to ensure that display text explained the intent of the displays and appropriately described the objects to all viewers. This effort was often at odds with the intention of the faculty members who were entirely focused on the needs of their classes. For example, one professor wanted no label text other than numbers identifying each object because students were expected to do some research to identify the artwork and would be tested on their research skills. We compromised by creating a handout with information about the objects that we kept at the desk for those who asked.

Complementary Exhibitions and Programming

We have also started to identify library exhibitions that connect to museum exhibitions. Once we identify and agree to a complementary exhibition, the museum handles all design and installation work. This is a major benefit to the library. Although the library has a staff graphic designer and the ability to contract with campus facilities management to install most library exhibitions, the fact that the museum manages these tasks frees up library resources significantly. This allows us to increase the number of teaching-focused exhibitions that we can install in a given year. An example of a recent successful complementary exhibition was *14 Black Classicists*,[10] a joint exhibition that focused on the lives of fourteen African American men and women who made groundbreaking achievements in education and the field of classics at the end of the Civil War. Each of the fourteen taught Greek or Latin at the college or university level and their academic accomplishments paved the way for future generations of African Americans who were entering universities. We displayed a selection of these scholars' portraits in the library's first-floor Mountain Gallery, with the balance, along with a book by one of the scholars and a selection of Greek antiquities from the museum's collection, on view at the museum. Explanatory text on the wall and a brochure referenced the separate installations. Expanding this initiative, the Classics Department organized a number of public lectures across campus, and the library hosted a lecture titled "'Let Us Go Upon the Acropolis': John Wesley Gilbert in Greece, September 1890–April 1891" presented by Professor John W. I. Lee. The library is able to draw an interdisciplinary audience to its events, and attendance was high at this lecture. Additionally, we promoted this exhibition to faculty in Classics and Black Studies, some of whom incorporated the exhibition into courses. The instructor for one undergraduate classics course with an enrollment of 740, for example, required students to attend exhibition programming, including the library-hosted event. The professor arranged that in lieu of attending one class section, students would visit the exhibition and included extra-credit questions on the exam that were developed from the introductory text. In the Department of Black Studies, a professor who taught an upper-division class on Black cinema shared a screening of Spike Lee's movie *Chi-raq* (whose story is based on Aristophanes' Classical Greek comedy play *Lysistrata*) and followed it with a discussion about the connections between Black experiences and the classics. Students in the class were also encouraged to visit the exhibition in both locations. We will continue to explore collaborations of this type because companion exhibitions that are tied to academic departments allow the library to deepen and expand connections across campus while reducing costs tied to installation and publicity.

Undergraduate Internships

Hurst, Thye, and Wise, among others, have written about the career benefits students gain by undertaking internships during their college years.[11] Although less studied, research shows that internships also have a crucial effect on subsequent academic outcomes and that this holds across all disciplines and for both advantaged and disadvantaged students.[12] In 2005, the library began to offer internship placements for students in the museum's internship program. The internships are open to all majors, with priority given to applicants who express an interest in the visual arts, cultural research, and educational outreach, and are designed to offer yearlong practical museum experience, professional development opportunities, and behind-the-scenes training. The internship is offered as part of an undergraduate museum studies emphasis within the Department of History of Art & Architecture. Each year, a curatorial fellow from the museum, typically a graduate student in the History of Art & Architecture Department, oversees the internship program. Recruitment of undergraduates begins in the spring quarter for the following academic year. Application packets include a four-page application form, résumé, list of references, and at least one letter of recommendation. Students indicate their top preferences for seven separate positions, including that of library Intern. The internship allows students to earn from one to four credits, with one credit unit corresponding to three hours of work per week. Students receive one credit for thirty hours of internship during UCSB's ten-week quarter, two credits for sixty hours, etc. The hands-on training in many aspects of exhibition work is attractive to applicants, and from its inception in the 2015–2016 academic year, the library has had no trouble attracting one to two interns each academic year. Even when working only six hours a week, interns attend curatorial meetings with Special Research Collection staff and conduct archival background research for exhibitions in development. For the exhibition *From Eunice Foote to UCSB: A Story of Women, Science & Climate Change*, a museum intern was involved at the planning stage over a year before installation. In the post-internship evaluation, she highlighted the value of working directly with the curator and graphic designer to learn how to develop historical exhibitions:

> I have mainly only worked on art exhibitions, so an historical exhibition that must be planned carefully to avoid overloading viewers with text was very educational. I learned how valuable graphic design is to exhibitions that emphasize text, and how important it is to learn to coordinate with many different individuals and departments. I also learned how to create a focused plan for an exhibition.

190   Chapter 13

For a recent Special Research Collections exhibition, *Nuestras Américas: An Exploration of Expressive Cultures in Latina and Latino America*,[13] an intern majoring in global studies conducted archival research for the section of the exhibition dedicated to the tango. In her post-internship evaluation, she stated that she had never done archival research before, and having the opportunity to do so was the most valuable part of the internship.

At the time of writing, two interns are working with the library's Special Research Collections staff, and their tasks include arranging and describing primary source collections and creating metadata. Given the library's need for such work and the positive learning opportunities it offers to students who are interested in archival work, we intend to update and expand the internship position description to include these options. In addition to curation, research, and exhibition installation activities, it will include tasks such as arrangement and description of primary source collections, including producing metadata and working with digital content. The museum requires that all interns, regardless of the location of their internship, attend additional learning seminars at the museum. These seminars are taught by curators, exhibition designers, the registrar, the museum director, and the art and architecture librarian, who instruct interns on information literacy and how to do research in support of curatorial work. Library goals for the internship program include working more closely with the curatorial fellow to learn more about the intern experience at the museum and capturing more complete feedback from the students at the end of the internship.

Next Steps: Challenges and Opportunities

Zorich, Waibel, and Erway laid out a useful continuum of steps for thinking about collaborations: contact, cooperation, coordination, collaboration, and convergence.[14] The collaborative efforts I have described here fall between cooperation (agreeing to work informally on an activity or effort that offers a small benefit) and coordination (when cooperation moves beyond the ad hoc basis and a framework is needed to organize efforts and make sure that participants are on the same page). Although the process is somewhat informal, the library and museum together coordinate the installation, label writing, promotion, and deinstallation/storage of the teaching exhibitions. Coordination also exists around the museum-library internship partnership; however, again, this is informal. I believe the intern experience would improve if the partnership were more integrated—for example, if the library mentors, museum internship coordinators, and interns meet together to establish internship goals and guideposts for success. Finally, collaboration around the complementary exhibitions is still on an ad hoc basis, as opportunities arise.

Using Exhibitions for Teaching and Learning   191

We do not expect that we will develop a combined museum-library exhibition program anytime soon because we have much invested in our autonomy and spaces. However, there is potential for deeper collaboration through the development of formal shared goals for collaboration and metrics for success and utilization of librarian subject expertise. Furthermore, I believe that our future is one of closer collaboration; the library at UCSB has become a true hub of campus, and greater integration with the library would help the museum achieve many of its goals. Campus-library partnerships at UCSB are on the rise as partners recognize and value the important place the library holds on campus. In the last several years, two new centers have been established within the library: UCSB's first Transfer Student Center to support its large transfer student population and the Center for Innovative Teaching, Research and Learning, a research unit that promotes and supports inclusive teaching and learning.

Students spend more time in the library than in any other campus building, and as UCSB's population expands and becomes more diverse, the demand for our services and spaces continues to grow. Our bookable group study rooms, presentation practice rooms, quiet places to study, instruction sessions, and public programming are in high demand. Art and other exhibitions in the library create opportunities for reflection and inspiration that students appreciate:

I left feeling inspired. Thank you. – Anonymous

There is something beautiful and admirable about the people in the photos. I see strength and will. Although their lives are harsher than I could ever imagine, it feels like looking at them, I feel courage. If I were to converse with them, there is no doubt that I would learn much about all that is important in life. At least that is the impression I get. Thank you for this gorgeous, inspiring art! I really needed it after this tiring year. That there are people out there with their strength as in these photos, I want to be strong too. – A lost UCSB student

Fun to look at while stressed with midterms! – Anonymous

The library has much to learn from the museum and values its greater expertise in exhibition design, curation, and installation. The museum's exhibition designer, registrar, and curatorial staff have been willing to share their knowledge and skills with the library and this has resulted in an overall improvement in the quality and impact of library exhibitions. The library values the companion exhibitions for the cultural enrichment they bring to library spaces and the library's physical spaces and established channels for publicity and promotion provide increased visibility for museum exhibitions. In addition, the library's research, teaching, subject expertise, and the relationships between subject librarians and academic departments provide added value to these partner exhibitions. Because of the mutual benefit and our shared dedication to student learning through exhibitions, I expect the collaboration to continue. We agree with the statement in the white paper resulting from the Academic Art Museum and Library Summit that "no longer simply repositories of knowledge and stewards of objects, academic libraries and museums play critical roles in the intellectual engagement, cultural enrichment, and personal as well as professional development of the many constituents they serve."[15] In partnership with the museum, the library will continue to explore a collaborative approach to exhibitions, exhibitions as learning tools, and ways in which the existing internship program can be strengthened to better serve students' academic and professional goals.

Endnotes

1. "About UC Santa Barbara," University of California, Santa Barbara, accessed December 1, 2019, https://www.ucsb.edu/about.
2. "Mission, Vision and Values," University of California, Santa Barbara, UCSB Library, accessed December 1, 2019, https://www.library.ucsb.edu/about-library/mission-vision-values.
3. "About the Museum," University of California, Santa Barbara, AD&A Museum, accessed December 1, 2019, https://www.museum.ucsb.edu/about.
4. *Art of Science 2019*, University of California, Santa Barbara, UCSB Library, https://www.library.ucsb.edu/events-exhibitions/art-science-2019.
5. *Helmets of the First World War: Battle, Technology, and Culture*, University of California, Santa Barbara, UCSB Library, https://spotlight.library.ucsb.edu/starlight/helmets-firstworldwar.
6. *Garimpeiros: The Wildcat Gold Miners of the Amazon Rainforest*, University of California, Santa Barbara, UCSB Library, https://spotlight.library.ucsb.edu/starlight/garimpeiros.
7. *Eunice Foote to UCSB: A Story of Women, Science and Climate Change*, University of California, Santa Barbara, UCSB Library, https://spotlight.library.ucsb.edu/starlight/eunice-foote-to-ucsb.
8. T. Tuckett and E. Lawes, "Object Literacy at University College London Library Services," *Art Libraries Journal* 42(2) (2017), 99–106.
9. "Object-based Learning Research," University College London, UCL Museums and Collections, accessed December 1, 2019, https://www.ucl.ac.uk/culture/teaching-object-based-learning.
10. "News," University of California, Santa Barbara, AD&A Museum, https://www.museum.ucsb.edu/news/feature/512.
11. J. L. Hurst, A. Thye, and C. L. Wise, "Internships: The Key to Career Preparation, Professional Development, and Career Advancement," *Journal of Family & Consumer Sciences* 106(2) (2014), 58–62.
12. J. F. Binder, T. Baguley, C. Crook, and F. Miller, "The Academic Value of Internships: Benefits Across Disciplines and Student Backgrounds," *Contemporary Educational Psychology* 41 (2015), 73–82.
13. *Nuestras Américas: An Exploration of Expressive Cultures in Latina and Latino America*, University of California, Santa Barbara, UCSB Library, https://spotlight.library.ucsb.edu/starlight/nuestras-americas.
14. Diaane Zorich, Günter Waibel, and Ricky Erway, *Beyond the Silos of the LAMs: Collaboration Among Libraries, Archives and Museums* (Dublin OH: OCLC Research, 2008), https://www.oclc.org/content/dam/research/publications/library/2008/2008-05.pdf.
15. J. Deupi and C. Eckman, "Prospects and Strategies for Deep Collaboration in the Galleries, Libraries, Archives, and Museums Sector," University of Miami, 2016, https://scholarship.miami.edu/discovery/delivery/01UOML_INST:ResearchRepository/12355386560002976?l#13355502670002976.

Bibliography

Binder, J. F., T. Baguley, C. Crook, and F. Miller. "The Academic Value of Internships: Benefits Across Disciplines and Student Backgrounds." *Contemporary Educational Psychology* 41 (2015), 73–82.

Chatterjee, H. J. "Object-based Learning in Higher Education: The Pedagogical Power of Museums." 2011. Published online at https://edoc.hu-berlin.de/bitstream/handle/18452/9349/behler.pdf?sequence=1.

Deupi, J., and C. Eckman. "Prospects and Strategies for Deep Collaboration in the Galleries, Libraries, Archives, and Museums Sector." University of Miami. 2016. https://scholarship.miami.edu/discovery/delivery/01UOML_INST:ResearchRepository/12355386560002976?l#13355502670002976.

Eyler, J. "The Power of Experiential Education." *Liberal Education* 95(4) (2009), 24–31.

Ford, E. "Bringing Town and Gown Together: Using Local History to Engage Students and Create Collaborative Partnerships." *Journal of Museum Education* 41(4) (2016), 262–74.

Hendrickson, L. "Teaching with Artifacts and Special Collections." *Bulletin of the History of Medicine* 90(1) (2016), 136–40.

Hurst, J. L., A. Thye, and C. L. Wise. "Internships: The Key to Career Preparation, Professional Development, and Career Advancement." *Journal of Family & Consumer Sciences* 106(2) (2014), 58–62.

Maloney, B., and M. D. Hill. "Museums and Universities: Partnerships with Lasting Impact." *Journal of Museum Education* 41:4 (2016), 247–49.

Rislow, M., and A. Nelson. "Artist Files and Art Students: Expanding Audience Through Collaboration Between an Art Museum Library and a Contemporary Art History University Course." *Journal of Museum Education* 45(2) (2020), 166–75.

Spanjaard, D., T. Hall, and N. Stegemann. "Experiential Learning: Helping Students to Become 'Career-ready.'" *Australasian Marketing Journal (AMJ)* 26(2) (2018), 163–71.

Tuckett, T., and E. Lawes. "Object Literacy at University College London Library Services." *Art Libraries Journal* 42(2) (2017), 99–106.

University College London. UCL Museums and Collections. "Object-based Learning Research." Accessed December 1, 2019. https://www.ucl.ac.uk/culture/teaching-object-based-learning.

University of California, Santa Barbara. "About UC Santa Barbara." Accessed December 1, 2019. https://www.ucsb.edu/about.

University of California, Santa Barbara. AD&A Museum. "About the Museum." Accessed December 1, 2019. https://www.museum.ucsb.edu/about.

———. "News." https://www.museum.ucsb.edu/news/feature/512.

University of California, Santa Barbara, UCSB Library. Art of Science 2019. https://www.library.ucsb.edu/events-exhibitions/art-science-2019.

———. *Eunice Foote to UCSB: A Story of Women, Science and Climate Change.* https://spotlight.library.ucsb.edu/starlight/eunice-foote-to-ucsb.

———. *Garimpeiros: The Wildcat Gold Miners of the Amazon Rainforest.* https://spotlight.library.ucsb.edu/starlight/garimpeiros.

———. *Helmets of the First World War: Battle, Technology, and Culture.* https://spotlight.library.ucsb.edu/starlight/helmets-firstworldwar.

———. "Mission, Vision and Values." Accessed December 1, 2019. https://www.library.ucsb.edu/about-library/mission-vision-values.

———. *Nuestras Américas: An Exploration of Expressive Cultures in Latina and Latino America.* https://spotlight.library.ucsb.edu/starlight/nuestras-americas.

Zorich, Diane, Günter Waibel, and Ricky Erway. *Beyond the Silos of the LAMs: Collaboration Among Libraries, Archives and Museums.* Dublin OH: OCLC Research, 2008. https://www.oclc.org/content/dam/research/publications/library/2008/2008-05.pdf.

CHAPTER 14

Collection-Centered Teaching, Learning, and Scholarship in St. John's University's Master's Degree Program in Museum Administration

Dr. Susan Rosenberg with Alyse Hennig

This chapter illuminates the dialogue between Dr. Susan Rosenberg, director of the Master of Arts (M.A). Museum Administration program, and university archivist Alyse Hennig in developing opportunities for collections-based, collaborative teaching and learning at St. John's University, a teaching-focused institution of over 20,000 students based in New York City. Three case studies highlighting student engagement with the university's Special Collections provide insight into the central role of collections-based teaching and learning in the M.A. Museum Administration program's mission and curriculum. Detailed discussion of the development and implementation of hands-on educational projects and programs devised by faculty and university archivists to utilize the unique collections available to students "in their own backyard" demonstrates how this teaching/learning model is embedded in the curriculum and professional training of graduate museum administration students, public history students, and archives studies students while benefiting the mission of the Special Collections Department.

Devised in response to the plethora of academic programs in the New York metropolitan area and beyond that exclusively focus on training students to become contemporary art curators, the M.A. Museum Administration program was launched in fall 2015 at St. John's University, New York.[1] This program educates students about collections-based institutions and the wide range of job opportunities available in the cultural sector. The program recognizes that today every aspect of the museum field requires professional expertise that can be gained through academic study, which includes practical, hands-on skills building. Students learn that a museum's mission is grounded in the identity of its permanent collection—the touchstone for all programming, including temporary exhibitions. As a participant in an academic consortium that includes master's degree programs in both public history[2] and library and information sciences,[3] the Museum Administration program emphasizes commonalities among collections-based institutions and how knowledge obtained in one program (and in relationship to one type of institution) is easily transferrable to another. Many students enrolled in the M.A. Museum Administration program come from undergraduate majors other than art history. Students enrolled in the program regularly benefit from courses offered by the public history program—such as "U.S. Monuments and Historical Sites," "Oral History Methodologies," as well as "Introduction to Public History." Within the Library and Information Sciences program, M.A. Museum students participate in courses such as Museum Informatics and Archives and Records Management, much as Public History and Library and Information Science students greatly contribute to M.A. Museum Administration courses that include, Writing for Museums, Introduction to Curating, Cultural Heritage Preservation, and Exhibition Controversies: Legal, Political and Ethical Issues, 1980s-Present.

All three programs are devised to enable students to draw their electives from among courses delivered in these content-adjacent degree programs. Embedding cross-disciplinary study in these programs enables graduates to attain positions in museums of any type or genre—not merely art museums, art galleries, and auction houses but also historic houses, archives, libraries, and in many other cultural institutions. The students come from a wide range of academic backgrounds and professional experiences. They are given great latitude to engage with the curriculum of the three related master's degree programs through the lenses of their discipline-specific interests and career goals. Because collections are at the core of each of the three programs, St. John's University Libraries' Special Collections have become an integral resource for research, teaching, and learning. Educational activities designed through faculty-archivist collaboration, including a condition reporting exercise and a student-curated exhibition capstone project, enhance the student experience in the M.A. Museum Administration program while benefitting Special Collections through knowledge creation and increased publicity.

Condition Reporting Exercise

As has been reported in analyses of object-based pedagogy, "faculty often don't realize that librarians and archivists can help them design interactions with primary sources based on their course learning objectives using active learning techniques that ask students to engage deeply in an interpretive activity."[4] As we have discovered at St. John's University, "Archivists and librarians can work with faculty to create assignments and active learning exercises that highlight their collections, and, more importantly, foster students' cognitive development and critical thinking skills."[5] One project initiated in the program's inaugural year has continued to remain a staple for incoming students' first semester. A required course, Introduction to Working in Museums, awakens students to the great variety of available museum jobs while addressing best practices, ethical standards, and most especially current issues and debates taking place in different arenas of the field. The class devotes significant time to subjects such as collections management, collections preservation, and collections use.[6] Students are introduced to these topics through an exercise in condition reporting using objects strategically selected from the Kathryn and Shelby Cullom Davis Library located at the university's Manhattan campus. This is a specialized library focused on the insurance industry and its history, most often used by industry professionals and lawyers or scholars working in these areas. The collection's esoteric focus and idiosyncratic holdings mean that many of its artifacts are not readily identifiable; this makes the collection an ideal laboratory for a pedagogical project aimed to hone students' skills in visual observation and written analyses.

To prepare for the exercise, students read several books that contain examples of condition reports. They are encouraged to borrow from among the templates these texts offer and are invited to create their own, which they then bring to the library. Meanwhile, the archivist selects from among the many fascinating artifacts and artworks in the Davis Library's collection, which contains portraits of insurance industry leaders, late nineteenth- and early twentieth-century advertising signs, engravings depicting scenes of disasters, and a wide array of quirky memorabilia and ephemera. One guiding principle is to choose objects made in a variety of materials: works on paper, oil paintings on canvas, ceramics, glass, textiles, wood, metals, and plastic.

Some items are in excellent condition; others show damage or deterioration. Some are sturdy while others are more fragile. Many of the objects are cataloged or described within an archival finding aid; others have little or no description. Students are discouraged from pursuing any type of research as part of the realization of their condition-reporting assignment so that they concentrate solely on the physical properties of the objects. "Objects can be viewed from many different perspectives to reveal multiple, and sometimes contradictory, meanings. On encountering an object, especially one they have never seen before, a learner may start by asking relatively basic questions; such as what is it, what is it made of and where did it come from? However, these questions will lead the learner on a path towards confronting ever more complex considerations, which may concern the historical contexts, social relationships and biography of the object, as well as its (multiple) cultural meanings and values. Students can discover these new investigative avenues for themselves, as they respond to the prompts the object raises and can begin to make their own meaning through their concrete experiences with it."[7]

The controlled environment of the classroom enables students to gain hands-on experience with rare and fragile artifacts where there is little risk for damage. In this scenario, the students are asked to view the objects through the eyes of a collections manager and/or conservator. Upon arrival at the library, students receive a basic introduction to proper handling procedures. Then they encounter objects that the archivist has placed next to, or left inside of, their storage containers. Since current storage conditions are not always ideal, especially for new acquisitions, students are encouraged to contemplate what type of container is most appropriate for preserving a particular object. Students select an object that compels them and then examine it for about forty minutes while taking extensive notes. Both the faculty member and archivist move around the room prompting students with questions and pointing out unnoticed aspects of the objects under review. The archivist suggests that students refrain from photographing their selected objects, at least until the end of the class session, ensuring that their attention remains focused on the materiality of the artifact—and so that students do not replace first-hand observation with reliance on photographs for later consultation when they write up their assignment.

Any description of the purpose of the objects, the creator or manufacturer, provenance, date of creation, or material types is only revealed after the students have sufficient time to complete their reports. At the end of the meeting, students briefly share observations about their objects with the class and are asked to transform their notes into a written condition report that includes detailed descriptive information about the object's appearance, its state of deterioration or preservation, suggestions for future conservation efforts, guidelines to follow should the object be requested for loan to another institution, and sketches or photographs that note any condition issues. Due to differences in librarian and archivist staff responsibilities and priorities, as compared to those typical of museums, St. John's archivist does not create detailed condition reports but rather notes condition issues on accession records or in finding aids. Therefore, students' submission of their completed reports to the archivist adds knowledge and documentation to the collection.

Having repeated this exercise over several years, the archivist knows that certain objects are favorites and fulfill unique pedagogical purposes. For example, a wooden cigar box containing insurance inspectors' badges propels student discussion as to why the metal badges were stored in the box, when they were placed there, if they should remain there long-term, whether the container offers clues regarding the objects' provenance, and the reasons why the badges might be of historical research value for the library's users. The ultimate purpose of the condition-reporting exercise is to promote detailed and prolonged observation as a method that produces research questions that may or may not be answerable. Students are educated to recognize when an object's condition is compromised and to learn basic conservation terminology as applied to describe typical condition problems of different materials. They are taught how to do a close reading of an artifact and its condition in preparation for transferring these facts into a condition report defined by clear, detailed descriptive writing and a structure that accounts for both the "big picture" overview of the object as well as discussion of important but smaller-scale aspects of its identity.

In addition to serving as a resource for the Introduction to Museums course, the Davis Library attracts work-study students and graduate assistants who obtain mentoring in various aspects of archival management while contributing to the library's ongoing activities. Graduate students in the Public History program conduct scholarly research on its collection materials, a work product that inevitably supports the library's ongoing efforts to catalog and digitize its holdings. At the same time, the St. John's University Libraries' Special Collections department, located on the university's main campus in Queens, New York, is an essential resource for other collections-based teaching and learning activities embedded in the Museum Administration program curriculum.

Student-Curated Exhibitions

During semester three of the four-semester program, all students are required to enroll in the Introduction to Curating class, which results in a student-curated exhibition that is presented each March in the university's Dr. M. T. Geoffrey Yeh Gallery. The class is overseen by Dr. Susan Rosenberg, a former curator of modern and contemporary art and founding director of St. John's University's M.A. Museum Administration program. The students are first asked to research and write about a group of artifacts that have been pre-selected from the St. John's University Libraries' Special Collections department. Next, they participate in curating the exhibition and work with the gallery director to install the artwork and labels. Finally, they create and execute educational programming that promotes the exhibition and serves the university community's academic environment. The accessibility of the Special Collections department as the source for a student-curated exhibition mitigates the complex and time-consuming effort to produce an exhibition that borrows works from outside institutions, requiring loan requests and legal paperwork, although in the 2020 iteration of the course, the exhibition relied on loans from another academic institution's special collections department.

In preparation for the Introduction to Curating class, students are required to enroll in a class called Writing for Museums, where virtual—rather than actual—collections are the center of semester-long projects. This prepares students to hit the ground running when they enroll in Introduction to Curating. In the writing course, students are asked to "curate" a package of objects that they believe can tell a story or illuminate some aspect of art history or history as if they were creating an actual exhibition. Students typically identify five objects about which they will research and write throughout the semester.

A major function of this class is "The teaching of verbal literacy... [i.e.] how words interact with objects and their installation to form persuasive arguments. [Students are instructed to analyze] the claims that verbal texts make and on how they are supported—[and to scrutinize] the agency of exhibitors, curators, educators, and administrators in producing both those texts and more broadly, the exhibit."[8] Owing to the diverse interests of students in the Museum Administration and Public History programs at St. John's, in past years, members of the class chose to write about topics ranging from the history of sneaker design to seventeenth-century Dutch regentesses portraits, the representation of psychoanalysis in 1940s films, the history of Henry K. Frick's collection of female portraits, contemporary photography, and the representations of homes in American paintings, among other subjects. Because students are working with virtual objects, they are encouraged to change the contents of their object package if their research takes them in different directions during the semester. One important goal of the class is to impart the experience of keeping research and writing "in-process" rather than sticking with a first thought or a first draft. For most students, this can be anxiety-producing at first, but they soon become accustomed to responding to requests for multiple revisions of submitted texts. This simulates the creative processes inherent to writing and curating, simulating situations when objects cannot be loaned and substitutes must be used instead, or, as is often the case in exhibition-making, when new research comes to light and changes the project's focal argument.

In the writing course, students study museum style guides to learn about different requirements with regard to navigation tools, graphic design prototypes, didactic and object label formats, and catalog entries. Throughout the semester, students are asked to generate these forms of writing in relation to the virtual objects in their "package." The most important lesson imparted in this class is that "objects do not speak by themselves... rather, exhibitors press them into speech through interpretive frameworks."[9] Students also produce an exhibition brochure discussing the objects that comprise their "exhibition." This allows them to consider how the scholarship and stories told in a brochure can be different from—and augment—those presented through objects and texts in the gallery context. Finally, the students are asked to produce a grant proposal, a press release, and a marketing strategy for their project. In every case, students learn by example, examining how different museums address these various writing forms and requirements and considering the appropriateness of typographical (font) choices and other graphic elements used in an exhibition display context. By the time students enroll in Introduction to Curating, they have a great deal of practice generating exhibition-ready texts that conform to writing conventions such as limited word counts, language styles, and interpretative strategies used to communicate with a general museum audience. Most of all, they become skilled in "analyzing the museum's means of persuasion, the ways in which the museum makes arguments through and about the objects that it displays" ...and are encouraged to deploy "the selection, organization, and exhibition of objects a[s] rhetorical acts."[10]

Because Introduction to Curating is taught during a single semester, it is more efficient if the faculty member, in consort with the archivist, identifies a group of objects that will form the basis of the student-curated exhibition in advance. Later, each student further winnows down the selection of objects assigned to them—the basis for their research, writing, and display decisions. During the first iteration of this class, the faculty member, in consultation with the archivist (whose knowledge base encompasses un-accessioned, un-cataloged holdings that range from a collection on the history of lawn tennis to first edition books with mid-century modern graphic design covers) drew attention to a group of photography portfolios that had not been previously exhibited together. The faculty member studied the photographs and made a selection. Then, six individual photographers and their portfolios were parceled out to the six students as the basis for the Introduction to Curating class.

The course begins with assigned readings on different methodological approaches to curating both art exhibitions and historical exhibitions. Students write a paper addressing how these articles and first-person accounts written by curators can inform how they will approach their individual curating projects. The class visited the New York Public Library's Photography and Print Department to study photographs identical to those held in the university's collections or other examples of the work of the photographers they were studying. One of the insights that students gained from this visit—apart from its function as an exercise in the connoisseurship of photography—was that professional curators do not know *everything* about the varied and extensive collections they oversee. In other words, observing a professional curator who had little knowledge of the objects she had graciously culled from the collection for student viewing is an educational opportunity that empowers students with the understanding that curators often come to study a particular aspect of their collection only when there is an imperative to do so, such as an exhibition. Thus, student curators come to see their situation as novice researchers as parallel to that of professional curators.

After reading *about* curating, students embark on research, visual assessment, and consideration of the physical properties of the university gallery. Each student narrowed down their selection to between five and seven photographs. These ultimately comprised each student's contribution to a thematically and/or visually based mini-exhibition presented within a larger exhibition of photographs from Special Collections. Each student made an in-class presentation of their research and plan for their photograph's display in the gallery. The remainder of the class closely followed assignments in the Writing for Museums course in which the students' study of individual photographs generates object labels. Based on this research, they wrote a didactic label to provide an overarching thematic discussion of the assigned photographer's work and the rationale for their selection of the five to seven photographs. Discussions in the gallery led to many debates about the use of wall colors and professional vinyl lettering applied to the gallery walls for the introduction to the exhibition content and to the individual student contributions. In addition, the students collectively selected a photograph for a promotional postcard. An opening reception was scheduled as was a roundtable discussion in which the student-curators discussed the experience of curating an exhibition. By this time, they were thoroughly imbued with knowledge of the "museum-based approach" in which "objects interact with their physical setting to form persuasive arguments that are primarily visual."[11]

Each student contributed two different educational programs to supplement the exhibition and targeted specific audiences with marketing materials, ensuring that they would not be speaking to a gallery devoid of visitors. For example, one student developed a program for the Public Safety Department, staff who are responsible for the university's gallery security but who had never been offered information about that gallery's contents. Student programming kept the exhibition alive throughout its six-week duration. Students used a free online survey tool to obtain reactions from guests they invited to visit. After the close of the exhibition, student research on the photographs was shared with the archivist. Their in-depth research and fact-checking about the objects selected for exhibition increased the Special Collections staff's overall knowledge about the collections for which they serve as custodians.

One unforeseen outcome of the student exhibition arose from a visit to the show by a St. John's University alumnus, who scrutinized the photographs' credit lines and made important corrections to the provenance records of these objects because he was witness to a friend's initial gift of these photographs to the university. This incident served as a concrete demonstration to students of a key but often overlooked outcome of curating: the way that bringing together and displaying a selection of objects can, in and of itself—apart from any published writing—generates new knowledge about specific artifacts. Another important outcome included publicizing the Special Collections holdings to the university and the public at large. Exhibitions also increase the potential number of researchers who may consult the collections.

This first student-curated exhibition garnered three reviews from the local press, and the university's marketing department visited the student roundtable discussion on curating to produce a report that appeared on the university's website. For the last class, the students met in the gallery and stood back to analyze their curatorial decisions and assess the overall outcome of their project. None intended to pursue careers in curating, which sometimes was a source of discomfort and even complaint by students resistant to the demands of this required course. However, all agreed that the experience was valuable, given the leading role that curators play in museums and the likelihood that students working in other museum departments would interact with curators and support curatorial projects through educational programs, social media campaigns, fundraising, development, and registrarial expertise. The students appreciate that their work on the exhibition contributes to their educational and professional portfolios.

Overall, the first use of the university gallery for a student-curated, academic-oriented exhibition established the template for future iterations of the Introduction to Curating class. Another course outcome was the identification of new functions for the Special Collections in relation to the M.A. Museum Administration program. To prepare for future student-curated exhibitions based on the university's permanent Special Collections holdings, the graduate program director assigned a graduate assistant to undertake research in the department with an eye toward identifying groups of objects whose depth and substance would make them potential subjects for future student research and exhibitions. The archivist aimed to show as many of the visually rich collections as possible over the course of several meetings, explaining the pros and cons of exhibiting each one, to allow the graduate student to make the final evaluations on his own. Meeting with the faculty member, the graduate assistant agreed that the most compelling collection that emerged from his research was a cache of World War II propaganda posters, which upon further research was discovered to be the among the most comprehensive concentration of such posters in any American archive or library. This process also led to further discussions between the archivist, the faculty member, and the graduate assistant about the challenges and opportunities for future collaborations. For example, certain objects are easier to display on the wall (with or without frames); others require wall or table-style display cases or other expensive supplies. Some of the objects in Special Collections have condition issues, which can be expensive to address, while others feature unique subject matter requiring more challenging and extensive background research or even research in foreign languages. Other considerations include relevance to educational programs and priorities of the university and possible concurrent events and celebrations on campus. Over time, new acquisitions will present additional possibilities for exhibition materials.

Together, the faculty member and graduate assistant (with the assistance of the archivist) then studied the collection of posters—with the faculty member quickly deciding to limit the exhibition's focus to wartime posters geared toward civilians on the home front—and deliberately eliminated the posters with violent content. Each student in the second Introduction to Curating class was assigned a group of posters on a single theme—"careless talk," food rationing, fuel rationing, nurse recruitment, victory gardens, war bonds, and an additional mix of posters to be presented in an introductory gallery. Students were first asked to create a checklist of every poster assigned to them—a project that was challenging since many of the posters' creators were unidentified, and the mediums and techniques used to produce each poster were often mysterious. Most students were also unfamiliar with the components and format used to generate a checklist, and so their semester began with a lesson about creating perhaps the most fundamental document on which museum staff rely during an exhibition's making.

The remainder of the semester was devoted to repeating practices established during the previous curating class whose goal was a photography exhibition—but with one exception. In this course, students were assigned more extensive and focused content-based reading on the subject of World War II propaganda posters, since this was the shared background for each students' contribution to the show. Following several units of reading devoted to case studies in the area of art-curating and the curating of historical exhibitions, each student was assigned to undertake research relevant to their posters and to use PowerPoint to present several possible options for their poster's ultimate display. One student invited a faculty member from the university's Public History program to offer a lecture that discussed World War II poster propaganda—a talk that introduced students to the common historical and artistic background informing each of their individual research projects.

In contrast to the first Introduction to Curating course—in which each student focused on an individual photographer—this class, because it centered on a common theme and historical period, demanded greater engagement by students. Each was responsible for leading a class meeting during the last two-thirds of the semester. The approach enabled the student curators to acquire a shared knowledge base while guiding them to hone their research contributions in coordination with those of their colleagues in the class. By the end of the semester, all written materials were complete, decisions about the display were completed, educational programming and marketing materials were assembled, and students were assigned specific tasks related to the exhibition's finalization.

One student assumed responsibility for securing rights to reproduce one poster for the exhibition's promotional materials, another student offered to create a checklist with thumbnail images of each poster on display, and in another case, a student who had discovered propaganda films and popular films directly related to the subjects of the exhibition assumed responsibility for creating a multi-media display to supplement the exhibition. Also important were the educational programs students devised to accompany the exhibition, which involved outreach to other departments of the university and fulfilled several important secondary goals of this project. These include bringing faculty, students, administrators, and the local community to the gallery, raising the gallery's profile on the university campus, and promoting awareness about both the existence of this relatively new M.A. Museum Administration program and about the significant artifacts that comprise the university's Special Collections.

Conclusions

The collections-based teaching models discussed in this article underscore the potential for creative and mutually advantageous collaborations between university faculty and the Special Collections department. Objects can be studied or utilized for their historical significance, artistic qualities, or a combination thereof. Other university faculty, especially in the departments of English, Fine Arts, and History, have used Special Collections objects as inspiration for poetry and fiction assignments, the creation of original artworks, or the production of historical research papers. These models of library-museum collaboration include both one-time classroom activities and semester-long projects. All fulfill one of the university's key strategic priorities—the use of "high-impact educational practices" that include "problem-based learning and culminate in applied projects."

"Increasing the use of primary sources helps archives demonstrate the relevance of their holdings to their parent organizations' missions [the education of students at St. John's University]. However, it is the instructional role of archivists [in collaboration with university faculty] that cements the relationships and demonstrates how archivists add value to courses and contribute to student learning."[12] Student research and exhibitions that use objects in special collections unearth new knowledge, which in turn contribute to the archivist's work, particularly since the administrative demands of the archivist position can prohibit in-depth research on the thousands of artifacts under her custodianship.

Eliciting the archivist to interact with graduate museum administration students through the condition-reporting exercise, through supervision of graduate research in the collections and through many contributions to the student-curated exhibition project, provides students with insights into the workings of a collection and its manager. As the archivist mentors students and supports their research, she also models expertise and job functions that support students in the Museum Administration program as they pursue internships as collection managers, registrars, and archivists—and as graduates enter the job market with demonstrable skills in these areas. Students' production of educational programming to accompany their exhibition introduces new audiences to the university gallery and brings attention to the gallery's potential educational role in other curricular activities besides those embedded in the M.A. Museum Administration program. Object-based learning imparts research techniques and students' use of resources that are not typically included in art history or history courses. Students learn to closely study and apply critical thinking to museum exhibitions, museum catalogs and brochures, navigation and program guides, press releases, and museum websites—all of which become models for their own work as budding museum professionals.

Endnotes

1. "Museum Administration, Master of Arts," St. John's University, https://www.stjohns.edu/academics/programs/museum-administration-master-arts.
2. "Public History, Master of Arts," St. John's University, https://www.stjohns.edu/academics/programs/public-history-master-arts.
3. "Library and Information Science, Master of Science," St. John's University, https://www.stjohns.edu/academics/programs/library-and-information-science-master-science.
4. Barbara Rockenbach, "Archives, Undergraduates, and Inquiry-Based Learning: Case Studies from Yale University Library," *The American Archivist* 74/1 (Spring/Summer 2011): 298.
5. Rockenbach, "Archives, Undergraduates, and Inquiry-Based Learning," 298.
6. Students can continue to study collections management through a class specifically devoted to that subject. They also often enroll in a Museum Informatics class offered in the Department of Library and Information Sciences, where students learn about different collection management databases and their various technological functions, while also partnering with a museum in New York for a final research project.
7. Thomas Kador, Helen Chatterjee, and Leonie Hannan, "The Materials of Life: Making Meaning through Object-based Learning in Twenty-first Century Higher Education," in *Developing the Higher Education Curriculum Book Subtitle: Research-Based Education in Practice Book*, eds. Brent Carnell and Dilly Fung (London: University College London Press, 2017), 61–62.
8. John Pedro Schwartz, "Object Lessons: Teaching Multiliteracies through the Museum," *College English* 71/1 (September 2008): 33.
9. Schwartz, "Object Lessons," 28.
10. Ibid., 31.
11. Ibid., 34.
12. Elizabeth Yakel and Doris Malkmus, "Contextualizing Archival Literacy," in *Teaching with Primary Sources*, eds. Christopher J. Prom and Lisa Janicke Hinchliffe (Chicago: Society of American Archivists, 2016), 5–67.

Bibliography

Kador, Thomas, Helen Chatterjee, and Leonie Hannan. "The Materials of Life: Making Meaning Through Object-based Learning in Twenty-First Century Higher Education." In *Developing the Higher Education Curriculum Book Subtitle: Research-Based Education in Practice Book*, edited by Brent Carnell and Dilly Fung, 60–74. London: University College London Press, 2017.

Rockenbach, Barbara. "Archives, Undergraduates, and Inquiry-Based Learning: Case Studies from Yale University Library." *The American Archivist* 74/1 (Spring/Summer 2011): 297–311.

Schwartz, John Pedro. "Object Lessons: Teaching Multiliteracies through the Museum." *College English* 71/1 (September 2008): 27–47.

St. John's University. "Library and Information Science, Master of Science." https://www.stjohns.edu/academics/programs/library-and-information-science-master-science.

———. "Museum Administration, Master of Arts." https://www.stjohns.edu/academics/programs/museum-administration-master-arts.

———. "Public History, Master of Arts." https://www.stjohns.edu/academics/programs/public-history-master-arts.

Yakel, Elizabeth, and Doris Malkmus. "Contextualizing Archival Literacy." In *Teaching with Primary Sources*, edited by Christopher J. Prom and Lisa Janicke Hinchliffe, 5–67. Chicago: Society of American Archivists, 2016.

CHAPTER 15

Collaboration and Convergence at the Consortial Level:

Museums10 and the Five College Library Consortium

Jennifer Gunter King, Simon Neame, and Jessica Nicoll

> The rules about everything from inter-institutional collaboration to public engagement are changing as libraries, museums, and repositories develop open frameworks and infrastructure, inviting new methods of engagement with art, scholarship, and archival materials. At times, libraries, archives, and museums respond to the changing rules collaboratively and at other times, independently. What factors inspire and sustain inter-institutional collaboration? This chapter addresses this question by reviewing the long arc of collaboration in the Five College Libraries, Archives, and Museums. Prospects for convergence among the repositories and museums in the Connecticut River Pioneer Valley in Western Massachusetts are especially promising, given the deep

history of collaboration among the Five College Library Consortium and Museums10. Of the myriad examples of collaborative initiatives that comprise cultural heritage work in the consortium, this chapter's focus is on four historic collaborative projects and two current collaborative projects, all of which represent infrastructure initiatives that are striking examples of convergence. Each is a case study of convergence: Five College Library Integrated Library System, Five College Digital Access Project, Five College Finding Aids Access Project, Five College Museums Database, Five College Compass Digital Collections Project, and Five College FOLIO project. The focus on these examples highlights the potential for academic libraries and museums to partner and develop shared technical infrastructure in support of cultural heritage stewardship within their academic communities.

Introduction

The Five College Consortium comprises four liberal arts colleges and one university totaling approximately 38,000 students. The campuses are geographically close and are linked by frequent bus service. The consortium was formally established in 1965, but its roots lay in cooperative efforts between the oldest four members of the consortium dating back to 1914. The consortium is composed of Amherst College, Hampshire College, Mount Holyoke College, Smith College, and the University of Massachusetts Amherst. Broadening the collaborative potential for the Five College libraries is Museums10, an allied museum collaborative that includes the Emily Dickinson Museum, The Eric Carle Museum of Picture Book Art, Hampshire College Art Gallery, Historic Deerfield, the Mead Art Museum and the Beneski Museum of Natural History at Amherst College, Mount Holyoke College Art Museum, Smith College Museum of Art, University Museum of Contemporary Art, and the Yiddish Book Center.

As the Five College Consortium passed its first quarter-century in 1993, it had an impressive track record of academic and administrative cooperation. Recognizing the far-reaching implications of new technologies, Five Colleges, Inc., prioritized expanding shared online information systems to include a course catalog, a calendar of events, and a museum collections database. At the center of this were efforts to link the libraries on the five campuses. As a proposal to the Davis Educational Foundation proclaimed, "Just as the library represented the symbolic, if not the actual, heart and soul of Five College cooperation in its first quarter-century, so will information systems play that role in the next quarter-century."[1] Shared information systems represent the deepest form of collaboration and convergence, as outlined in the 2008 OCLC report, "Beyond the Silos of the LAMs: Collaboration Among Libraries, Archives and Museums."[2] While the Five College Libraries and Museums10 consortium offer examples of collaboration at every stage of the continuum, including contact, cooperation, coordination, collaboration, and convergence, the focus of this chapter is on convergence.

Convergence is "a state in which collaboration around a specific function or idea has become so extensive, engrained and assumed that it is no longer recognized by others as a collaborative undertaking. Instead, it has matured to the level of infrastructure and becomes, like our water or transportation networks, a critical system that we rely upon without considering the collaborative efforts and compromises that made it possible." It appears likely that those initiatives that have administrative oversight and directive may be most likely to achieve convergence. While the Five Colleges Consortium is rich with examples of practitioner-led cooperative and coordinated initiatives, those that we review are top-down initiatives, driven by library and museum administration and told from that perspective. Given the differences between the institutions—large versus small, private versus public, liberal arts focus versus broad research agenda—the project goals and outcomes must strike a balance between differing missions, funding models, governance structures, and institutional cultures. Each of the following six infrastructure initiatives provides case studies of convergence that span 1981 through 2018: Five College Library Integrated Library System, Five College Digital Access Project, Five College Finding Aids Access Project, Five College Museums Database, Five College Compass Digital Collections Project, and Five College FOLIO project.

Five College Library Cooperation and Resource Sharing: Integrated Library Systems

As one of the oldest library consortia, the Five College Libraries have been on the vanguard of collaboration throughout its history. The Hampshire Interlibrary Center (HILC) was established in 1951 to foster library cooperation and resource sharing. The libraries today provide unified access to integrated library systems, actively steward digital resources consistent with national and international efforts to reduce the cost of scholarly information and promote open access, expand shared uniform access to electronic resources, manage less commonly used materials, and increase the accessibility of physical and electronic resources. The unification of library resources has been iteratively developed. In 1981, the Librarians Council submitted a Library Automation proposal to the directors of Five Colleges, Inc. (the Presidents of the Colleges and Chancellor of the University). Seven years later, in 1988, the first Five College online library catalog was launched—OCLC's LS/2000. A review of contemporaneous minutes from the

Five College Library Directors council reveals significant concern about the value of building a shared integrated library system, especially among individual library staff and cultures. The investments needed to achieve an integrated library system, with its contingent agreements on standards and lending policies, while not insignificant, have proven the value, over time, of surmounting challenges and barriers to convergence across allied institutions. Today, the Five College library system's ten million volumes would make the Five Colleges the tenth-largest library in the United States. Faculty, students, and staff all have access to the combined resources of the libraries, an important factor for the recruitment and retention of students and faculty.

The convergence into a shared library system has led, over the years, to the formation of governance to support ongoing collaboration. Nine advisory groups and committees are comprised of representatives from each library, reporting to the Five College Librarians Council in the following areas: access, discovery, innovative learning, user experience, archives and special collections, and digital stewardship along with working groups on time-limited topics.

Five College Library Cooperation and Resource Sharing: Digital Access Project

The Librarians Council and Five College library committees have launched consortia initiatives with foundation support, allowing the libraries to advance further together than they could on their own. In 1999, The Andrew W. Mellon Foundation awarded the Five Colleges funds to bring faculty, librarians, and technical staff together to develop a shared infrastructure. The resulting pilot project—the Five College Digital Archives Access Project—involved digitizing select archival documents from each of the Five College libraries and presenting them together through an online website. The digital archive drew from forty-one collections, including 35,000 scanned pages related to the topic of the history of higher education for women. Analogous to a shared integrated library system, the project provided the groundwork for shared or centralized operations in digitizing print and image sources.[3] The project was concerned both with a desire to enhance access to resources and to control rising costs associated with the realities of curating collections in the digital age. The grant recognized "the tremendous pressures on libraries and information services to contain costs while meeting burgeoning needs.... We believe that only if libraries create a new culture of sharing and cooperation, one that extends to archival and collection policies as well as to training, can we rein in some of these growing costs without sacrificing quality."[4]

Five College Library Cooperation and Resource Sharing: Five College Finding Aids Access Project

With funding from The Andrew W. Mellon Foundation, the libraries oversaw the development of a shared archival finding aid system in 2004. The Five College Finding Aids Access Project provides access to finding aids representing collections of historic records held by Amherst, Hampshire, Mount Holyoke and Smith Colleges, and the University of Massachusetts Amherst. The project's goal to improve access to the manuscript and archival collections of the Five Colleges was achieved by publishing more than 1,500 finding aids for these collections online. The finding aids included in this site are marked up in XML according to the Encoded Archival Description (EAD) standard. The finding aid access project enabled cross-collection searching by harmonizing metadata standards for archival description and creating a single portal for searching across finding aids for collections held in the archives at each of the Five Colleges. The project also embedded archival collections for discovery in the integrated library system with a MARC record linking to Encoded Archival Description finding aids, helping to integrate archival resources with library holdings.

Five College Museums Database

The history of deepened collaboration among the Five College museum collections dates to the 1990s and a visionary project to automate collections record management in a shared database. Driving the museum initiative was Suzannah Fabing, who assumed the directorship of the Smith College Museum of Art in 1992. She came to Smith after a decade at the National Gallery of Art as the managing curator of records and loans, where she had been integral to the National Gallery's project to automate its records, one of the first projects of its kind in this country. She had served as the gallery's representative on the J. Paul Getty Trust's Museum Prototype Project, a forum of six leading art museums and two academic museums created to develop shared practice around the computerization of art museum collections.[5] As such, Fabing was part of the elite team of museum professionals who developed the standardized records format and controlled vocabularies that provided the foundation for the automation of collections records.

Fabing arrived at Smith with deep knowledge of the emerging best practices for the computerization of collections records and of the benefits of inter-institutional collaboration in developing these new processes and systems. In 1992, the Smith College Museum of Art, like its peers within Five Colleges, was working with manual record-keeping systems and was in the first stages of contemplating automation, a project that seemed out of scope for a small staff with limited technical expertise. Fabing quickly engaged her peers at the Mead Art Museum at Amherst College, the Hampshire College Gallery, the Mount Holyoke College Art Museum, the University of Massachusetts Gallery (now the Museum of Contemporary Art), and Historic Deerfield, an affiliated institution, to discuss pooling resources to advance this goal. A feasibility study commissioned that same year affirmed that the creation of a Five College/Historic Deerfield networked collections database would improve each institution's internal collections management practices, make information about the 80,000 artworks and artifacts in these collections more widely and easily available to students and faculty, make more efficient use of museum staff time when the expansion of permanent staff seemed unlikely, and facilitate the exchange of information among the institutions, opening up further opportunities for cooperation.[6]

This initiative dovetailed with the priority that Five Colleges, Inc. was placing on the expansion of shared online systems among its five member institutions. In 1993, a Five College Information Systems Task Force was appointed with the mandate to oversee and coordinate development of new consortial systems, with the goals of containing costs, expanding the pool of available expertise, and working to ensure compatibility across new information systems. The Five College/Historic Deerfield Collections Database was one of five projects prioritized by the task force in its first year and administered by two newly established positions of Five Colleges director of information technology and information technology projects coordinator.

This project unfolded over the next decade in phases. The collections management system was conceived to work on two levels, with each institution maintaining local control for internal management purposes while publishing data through a web portal to facilitate discovery of the collective holdings of the Five College museums. Early in the process, Multi MIMSY from Willoughby Associates was chosen as the collection information system because it was designed to work on multiple hardware platforms, it could accommodate images, and Willoughby had substantive experience working with museums. During the first phase of the project, data from the museums' collections were transferred onto the Multi MIMSY database, a rigorous process that was preceded by close collaboration to develop shared cataloging standards and descriptive vocabularies. Once the database was populated and had been integrated into museum operations, the second phase developed the public web portal to provide access to the data for students and researchers. The final phase, completed in 2005, added digitized collection images to the database.

This project laid the foundation for deepened collaboration among the campus museums and transformed the discovery and use of their collections to support teaching and learning. What began as a database of some 80,000 artworks and artifacts now holds information for more than 110,000 unique items representing an extraordinary record of human creativity spanning media, time, geography, and world cultures. The database has revealed connections and synergies across our collections and facilitated collection development strategies that consider the breadth of Five College holdings, allowing us to make complementary acquisitions, develop distinctive areas of strength, and avoid redundancy. Faculty, students, and scholars are able to find and access related materials held across the six collections, which has catalyzed exponentially growing use and broadened the range of academic partners to include not only the humanities but also the sciences and social sciences. Through their practice, Five College faculty and their museum colleagues have contributed significantly to the development of integrative object-based pedagogy. This innovation has been facilitated by making the scope and depth of the collections, previously understood by only a few knowledgeable stewards, broadly discoverable.

It is not coincidental that as the final phase of the database project was being completed in 2005 that an expanded museum partnership began to take shape. The power and potential of cross-institutional collaboration demonstrated by the database inspired the formation of Museums10, which includes the six original partner museums plus the Emily Dickinson Museum, the Beneski Museum of Natural History (both at Amherst College), the Eric Carle Museum of Picture Book Art, and the National Yiddish Book Center (the latter two located on the campus of Hampshire College). Just as the museums' collections become much more powerful when aggregated, Museums10 recognizes that we can do more when our staffs work together. Representing a network of more than 100 museum professionals, Museums10 has facilitated coordinated planning, communications, and collaboration in such areas as joint curatorial projects and workshops for regional teachers. Staff members meet regularly around areas of shared practice and responsibility, and the consortium hosts an annual summit that serves as a professional development opportunity for all staff on a topic of current relevance to the field. The varied work of Museums10 has deepened the patterns and pathways of collaboration across our museums and created an appetite for thinking more expansively about what we can achieve together and with other stewards of research collections across the Five Colleges, including the libraries.

Five College Compass Digital Collections Project

The Five College Compass Digital Collections officially launched in 2017 as a partnership between the Mount Holyoke College, Smith College, and Hampshire College libraries. Compass provides a platform for the discovery and stewardship of digital collections from the participating libraries and offers the opportunity to search across a broad range of materials. The genesis of the project came from a need to have better discovery and stewardship of digital collections, a priority that was not shared by all five libraries at the time of the project's inception. Amherst College had developed its own Islandora-based digital repository, and UMass Amherst managed its digital collections through a locally developed, Fedora-based digital repository called Credo. Since both Amherst and UMass already had solutions in place to manage their digital collections, neither institution chose to participate in the Compass project. However, the project was still seen as a Five College initiative, and all member libraries contributed to the development of Compass. In addition, the project's development factored in the possibility of the other two schools joining Compass in the future. The approach taken by the Compass project team, with support from the Five College Librarians Council, demonstrates an important aspect of how collaboration within the consortium is not dependent on all members participating in a project. This degree of flexibility recognizes that, even in a small consortium, not all institutions will have the same needs at the same time. Accommodating these differences as a component of partnership development contributes to the overall health of the group.

Five College FOLIO Project

The FOLIO (Future of Libraries is Open) project represents a renewed commitment to integration for the Five College libraries. A foundational component of the Five College partnership has long been the inter-library lending and borrowing between the five member libraries. For much of the Five Colleges' history, this has meant physical items, mainly books. The sharing of the physical materials continues to be an important service the libraries provide to the Five College community, and in recent decades this has been managed via an integrated library system (ILS), currently Ex Libris' Aleph ILS. Like many libraries, the Five College libraries have been thinking about a next-generation ILS to meet changing user and collection management needs. In exploring available options, it seemed only natural to consider an open-source solution as one possible way forward, given that the concept of "open" is a common value across member libraries. In early 2018, the consortium was approached by EBSCO Information Services to join a small group of libraries as a beta partner in developing a new Library Service Platform (LSP) based on the FOLIO open-source software. Discussions around whether to join the project as a beta partner surfaced many important differences between the libraries, such as varying levels of staffing, technical expertise, and infrastructure capacity that needed to be considered in balancing the shared contributions to the project. In addition, an important component of moving forward was establishing a governance structure that would ensure all member institutions had a forum for raising concerns or issues for discussion and resolution. The FOLIO project is overseen by the FOLIO Implementation Team (FIT), a group that includes member representatives from each library. User testing and development for the functional areas of the Five College FOLIO instance falls to various working groups, comprised of staff who have particular areas of functional expertise. These teams work closely with EBSCO and the broader FOLIO development community, and representation is based on a careful balance between organizational capacity and local expertise.

As of this chapter's writing, the Five College FOLIO project continues to make progress. The project represents an opportunity to further integrate staff workflows in a number of areas, including acquisitions, circulation, and resource sharing. It also presents an opportunity to improve the user experience across the Five Colleges. The potential for greater interoperability with other systems is an important feature of FOLIO that could allow for the discovery of other collections, such as those held by the various campus and local museums. In addition, many campuses include collections that are not housed in libraries, archives, or museums, such as entomology and anthropology collections. Although the initial focus is to develop an LSP with functionality for core library services, this broader potential is bringing heightened attention to improving access and discovery across many diverse collections. Even as the museum community begins to think about its next-generation collections management tool, FOLIO and the open source community may provide a way forward for interoperability and sharing across platforms.

2018 Summit: Libraries, Museums, Collections and "The Network Turn"

To inspire renewed collaboration, the Five College Libraries and Museums10 hosted a Summit on October 4–5, 2018, titled, "Libraries, Museums, Collections and 'The Network Turn.'" The goal of the summit was to actively explore our history of collaboration in the context of new and emerging challenges and opportunities in order to identify shared goals that would inform our partnership moving forward. The summit represented an important opportunity to explore new approaches to access and discovery that leverage the combined expertise, knowledge, and infrastructures across the Five College libraries, archives, and museums. The seventy-five participants in the summit came from all five campuses and included librarians, information and educational technologists, stewards of special collections (including archivists, curators, educators/ academic liaisons, and collection managers), and administrative leadership. The summit tapped into the growing interest in the collaborative potential of libraries, archives, and museums. Our effort was framed by national conversations that include a January 2016 symposium, "Prospects and Strategies for Deep Collaboration in the Galleries, Libraries, Archives and Museums Sector," hosted at the University of Miami[7] and supported by the more recent report, "Research and Learning Agenda for Archives, Special, and Distinctive Collections in Research Libraries" (2017).[8]

The diversity of expertise, responsibility, and perspective at the summit modeled the evolving way that we understand collaboration to be broader and more inclusive, reaching across silos with the goal of creating a more unified experience for our users. The structure of the day included a welcome that reviewed the history of collaboration, much of which is outlined above. Clyfford Lynch, Executive Director of the Coalition for Networked Information, presented the Keynote Address "Libraries, Museums, Collections and the Network Turn." Clifford began his remarks with the admission that this has been a topic of importance for him during the last thirty years. He shared a vision of one of his favorite spots in the world—the Enlightenment Room at the British Museum—"a very special kind of a room because it's really about the history of collecting and museums and organizing and thinking about collections. [It] traces stories of early collectors, like Hans Sloane, who were central to the establishment of the museum collections and much of the thinking of the time, of moving beyond wonder cabinets to genuine museum collections; it tries to capture the unity and continuity of knowledge as it was viewed at the time: you see books, works of art, anthropological collections, natural specimens, manuscripts that are all intermixed. It gives a sense of the way these folks thought about knowledge not as a series of stovepipes but as a genuine web and continuity." Lynch then moves from this realm of continuity to the present day, where most scholars, faculty, and students have to navigate collections that are organized by format and divided into libraries, archives, and museums. He shares, "We've lost some of that as things have become large and specialized. [It] falls to the individual scholar to make the effort to go across those silos. [It's] tough for students and researchers to move across silos of disciplines and different types of collections. Our challenge and our opportunity is to get back to what's captured in that Enlightenment Room in the British Museum, to make our LAMS and scholarship that our researchers produce into a much more unified whole. This is much more than finding and viewing; it is *linking*. This is hard, but it is the great opportunity."[9] The message was well delivered and was followed by a contemporary example that is a virtual version of the Enlightenment Room.

Depaul University librarian Scott Walter discussed with attendees "Explore Chicago Collections," a free, centralized, web-based search engine and record-finding tool where researchers, teachers, and students are able to locate and access more than 100,000 maps, photos, and letters held by its twenty-eight member institutions. Providing unparalleled access to primary source materials, users can explore art, artifactual, archival, digital, and manuscript collections by topic—from government to everyday life, and beyond— and interact with library guides, digital exhibits, and educational materials. It was quite easy for summit attendees to see the parallels between cohesive access to collections in Chicago and what that cohesion could look like for the Five College libraries and museums. The summit then explored in more depth the examples of the substantive Five College convergences that include the Five College Museums Collections Database, Compass, and the FOLIO platform.

With this as context, summit attendees had the opportunity to talk directly with representatives from foundations and granting agencies. Alison Gilchrest, former program officer for arts and cultural heritage for The Andrew W. Mellon Foundation, and Paula Gangopadhyay, deputy director of museum services, Institute of Museum and Library Services, described their funding priorities for library, archive, and museum collaboration. This conversation was essential given the crucial role foundation support has played in leading change in this area.

In reflecting on the value of the summit, participants reported that it reinforced their appreciation of the benefits of inter-organizational collaboration. Further, many felt inspired to nurture new connections across departments and between institutions in order to lay the foundation for taking our collaborative work to the next level. Two areas of focus that emerged in breakout discussions were: (1) the recognition that the museum collection database is an outmoded system that is inhibiting broader cross-collection discovery; and (2) our shared desire to build our capacity for efficient, productive, and sustainable cross-divisional and cross-institutional collaboration. The overarching theme that emerged from the summit is that the nature of collaboration has changed. It is broader and reaches beyond libraries and information technology to include stewards of myriad collections that are physically distinct but intellectually related. We have the opportunity and potential at the beginning of this century to unify discovery across collections and institutions, which stands in stark contrast to the investments made in these fields at the dawn of the last century to separate collections by format and formalize research processes independently. The mandate going forward is not to build a new institution, but to provide a unified and coherent service across our established institutions.

The insight and energy coming out of the summit have catalyzed a new chapter in the history of Five College collaboration. With the support of The Andrew W. Mellon Foundation, the consortium has embarked on a new project, the Museum Collections Management Commons (MCMC), to identify the requirements for the next-generation museum database. At its core, this project will maintain and improve the integrity of the museums' data and collection management processes. More broadly, it will define requirements for a solution that will be responsive to the needs of our users, will allow for the integration of museum data with other collection discovery systems, and will be undergirded by a sustainable vision for coordinated oversight, staffing, and support. To achieve this, the project has a significant focus on organizational development, mapping new cross-collection systems of governance, planning, and communication to facilitate increased coordination across museums, libraries, and archives. This work seeks to break down silos that impede collaboration and to diagnose the imbalanced distribution of expertise and capacity across the colleges and their special collections to build and sustain a more robust cross-collection network of knowledge and discovery.

MCMC was launched by a planning grant awarded to Five Colleges, Inc. by The Andrew W. Mellon Foundation in October 2019. The first phase of the project has focused on hiring dedicated project staff and setting up a working group and a steering committee to coordinate research, communication, and decision-making across the partner museums and the five campuses. The project manager brings deep expertise in museum collection management systems and practices while the data specialist, trained in library science, brings much-needed knowledge of controlled vocabularies, metadata frameworks, and data governance. They are working closely with the project Working Group, which includes the collection managers of the six museums, curatorial representatives, and the Five Colleges information technology analyst. The Project Steering Committee has been constructed to ensure coordination and communication across museums and libraries, to facilitate reporting to and decision-making by the leadership of the five campuses, and to include a range of expertise and perspectives. All five campuses are represented on the steering committee by museum and library leadership, specialists in collections management and digital services, and, valuably, the chair of the Five College FOLIO Implementation Team.

Extending this commitment to cross-institutional and cross-collection exchange is a plan for programming to bring together stewards of collections housed in galleries, libraries, archives, and museums on the five campuses. Building on the 2018 summit, this was originally imagined as an annual, in-person convening; however, with the disruption caused by the COVID-19 pandemic and the pivot in March 2020 to remote instruction and work, this has been re-conceived as an extended series of digitally delivered sessions offered at regular intervals throughout the 2020–21 academic year. This series of synchronous and asynchronous digital experiences is providing a forum for MCMC project staff and committees to report on the project. Additionally, the program aspires to ensure that knowledge is created, gained, retained, and implemented among stakeholders, to create and sustain permeable boundaries across the library, archives, museum, and information technology silos, and to promote reflection on what the upheaval of 2020 means for this project's immediacy and importance. Crucially, this work acknowledges the necessity of building and sustaining community among practitioners as a pre-condition to effective collaboration.

A critical component of the MCMC project is a study of users of the museums' Collection Database Public Portal. The user study will provide demographic information about web portal users and information about their expectations and perceptions of the discovery experience. This will inform planning for future improvements to the collection management system, metadata, metadata transparency, linked data, and the public discovery platform. Additionally, the study seeks to understand non-users and their perceptions regarding the potential of art and humanities collections to support scholarship, teaching, and learning in a wide array of academic disciplines. The study will provide baseline information that can be compared against future studies. It is anticipated that the study results will be published in support of field-wide learning.

It's too early to know fully what the outcomes of the MCMC project will be. The project aims to address significant challenges posed by the unique and still pioneering shared database model, such as instituting a formal metadata governance system across very different kinds of collections and institutions, while developing specifications for a new collection management system that incorporates linked data across many managed collections at the five campuses. The concurrent and collaborative planning that is occurring, particularly with the FOLIO and MCMC projects, points tantalizingly to the possibility of a federated discovery experience for internal and external users. There is serious momentum in the work happening across museums and libraries in the Five Colleges that merits ongoing attention for the contribution it can make to broader learning in the field.

Conclusion

Thinking back to the history of collaboration in the Five Colleges, the major infrastructure advances and the moments where the collective has achieved convergence or coherence have been driven by administration and have led to new understandings of the potential cultural heritage institutions can play together in the networked age. Notably, the convergence has been achieved separately across the libraries and museums but not spanning both. The summit revealed that the libraries, archives, and museums have both the *opportunity* to do collaborative work as well as the responsibility to create new and networked ways of doing our work and acknowledging the power and potential of being an academic consortium—comprised of libraries and museums—in the twenty-first century. Our future efforts are supported by the long history of collaboration and the new ways of thinking that have emerged.

Endnotes

1. Proposal to the Davis Educational Foundation from Five Colleges, Incorporated, October 27, 1994.
2. Diane Zorich, Günter Waibel, and Ricky Erway, *Beyond the Silos of the LAMs: Collaboration Among Libraries, Archives and Museums* (Dublin OH: OCLC Research, 2008), https://www.oclc.org/content/dam/research/publications/library/2008/2008-05.pdf.
3. The Five College Archives Digital Access Project, http://clio.mtholyoke.edu/.
4. Proposal to The Andrew W. Mellon Foundation from Five Colleges, Incorporated, 1996.
5. Nancy S. Allen, "The Museum Prototype Project: A View from the Library," *Library Trends* 37, no. 2, Fall 1988, 175–93.
6. Memo to Lorna Peterson, Executive Director, Five Colleges, Inc., from Five College/Historic Deerfield Museum Directors, December 15, 1993.
7. Jill Deupi and Charles Eckman, *Prospects and Strategies for Deep Collaboration in the Galleries, Libraries, Archives, and Museums Sector* (Coral Gables, FL: University of Miami, 2016).
8. Chela Scott Weber, *Research and Learning Agenda for Archives, Special, and Distinctive Collections in Research Libraries* (Dublin, OH: OCLC Research, 2017), https://doi.org/10.25333/C3C34F.
9. Clifford Lynch, "Libraries, Museums, Collections and the 'Network Turn,'" (speech, Amherst, MA, October 5, 2018.)

Bibliography

Allen, Nancy S. "The Museum Prototype Project: A View from the Library." *Library Trends* 37, no. 2 (Fall 1988), 175–93.

Deupi, Jill, and Charles Eckman. *Prospects and Strategies for Deep Collaboration in the Galleries, Libraries, Archives, and Museums Sector.* Coral Gables, FL: University of Miami, 2016.

Five College/Historic Deerfield Museum Directors. Memo to Lorna Peterson, Executive Director, Five Colleges, Inc., December 15, 1993.

Lynch, Clifford. "Libraries, Museums, Collections and the 'Network Turn.'" Speech, Five Colleges, Inc., Amherst, MA, October 5, 2018.

Proposal to The Andrew W. Mellon Foundation from Five Colleges, Incorporated, 1996.

Proposal to the Davis Educational Foundation from Five Colleges, Incorporated, October 27, 1994.

Weber, Chela Scott. *Research and Learning Agenda for Archives, Special, and Distinctive Collections in Research Libraries.* Dublin, OH: OCLC Research, 2017.

Zorich, Diane, Günter Waibel, and Ricky Erway. *Beyond the Silos of the LAMs: Collaboration Among Libraries, Archives and Museums.* Dublin OH: OCLC Research, 2008. https://www.oclc.org/content/dam/research/publications/library/2008/2008-05.pdf.

CHAPTER 16

How History and a Commitment to Social Justice Informed Library-Museum Collaboration at Oberlin College

Alexia Hudson-Ward

In December 2016, the Oberlin College Libraries Director Alexia Hudson-Ward and Oberlin College's Allen Memorial Art Museum Director Andria Derstine, PhD, in partnership with the college's Executive Director of Foundation, Government, and Corporate Grants Pamela Snyder, submitted a successful library-museum collaboration planning grant proposal to the Andrew W. Mellon Foundation. The planning grant resulted in a four-year partnership during my tenure at Oberlin College, which included hosting a summit of academic library and museum directors in June of 2018. The planning grant was extended twice due to senior level administration changes and the college's one year intensive strategic planning process of 2018-2019.

Oberlin College is located in Oberlin, Ohio, and is considered one of the nation's premier liberal arts colleges. The institution is two distinct schools— a college of arts and sciences and a conservatory of music. Oberlin College was founded as the Oberlin Collegiate Institute in 1833 by a Presbyterian minister and a missionary (Reverend John J. Shipherd and Philo P. Stewart). Shepherd's and Steward's initial intention was to establish a college and a colony based on their religious beliefs. Deeply influenced by French Alsatian pastor John Frederick Oberlin, Shipherd and Steward established a service-learning curriculum that elevated "learning and labor" (a phrase that would later become the college's motto).[1]

From its early beginnings, Oberlin College emphasized a commitment to equality and social justice. African Americans and women were admitted as full students in 1835 and 1837, respectively. The town of Oberlin was a stop on the underground railroad and active in abolitionism. A group of citizens from Oberlin and the nearby town of Wellington, Ohio, made history in 1858 when they rescued an enslaved man (John Price) who ran away from his capturers. The liberators took Price to Canada and were later jailed in Cleveland for violating the "Fugitive Slave Act." Their case (referred to in the media as the Oberlin-Wellington Rescue) drew national attention and was considered the historical tipping point that led to the American Civil War.[2]

Oberlin College and Conservatory boasts distinguished alums comprised of leaders within various sectors. Among its alumni ranks are several Nobel Laureates, Pulitzer Prize winners, Academy, Grammy, Tony, Emmy, and Golden Globe award recipients, and MacArthur Foundation "Genius" Grant award winners. Around 2006-2007, Oberlin College adopted the marketing tagline "Think one person can change the world? So do we" to elevate the college's international stature more distinctly.

From nearly its inception, Oberlin College promoted itself as committed to cultural heritage, libraries, museums, materiality, and objects-based pedagogy. The Oberlin College Libraries and the Allen Memorial Art Museum share high levels of distinction due to the tradition of collection care embedded within the college's DNA. The college's first objects collection was the anti-slavery collection, created in 1834. Many institution graduates elect to pursue graduate degrees and career pathways into librarianship and various museum roles, serving as cultural heritage sector influencers regarding library-museum partnerships.

During the period covered within this book chapter, the institution's two deans—the dean of the college of arts and sciences and the dean of the conservatory—acted as the principal leads for the majority of academic and educationally centered administrative activities (Oberlin College does not have a provost). The Director of Libraries and the Museum Director's roles are endowed as the Azariah Smith Root Director of Libraries and the John G. W. Cowles Director of the Allen Memorial Art Museum, providing both leaders with funding to support a wide range of educational and administrative initiatives.

The Director of Libraries reported to both deans. The Museum Director reported to the Dean of the College of Arts and Sciences. Both directors were voting members of the institution's general faculty body, and the library director was also a voting member of the conservatory faculty body. The reporting structure and voting status within the faculty bodies elevated the importance of the Director of Libraries and the Museum Director as pedagogical partners, champions of faculty research pursuits, and supporters of innovative object-centered approaches to student learning.

Against the backdrop of many academic library and museum collaborations are stories of the behind-the-scenes work of the library director and the museum director to situate organizational infrastructure elements vital to shared endeavors' success. These organizational infrastructure elements include staffing composition and designing staff roles; institutional negotiations for financial resources in support of library-museum collaboration; and partnership with faculty on advancing traditional and experimental objects-based pedagogy.

The Oberlin College story of the library-museum collaboration from 2016 to 2020 fits within this experience. While the work of the library director and the museum director is informed by rich traditions and historical legacies, serving in these roles is often a delicate balancing act for the directors. Leading at the nexus of the institution's academic and administrative enterprises requires adroitness. Academic library directors and museum directors work in multiplicities, which is tantamount to the code-switching that many people of color report as essential for their daily existence. One must ensure that curatorial and pedagogical activities are supported while leading staff through myriad initiatives, including reskilling and applying a new lens to how the library-museum partnership becomes a priority for all library and museum staff.

This chapter will highlight the unique and enriching collaboration between the Oberlin College Libraries and the Allen Memorial Art Museum from 2016-2020, as supported by the Andrew W. Mellon Foundation's planning grant. The histories of the libraries and the museum are shared to underscore the solid foundation upon which the two organizations met in the middle to advance a new form of inclusive objects-centered pedagogy.

The History of Collaboration Between The Oberlin College Libraries and the Allen Memorial Art Museum

The Libraries and AMAM has historically cross-promoted and jointly supported various educational activities. While pinpointing the exact date of when joint library-museum activities began is difficult, a history of collaboration between the two entities appears to have started in the late 1930s with the appointment of Ellen Johnson as the art librarian. Johnson, a prolific historian of contemporary American Art, helped to build the Clarence Ward Art Library's collection and, in doing so, weaved together art history and library pedagogy in her popular museum history courses. Johnson is widely believed to be among the first faculty members in the United States to offer such courses.[3]

The connection between the Oberlin College Libraries and the Allen Memorial Art Museum continued relatively seamlessly through the term for the Mellon Foundation planning grant (2016-2020). The Allen Memorial Art Museum director and I met multiple times each month to plan grant execution and to keep each other apprised of activities within our organizations. The head of the Clarence Ward Art Library, the college archivist, the libraries' head of special collections, the libraries' visual resources curator, the libraries' academic engagement coordinator, and the museum's curators partnered with faculty to support objects-based pedagogy across the disciplines. Some collaborations included faculty-led exhibitions supplemented with library resources to contextualize exhibition themes further.

The Libraries manages a sustainable art collection and several historical artifacts loaned for museum exhibitions with visiting artists. One of the most creative examples of this collaboration was the AMAM/OCL partnership for African American artist Fred Wilson's exhibitions "Wildfire Pit Test" and "Black to the Powers of Ten" held at AMAM from August 30, 2016, through June 12, 2017. Wilson explored race, time, and memory in American culture by combining his works with loaned artifacts and items from the College Archives and libraries' special collections, including actual slavery chains. The Fred Wilson exhibition programs of 2016-2017 captured materiality, cultural memory, diversity, equity, inclusion, and social justice and perfectly aligned with the histories of the college, the libraries, and the museum.[4]

An Abbreviated History of the Allen Memorial Art Museum and the Oberlin College Libraries

The Oberlin College Libraries and the Allen Memorial Art Museum have storied histories within the institution and the cultural heritage community. Both institutions are internationally acclaimed for their collections and commitment to diversity, equity, and inclusion (DEI). The collection's strength, coupled with decades of social justice and DEI endeavors—including library diversity fellowships and a focus on Black, Indigenous, and People of Color (BIPOC) artists—helped to simplify the approaches through which the museum and the libraries collaboration could thrive.

While Oberlin College's first art class was "a course in linear drawing for young ladies in the Junior Class of the Preparatory College" in 1836, the institution did not open the Allen Memorial Art Museum until 1917. The museum is named after former Oberlin College Trustee and alumni Dudley Peter Allen (Oberlin class of 1875), whose first wife, Elisabeth Severance Prentiss, provided a substantial bequest to the museum. Prentiss' bequest included a portion of her art collection and a $100,000 financial contribution (approximately $2 million in 2022).

The museum was conceived as a teaching museum from its founding. Over the century of its existence, the museum's collection (estimated to contain more than 15,000 works) grew to include items from the fifteenth century to the modern era. Some of the museum's collection foci include masterpieces in African, African American, Ancient Egypt, Greece, and Roman art by legendary artists such as Hendrick Ter Brugghen, Pompeo Batoni, Claude Monet, Ernst Ludwig Kirchner, Chagall, Amedeo Modigliani, Ad Reinhardt, and Arshile Gorky. The museum's first director was Clarence Ward, for whom the Clarence Ward Art Library is named.[5]

Multiple museum directors and art faculty contributed to the depth of the museum's collection and how the collection is incorporated into the curriculum. Among the most influential faculty who left a significant imprint on the museum was Ellen Hulda Johnson, a historian and professor of modern art from 1945 to 1977. Johnson, an Oberlin College alum who earned a bachelor's and master's degree in art history (Oberlin College class of 1933 and 1935, respectively), was a Contemporary American art critic who provided guidance and mentorship to artistic luminaries Andy Warhol and Roy Liechtenstein in the early part of their careers.[6]

A champion for creating a women's studies program in the 1970s, it is believed that Johnson planted the seeds of collaboration between the museum and the libraries that sprouted throughout the twenty-first century. Johnson served in the dual capacity of art librarian and faculty at one point during her tenure. The college's famed art rental program, in which current students may rent museum artwork each semester to hang in their dorm rooms for $5.00, was conceived by Ellen H. Johnson. In 2017 on the occasion of the museum's centennial, the late Ellen H. Johnson was honored with a gallery named in her honor and an exhibition entitled "This Is Your Art: The Legacy of Ellen Johnson."[7]

Andria Derstine, PhD, serves as the museum's current director, a role she has held since 2012. Derstine graduated magna cum laude from Harvard University with a bachelor's degree in history and literature and earned a master's degree and PhD in art history from the New York University Institute of Fine Arts. Prior to her appointment as director, Derstine served for six years as the museum's curator of collections and curator of European and American Art. Her knowledge of the museum's collection was described as "encyclopedic" by former Oberlin College president Marvin Krislov. Derstine attended the first library-museum summit with Alan Boyd, interim director of the Oberlin College Libraries, in 2015. This summit was funded by the Andrew W. Mellon Foundation and hosted by the University of Miami.

The Oberlin College Library was founded in 1834, one year after the college. The library's first major collection was the Anti-Slavery Collection (currently searchable via the Internet Archive). The Oberlin College Libraries (a change from "Library" to "Libraries" took place in 2016) are comprised of four libraries—the Mary Church Terrell Main Library, the Clarence Ward Art Library, the Conservatory Library, and the Science Library. Azariah Smith Root, the institution's first professionally trained library director, is credited for creating bibliographic instructional methods and college-community collaboration through managing a shared library for the town of Oberlin, Ohio, and the institution. Hired in 1887, Root later rose to distinction in librarianship as a president of the American Library Association, the Ohio Library Association, and a founder and president of the Association of College and Research Libraries.

According to his personal account, Root (Oberlin College class of 1884) inherited an organization in shambles. The libraries were inadequately funded, the staff suffered burnout, and the collection was extremely small relative to the size and prestige of the college. Root grew the library's endowment to $250,000 (approximately $4.25 million in 2022). By the time Root's fifty-year tenure concluded, the library's collection grew to more than 500,000 items and included various artworks. In 1923, Oberlin College Library was the largest college library in the country and ranked sixteenth among university libraries.

Root trained his young brother-in-law Keyes Metcalf (who served as the library's first official student worker) to become an academic library leader.

Root's mentorship paid off as Metcalf would later become the Dean of Libraries at Harvard University and the author of the seminal work on academic library space, 1965's *Planning Academic and Research Library Buildings*. Metcalf endowed a fund to host an annual celebration in recognition of the libraries' graduating student employees—a tradition that continues today.[8]

The Oberlin College Libraries had nine directors prior to my arrival. The past Directors of Libraries exercised great care over the libraries and their historical records. This duty of care afforded me the unique ability to understand the context and possibilities of expanding library-museum collaboration. When I assumed leadership of the Oberlin College Libraries in July 2016, I was the second woman and the first person of color to assume the directorship. My directorship was supported by the campus leadership and community along with the libraries' patron group—the Friends of the Oberlin College Libraries.

Aiming Towards a Systems-Approach within the Libraries & the Naming of the Mary Church Terrell Main Library

One of my first administrative declarations was to officially change the name of the "Oberlin College Library" to the "Oberlin College Libraries." Changing the libraries' name was a critical step toward harmonizing a systems approach to our work while further promoting the strength of the three "branch" libraries (Art, Conservatory, and Science). The system name change was only the beginning of naming changes for the Oberlin College Libraries. In 2018, the main library was named for a Black woman civil rights leader Mary Church Terrell (Oberlin College class of 1884), as a part of the presidential inaugural celebration of Carmen Twillie Ambar. The fact that President Ambar was appointed as the college's first Black president was purely consequential in how her appointment intersected with the main library's naming process.

The main library's name changing was the culmination of several years of groundwork initiated by two Oberlin College faculty members: Carol Lasser, emeritus professor of history, and Pamela (Pam) Brooks, Jane and Eric Nord Associate Professor of Africana Studies. The concept was proposed to me in late 2016 by former college president Marvin Krislov and former college dean Timothy (Tim) Elgren . Former Vice President of Development William (Bill) Barlow and I met to research to ensure that there were no existing naming agreements for the main library.

While the preliminary planning discussions were in progress, former Oberlin president Marvin Krislov announced he was transitioning into his new appointment as president of Pace University. Krislov's departure prompted the decision to postpone the main library's name-changing ceremony until the new president was appointed—and if this new leader approved this activity. On May 30, 2017, Carmen Twillie Ambar, JD, was announced as the new Oberlin College president. After a few months, I met with her to discuss the possibility of naming the library after Mary Church Terrell. She agreed, and we proceeded with a request to the Board of Trustees to officially ratify the main library naming. The trustees voted unanimously and with enthusiasm to proceed with naming the main library.

With the official go-ahead from the college president and trustees, I assembled a libraries-wide planning committee to create Mary Church Terrell-related educational and communication components in honor of the main library's naming. The components included a commissioned artwork, collectible bookmarks, a commemorative calendar, a digital exhibition, and a large-scale traveling exhibition. An endowed book fund established in Terrell's honor ensures earmarked money is available for diversity-centered library resources to support disciplines such as Africana Studies, Women and Gender Studies, and American Studies.

Using the Smithsonian Museums as our inspiration, we consulted ongoingly with our Allen Memorial Art Museum colleagues on visual representation, exhibition management, and prospectus development for the educational components of the soon-to-be-named Mary Church Terrell Main Library. Our principal objective with the Mary Church Terrell educational components was to weave together narratives of learning, labor, leadership, and legacy that celebrated Terrell as "an original Oberlin activist." The main library naming also allowed the Oberlin College Libraries to showcase the holdings of the college archives and its expanded corpus of digital resources.

Having all elements and team members in place and in the right roles to support a historically significant activity like the Mary Church Terrell Main Library naming ceremony was a major undertaking that required many proverbial "hands on deck." In some ways, the main library naming ceremony and all educational activities were the successful culmination of the libraries restructuring process.

How the Oberlin College Libraries Restructuring Plan Further Enhanced Libraries-Museum Collaboration

Oberlin College offered a retirement program entitled the Voluntary Separation Incentive Program (VSIP) in the spring of 2016 to relieve the institution of some financial pressure. To qualify, an employee had to be at least 52 years old with a minimum of 10 years of service. Those who accepted the offer received 100 percent of one year's salary, paid in equal monthly payments over 12 months. Ninety-eight employees accepted the offer, with the highest number (7) departing the libraries in December 2016.

I learned about the VSIP program and the pending libraries departures upon my arrival at Oberlin College in July 2016. The libraries had the highest number of retirees (7) of any division or department on campus, and all of them were leaving the institution in December 2016.

The departures allowed me to quickly restructure technical services, reference, and instruction services—formalizing some roles and duties that were not expressed within existing job descriptions. Consequently, roles that supported academic engagement, outreach, information literacy, emerging technologies and systems, metadata and discovery, and user experience were created. Only vacant positions were eliminated so that no current staff person would lose their job.

The Visual Resources Curator was one of the most essential of the new roles created to serve as a bridge to further strengthen collaborations between the libraries and the museum. Reporting to the College Archivist, this position was conceived to have a close partnership with the Head of the Art Library, the Libraries Head of Special Collections, and the museum curators.

I would be remiss not to state that the restructuring was difficult on the libraries' staff and on me. Fear and concerns ran rampant—not just within the college but also within the town of Oberlin. The library support staff's union raised concerns about position eliminations and workflow distributions. Some staff felt I needed to inform them about every decision and action in real-time.

For many, the term "restructuring" automatically harkens notions of massive job loss. While this was not the case for the Oberlin College Libraries' restructuring process under my leadership, I realized that it was tough to break through that perception until the process was completed. As a new director, I did not have time to establish trust with the library staff or many influential Oberlin residents who were concerned about how the restructuring would impact themselves, family members, and friends.

Without a doubt, the restructuring process of the libraries was a very complicated circumstance. It was not an instant remedy for unclear job duties, workflow distributions, or strategic initiatives. Nevertheless, while the circumstances that led to the need to restructure were not ideal, the libraries' restructuring plan was essential for the short-term and long-range strategic objectives of Oberlin College. Restructuring better positioned the libraries in support of increasing library-museum collaborations.

The Allen Memorial Art Museum's and Oberlin College Libraries' Andrew W. Mellon Foundation Planning Grant Activities

The Andrew W. Mellon Foundation notified Oberlin College of its successful grant application on December 8, 2016, for $150,000. The primary purpose of the planning grant was to:

- Develop foundational groundwork to expand curricular collaboration
- Deepen organizational alignments between the Oberlin College Libraries and the Allen Memorial Art Museum
- Engage three subject matter expert consultants in library-museum collaboration and technological platforms
- Host the second summit of academic library and museum directors and staff from leading institutions with experience in stewarding successful library-museum collaboration on their campuses
- Meet with library and museum leaders that had experience in objects-centered pedagogy
- Explore the creation of a searchable digital platform to enhance the discoverability of libraries and museum collections for faculty and students

Upon receiving the Mellon Foundation planning grant, the Allen Memorial Art Museum director and I immediately got to work. Among our first activities was co-designing a job description for our first shared post-baccalaureate library-museum fellow. We created a post-baccalaureate fellow rather than a more commonly offered post-doctoral fellowship to offer a cultural heritage role to an early careerist. Elizabeth (Lizzie) Edgar (Oberlin College class of 2015) was the successful candidate for the fellowship. Edgar was a recent graduate of the University of Michigan School of Information. She held a master's of science degree and had internship experience at the Folger Shakespeare Library in Washington, D.C.

Edgar's job duties were the following: to manage several focus groups comprised of faculty, staff, and students; co-design focus group and faculty survey questions with me, the museum director, and the executive director of grants; coordinate the consultants' visits to Oberlin; and plan the site visits to other institutions by teams of the libraries and the museum staff. Edgar was also a central organizer for the summit of academic library and museum leaders held on Oberlin College's campus. The role of the fellow was essential in ensuring all of the logistical elements converged on time.

Extending invitations to faculty within various disciplines to join a small libraries-museum faculty advisory committee (8-10 people) was the next major task for the museum director and me. Comprised of junior and tenured faculty from various disciplines, the committee provided advice and recommendations regarding how Oberlin College Libraries and Allen Memorial Art Museum could strengthen collaborations. In order to receive frank feedback, an anonymous survey was given to the faculty advisory committee. The survey results identified future-centered pedagogical skills-building opportunities for libraries staff and outreach skills-building for the museum curators.

We selected three consultants (Irene Herold, PhD, Wooster College's former director of libraries and current Dean of Libraries and University Librarian at Virginia Commonwealth University; Meredith Evans, PhD, director of the Jimmy Carter Presidential Library and Museum; and Terry Reese, Ohio State University Libraries professor and head of infrastructure support and digital initiatives) to meet with me, the museum director, key libraries and museum staff, and campus IT leadership to provide advisement on how to proceed with our collaborative efforts successfully. We also hosted each consultant for a campus-wide lecture on strategic outreach, library-museum collaboration, and building digital infrastructure supporting objects-based pedagogy.

Site visits to the New York Public Library, Columbia University Libraries, Yale University Libraries, University of Michigan Library, and University of Michigan Museum of Art were conducted within the first year of the grant. We interviewed library and museum staff and administrators to learn best practices and gain insights on making collaborations sustainable. Oberlin College Libraries and Allen Memorial Art Museum staff rotated for each trip for professional development purposes (myself and museum director Andria Derstine attended each trip). After each site visit, we placed all of our meeting notes in a shared Google document for easy reference.

These activities—the faculty advisory committee meetings, focus groups, surveys, consultants' meetings, and site visits—helped us plan for the second summit of academic library and museum professionals. There were consistent themes of emphasis from the faculty's focus on enhancing more outreach efforts from the museum and future-focused pedagogical support from the libraries. Object provenance and how to reconcile hard histories that arise from acquisitions with libraries and museums were discussed during every site visit. From this detail, museum director Andria Derstine and I decided that focusing the summit on DEI was appropriate.

The Second Summit of Academic Library and Museum Leaders Hosted at Oberlin College

The second summit of academic art museums and libraries was hosted at Oberlin College from June 13th to 15th, 2018. The summit was held approximately seventeen months after the University of Miami's inaugural event. From the initial summit, a round of planning grants was provided by the Andrew W. Mellon Foundation to various institutions, of which Oberlin College was one. Incorporated into the Oberlin College grant was financial funding in support of the second summit.

Eighteen American colleges' and universities' library and museum leadership were bought together (institutions listed below) to engage in deeper conversation regarding how to scale library-museum collaborations beyond joint programming efforts. Of the eighteen institutions represented, nine teams came from institutions represented at the inaugural summit. To ensure representational balance regarding institutional size and compositional diversity, institutions selected to attend the second summit were a blend of public and private universities, liberal arts colleges, and Atlanta University Center—the oldest consortium of historically black colleges and universities (HBCUs). Teams were also curated to represent newly formed partnerships and multi-year collaborations between academic museums and libraries.

The Mellon Foundation, Oberlin College, and the Oberlin College Office of Foundation, Government, and Corporate Grants provided support for the event. Each supporting entity sent representatives as observers, participants, and/or speakers. Additionally, representatives from the Samuel H. Kress Foundation, the American Alliance of Museums, and Ithaka S + R joined the summit as observers. Our welcome reception included remarks from Oberlin College's president Carmen Twillie Ambar, who expressed delight and enthusiasm for the pedagogical possibilities of strengthening library-museum collaborative efforts.

A significant portion of the summit's design included input from the invited attendees. Each team was asked to submit discussion topics centered upon their respective institutions' proposed or existing collaborative activities. Attendees were also asked to share their thoughts about opportunities and barriers regarding collection discoverability and advancing DEI-centered cultural heritage educational efforts on their campuses. Their responses shaped the summit's framework and guided me and the Allen Memorial Art Museum director's thinking about how to craft the plenary sessions and who would be most suited to serve as keynote speakers.

Attendees were most interested in five broad categories: developing shared vocabularies, understanding cultural norms, differences between academic libraries and museums, managing increasing demand for both digital and objects-centered collections skillfully, and overcoming Western hegemony within our institutional practices. From these broad topics, four plenary sessions were designed:

Constructing Narratives through Object-Based Teaching
Atlanta University Center
University of Miami
Smith College
University of Utah

Interactive Learning with Objects
Cornell University
University of Kansas
University of Oregon
Vassar College
University of Washington

Fostering Community and Encouraging Dialogue
Colby College
Northwestern University
Oberlin College
Princeton University
Skidmore College

Digital Transformation of Cultural Heritage Objects
Dartmouth College
Indiana University
University of Notre Dame
Yale University

Dr. Johnnetta B. Cole (Oberlin College class of 1957), who served as a two-time HBCU president and is a former Director of the Smithsonian Institution's National Museum of African Art, was the summit's opening keynote speaker. She delivered a powerful talk on diversity's value in library-museum collaboration, urging summit attendees to look to each other for best practices in access and public education. Cole also encouraged attendees to strive to form authentic relationships that help make one's workplace a joyful experience. The second-day keynote speaker was Dr. Mia Ridge, Western Heritage Collections Digital Curator at The British Library. Ridge urged the summit attendees to serve as thought leaders in addition to service providers. She also provided rich examples of a metric-centered approach to digital assets management and advocated for the need for library and museum collections to be open access.[9]

After the summit, attendees reported feeling excited and hopeful. The post-event survey indicated general enthusiasm to continue down the path of scaling and supporting more collaborative efforts between their respective libraries and museums. Following the summit, two participating institutions launched ambitious projects: The University of Notre Dame Libraries and the Snite Museum of Art at the University of Notre Dame began developing a new search platform (Marble) to enable streamlined wayfinding of libraries and museum materials, and The University of Miami developed plans for producing a shared library-museum catalog for a specific collection.

Both projects were successfully launched in later years. The University of Miami Libraries and University of Miami Lowe Art Museum won the 2019

American Library Association's Katharine Kyes Leab and Daniel J. Leab American Book Prices Current Exhibition Catalogue Award for "Antillean Visions; or, Maps and the Making of the Caribbean: An Exhibition of Cartographic Art at the Lowe Art Museum, University of Miami," curated by William Pestle and Ashli White, with additional contributions by Casey Elinor Lue, Timothy Norris, Diana Ter-Ghazaryan, and Nathan Timpano.[10] Marble was launched in June of 2021.[11]

Launching of the Oberlin College Libraries and the Allen Memorial Art Museum's New Website Platforms to Enable More Meaningful Searching

One key barrier to more library-museum collaboration at Oberlin College was the aged websites of both institutions. The libraries website was at least eight years old, and the museum's website was no less than a decade old. Both the libraries and the museum received scores of complaints from faculty and students about the older interfaces and how complicated it was to navigate both systems. One faculty member lamented anonymously in an internal survey that neither website accurately reflected the richness of the libraries' and museum collections nor showcased the talent of museum and libraries staff.

The museum director and I took charge of redesigning our websites, eliciting the help of The FORM Group (a web design firm based in Greater Cleveland, Ohio). The FORM Group had experience working with cultural heritage organizations and higher education institutions to elevate their distinctiveness while making key elements and assets findable. A joint team from the libraries and museum met to discuss plans and then worked independently to develop and design the respective websites. Similar to second summit institutions—the University of Notre Dame Libraries and Snite Museum of Art—it took the Oberlin College Libraries and Allen Memorial Art Museum four years to redesign and relaunch the websites.

Part of the time invested in this project meant getting the right people with experience in systems and user experience skills in place. Reimaging the information architecture for two extremely old websites was no small feat. Testing, gathering internal key stakeholders' input, and prioritizing this project in the growing portfolios of libraries and museum staff took much time. Fortunately, persistence and dedication ruled as both the libraries and the museum's new websites were launched to rave reviews on campus in 2020.

Conclusion

The Oberlin College Libraries and the Allen Memorial Art Museum have shared a rich history of collaboration for over seventy years. Building upon this legacy meant honoring the essence of what mattered from the past while keeping attention toward the future together to strengthen culturally relevant objects-based pedagogy on campus. As demonstrated by the array of activities we pursued in four years (2016-2020) as enabled by a planning grant from the Mellon Foundation, a firm foundation is in place to further catalyze more library-museum collaborations.

At the heart of Oberlin College, its libraries, and the museum is a deep commitment to infusing social justice and DEI in its pedagogical and programmatic efforts. This commitment informed all aspects of our collaborative work during my time as director of libraries. It is important to emphasize that no partnership or commitment to social justice is one-sided. The museum director Andria Derstine, PhD, was in proverbial lockstep with me during our entire time working together. We learned the power of our collective strength on campus and strategically advanced several efforts due to our shared commitment for joint success. Embodying Dr. Johnnetta Cole's advice during the second summit, Andria Derstine and I also became friends during this project. We learned much from each other, enriching how we approach leadership in our respective fields.

Notes

1. "Oberlin History," Oberlin College, accessed October 15, 2022, https://www.oberlin.edu/about-oberlin/oberlin-history.
2. "Oberlin Wellington Rescue," Oberlin College Archives, n.d., accessed October 15, 2022, https://www2.oberlin.edu/archive/wellington_rescue/rescue.html.
3. "Exhibition Honors Ellen Johnson, Who Championed Modern and Contemporary Art at Oberlin," January 8, 2018, accessed October 15, 2022, http://www.loraincounty.com/oberlin/feature.shtml?f=41018.
4. "Wildfire Pit Test," Allen Memorial Art Museum, n.d., accessed October 15, 2022, https://amam.oberlin.edu/exhibitions-events/exhibitions/2016/08/30/wildfire-test-pit.
5. Laurine Bongiorno, "The Fine Arts in Oberlin, 1836-1918," *AMAM Bulletin*, Spring 1958.
6. Carol Lasser, "'You Were Made of the Stuff That Makes Legends': The Life and Legacy of Ellen H. Johnson," *Digitizing American Feminisms*, n.d., accessed October 15, 2022, http://americanfeminisms.org/you-were-made-of-the-stuff-that-makes-legends-the-life-and-legacy-of-ellen-h-johnson/.
7. "Allen Memorial Art Museum celebrates 100 years of art for the people," n.d., accessed October 15, 2022, https://artdaily.com/news/98554/Allen-Memorial-Art-Museum-celebrates-100-years-of-art-for-the-people#.Yztv--zMLJ8.
8. Azariah Smith Root, personal papers, Oberlin College Archives.
9. Andria Derstine, Alexia Hudson-Ward, Elizabeth Edgar, and Pamela Snyder, "Academic Art Museum and Library Collaborations: Current Practices and Future Directions," 2018 Academic Art Museums and Libraries Summit, accessed October 15, 2022, https://digitalcommons.oberlin.edu/cgi/viewcontent.cgi?article=1065&context=ocl_works.
10. ALA Awards and Grants webpage, accessed October 15, 2022, https://www.ala.org/awardsgrants/university-miami-lowe-art-museum-and-university-miami-libraries.

238   Chapter 16

11.   "Notre Dame launches platform for online access to library, museum holdings," Notre Dame News, July 21, 2021, accessed on October 15, 2022, https://news.nd.edu/news/notre-dame-launches-platform-for-online-access-to-library-museum-holdings/.

Bibliography

ALA Awards and Grants webpage. Accessed October 15, 2022. https://www.ala.org/awardsgrants/university-miami-lowe-art-museum-and-university-miami-libraries.

Allen Memorial Art Museum. "Wildfire Pit Test." n.d. Accessed October 15, 2022. https://amam.oberlin.edu/exhibitions-events/exhibitions/2016/08/30/wildfire-test-pit.

Artdaily.com. "Allen Memorial Art Museum celebrates 100 years of art for the people." n.d. Accessed October 15, 2022. https://artdaily.cc/news/98554/Allen-Memorial-Art-Museum-celebrates-100-years-of-art-for-the-people#.Yztv--zMLJ8.

Bongiorno, Laurine. "The Fine Arts in Oberlin, 1836-1918." *AMAM Bulletin*. Spring 1958.

Derstine, Andria, Alexia Hudson-Ward, Elizabeth Edgar, and Pamela Snyder. "Academic Art Museum and Library Collaborations: Current Practices and Future Directions." 2018 Academic Art Museums and Libraries Summit. Accessed October 15, 2022. https://digitalcommons.oberlin.edu/cgi/viewcontent.cgi?article=1065&context=ocl_works.

Lasser, Carol. "'You Were Made of the Stuff That Makes Legends': The Life and Legacy of Ellen H. Johnson." *Digitizing American Feminisms*. n.d. Accessed October 15, 2022. http://americanfeminisms.org/you-were-made-of-the-stuff-that-makes-legends-the-life-and-legacy-of-ellen-h-johnson/.

Loraincounty.com. "Exhibition Honors Ellen Johnson, Who Championed Modern and Contemporary Art at Oberlin." January 8, 2018. Accessed October 15, 2022. http://www.loraincounty.com/oberlin/feature.shtml?f=41018.

Notre Dame News. "Notre Dame launches platform for online access to library, museum holdings." July 21, 2021. Accessed on October 15, 2022. https://news.nd.edu/news/notre-dame-launches-platform-for-online-access-to-library-museum-holdings/.

Oberlin College. n.d. "Oberlin History." Accessed October 15, 2022. https://www.oberlin.edu/about-oberlin/oberlin-history.

Oberlin College Archives. n.d. "Oberlin Wellington Rescue." Accessed October 15, 2022. https://www2.oberlin.edu/archive/wellington_rescue/rescue.html.

Root, Azariah Smith. Personal papers. Oberlin College Archives.

ABOUT THE EDITORS

Alexia Hudson-Ward is Associate Director of Research & Learning of the Massachusetts Institute of Technology (MIT) Libraries. Her past roles include the Azariah Smith Root Director of Libraries for Oberlin College, Penn State University tenured librarian, award-winning entertainment editor, public radio promotions coordinator, and Coca-Cola Company marketing manager. She contributes service to the cultural heritage & higher education communities as a trustee of the Corning Museum of Glass & on the Board of Directors for The Center for Research Libraries, LYRASIS, and *The Conversation* U.S. Edition.

Alexia is a member of the American Antiquarian Society, the MIT Press Editorial Board, and an Advisory Board member of the Andrew W. Mellon Society of Fellows in Critical Bibliography. She is also Editor-in-Chief of *Toward Inclusive Excellence,* a popular multimedia blog dedicated to illuminating diversity-centered research. She holds an MLIS degree from the University of Pittsburgh and a BA in English Literature and African American Studies from Temple University. Alexia is currently a Simmons University doctoral candidate in the Managerial Leadership in the Information Professions program and holds several professional certificates.

Julie Rodrigues Widholm is the Executive Director of UC Berkeley Art Museum and Pacific Film Archive (BAMPFA), where she leads the strategic and artistic vision to promote community building, new scholarship, equity, and interdisciplinary learning in exhibitions, collections, and programs. Prior to BAMPFA, Rodrigues Widholm was director and chief curator at DePaul Art Museum, where she launched a multiyear Latinx Art Initiative, and a curator at the Museum of Contemporary Art Chicago specializing in global contemporary art and artists from Latin America. Her curatorial projects have been presented at museums across the United States, such as Solomon R. Guggenheim Museum, Perez Art Museum Miami, Nasher Museum at Duke University, MIT List Visual Arts Center, among others. She holds a BA in Art History and Political Science from the University of Illinois at Urbana-Champaign and MA in Art History, Theory and Criticism from the School of the Art Institute of Chicago.

Scott Walter is Dean of the University Library at San Diego State University. Prior to coming to SDSU, he served in senior library leadership positions at Illinois Wesleyan University, DePaul University, and the University of Illinois at Urbana-Champaign. At DePaul, he provided leadership for strategic collaboration with the DePaul Art Museum, as well as with libraries, archives, and museums throughout the City of Chicago as part of the Chicago Collections Consortium. At SDSU, he continues to champion collaboration among academic libraries, public libraries, and museum collections, including the San Diego History Center and the Comic-Con Museum. Dr. Walter received his MLS and MS in History and Philosophy of Education from Indiana University Bloomington, and his PhD in Higher Education Administration from Washington State University.

ABOUT THE AUTHORS

Kayla Birt Flegal is the Access and Outreach Services Librarian, with rank of associate professor, at DePauw University, where she is responsible for circulation, reserves, and campus and community outreach, as well as engaging in library instruction, reference, and virtual services. Kayla is also embedded in the complete renovation and expansion project of DePauw's main Roy O. West Library, scheduled for a Spring 2023 completion. Courses taught at DePauw include UNIV135 Academic Excellence Seminar; ENG183 Children's Literature in London & Paris; UNIV183 Proposing the Future of Tech for Tenzer at DePauw; and UNIV300 Introduction to Librarianship. She holds a BA in English Literature from Taylor University and an MLS from Indiana University (Bloomington).

Sally Brown (formerly Deskins) is an artist, curator, and writer currently based in Morgantown. Her artwork including drawing, painting, and performance explores womanhood, motherhood, and the body. She has exhibited her work in spaces nationally and in the UK. She has won two awards for illustration for *Intimates and Fools* and *Leaves of Absence*, both with poetry by Laura Madeline Wiseman. Her writing has been published in *Hyperallergic, Women's Art Journal,* and *Artslant*, among others. She has curated group shows in Omaha, Nashville, Pittsburgh, and Morgantown. She holds a Bachelor of Arts-Studio Art, a Master of Public Administration, and Master of Arts-Art History and Feminist Theory. She is a former member of the College Art Association National Committee on Women in the Arts, edited the online journal *Les Femmes Folles*, and currently serves as Exhibits Coordinator for West Virginia University Libraries.

Mary Anne Caton joined Wikipedia in 2014 as Wikipedian-in-Residence at Vanderbilt Libraries. She develops Edit-a-Thons and teaches Wikipedia in campus classes and for community groups on local history and visual culture. She holds a BA from UCLA in European history and an MA in American Material Culture from the Winterthur Program at the University of Delaware and she is a reader at the Folger Shakespeare Library. Following curatorial and directorial positions in Virginia and New York City, she teaches curatorial practice in the Buchanan Library Fellowship program at Vanderbilt University Libraries, where she serves on the Collections Committee and the National Museum of African American Music Project Committee. After joining the Vanderbilt Fine Arts Gallery in 2021, she recently became Senior Associate Curator of Campus &

Community Engagement. She has curated exhibitions on American women book collectors, Tsuguharu Foujita, and recent acquisitions to the gallery collections including works by Luis Manuel Otero Alcantara, Yusef Lateef, Emily Arthur, and Adger Cowans.

Alexandra Chamberlain is the Director of Operations for the Association of Academic Museums and Galleries (AAMG). In this role, Alexandra manages all day-to-day operations for AAMG, including financial, programming, and membership related duties. Additionally, she is the Director of Relationship Management for a new arts non-profit, ViVA-Virtual Visiting Artists, that platforms women, BIPOC, LGBTQ+, and social justice artists. She is also a part of a small volunteer working group, the Putnam County Mural Project. This group is responsible for creating and producing seven murals in their home county, including one of the largest in the state of Indiana. Chamberlain holds a BA in Art History and English Literature from DePauw University, an MA in Arts Administration from the Savannah College of Art and Design, and a School of Professional Studies certificate in Museum Studies from Northwestern University.

Elizabeth Constantine directs the Grant and Research Services Office (GRSC) in the UI College of Education. In this role, Constantine works with faculty and staff to find funding to support projects that enhance the College's research, training, and service missions. She previously served as the assistant director for policy analysis and program officer for the Stanley Foundation based in Muscatine, Iowa, where she managed the Asia-Pacific Initiatives (API) program. Constantine also worked for four years in the Office of International Programs at the UI, where she served as the grants and development officer. She spent three years studying and working in China, two years in Uzbekistan, and a year each in Austria and Poland. Constantine received her BA degree from the University of Wisconsin, MA from the Monterey Institute of International Studies, and PhD in Central Eurasian Studies from Indiana University.

Jane Garrity is Director of Strategic Initiatives for the Office of the Vice President for Research (OVPR) at Iowa State University, where she leads the Grants Hub research development office and oversees the OVPR researcher success function. Prior to joining Iowa State University in 2018, she spent ten years in technology transfer, holding senior licensing positions at the University of Iowa Research Foundation (UIRF), the University of Delaware Office of Economic Innovation and Partnerships (OEIP), and NUtech Ventures at the University of Nebraska – Lincoln. She holds a BS in Biology from the California Institute of Technology and a PhD in Microbiology from the University of Wisconsin – Madison.

She is also a registered U.S. Patent Agent and a Registered Technology Transfer Professional.

Corinne Granof is Academic Curator at The Block Museum of Art, Northwestern University, where she directs the museum's curatorial initiatives involving student and faculty collaboration and the museum's publishing program. Working with students and faculty, Granof has curated, co-curated, and collaborated on such exhibitions as *Up is Down: Mid-Century Experiments in Advertising and Film at the Goldsholl Studio* (2018), *William Blake and the Age of Aquarius* (2017), *A Feast of Astonishments: Charlotte Moorman and the Avant-Garde, 1960s-1980s* (2016), *The Left Front: Radical Art in the "Red Decade," 1929–1940* (2014), and *The Last Expression: Art and Auschwitz* (2002), and edited the related companion publications. Granof has a PhD in art history from the University of Chicago, and BA and MA degrees from the University of Wisconsin-Madison.

Kelsey T. Grimm is the Librarian and Archivist for the IU Museum of Archaeology and Anthropology (formerly the Glenn A. Black Laboratory of Archaeology), where she manages the Reading Room collections and provides reference, instruction, outreach, and digitization services. She received her master's degree in Information and Library Science specializing in rare books and special collections from Indiana University in 2013. Since working at the IUMAA, Kelsey has helped digitize and make freely available over 18,000 documents related to the Native experience in the Midwest. She is interested in bridging the gap between special collections and Indigenous communities and wants to continue to learn and grow across the profession.

Jennifer Gunter King serves as the Director of the Stuart A. Rose Manuscript, Archives, and Rare Book Library at Emory University, a position she has held since 2018. Prior to this role, King served as Director of the Harold F. Johnson Library and Knowledge Commons at Hampshire College from 2012-2018, where she oversaw the library, media services, and archives; and as Director of Archives and Special Collections at Mount Holyoke College from 2004-2012. King is professionally active and holds appointed positions with the Society of American Archivists, Association of College and Research Libraries, and formerly with the New England Archivists. She is passionate about user-centered library design and advancing the accessibility of archival and library resources through digital strategies that elevate access to art, archives, and object-based collections. King holds a bachelor's degree from the University of Maryland, Baltimore County, and a Master of Art's degree in history and a Master of Library Science degree from the University of Maryland.

About the Authors

Megan Hammes is Senior Director of UI Wellness at the University of Iowa, where she provides leadership for initiatives and policies designed to support the well-being of 20,000+ faculty and staff including an academic medical center. The live*WELL* program at the University of Iowa is a Blue Zones Certified Worksite, C. Everett Koop National Health Award Honorable Mention, and National Wellness Challenge Winner in 2019 from the Building Healthier Academic Communities (BHAC) organization. Megan is as a planning co-chair for the Health Enhancement Research Organization (HERO) University Summit. She is certified as a Health and Wellness Coach, a Make it Okay Ambassador, and is a Master Certified Health Education Specialist (MCHES). Megan has a background in athletic training with an undergraduate degree from the University of Iowa, and her master's degree is in health promotion management from American University in Washington, D.C.

Alyse Hennig is a freelance archivist, librarian, and genealogist. One of her current projects is building a new digital archive for the Voices Center for Resilience and organizing two decades of their digital and physical collections. Her prior role as an archivist at St. John's University in Queens, New York included archival management, reference, instruction, processing, digitization, and outreach. She had the honor of leading the historical exhibition for the university's 150th anniversary celebration. Alyse holds a Master of Library Science and a Master of Arts in Public History from St. John's University, and a Certificate in Archival Studies from Queens College, New York.

Jennifer E. Knievel is a Professor and Department Director of Researcher & Collections Engagement at the University of Colorado Boulder Libraries. She oversees the services, collections, and support for scholars at all levels in many subjects at the university. She has held several roles at the university over nearly 20 years, including three interim Associate Dean roles over 2.5 years, during which time she was the administrator responsible for the Special Collections, Archives, & Preservation department, and a contributing team member to various proposals for shared libraries and museums spaces. Her research interests include organizational climate in libraries, especially related to sexual harassment, mentoring, staffing, and diversity, the research practices of humanities scholars, and library instruction.

John Patrick Kociolek is a Professor in the Department of Ecology and Evolutionary Biology at the University of Colorado Boulder. His research addresses questions on the taxonomy, systematics, biogeography and evolution of freshwater diatoms. He is interested in museum organizational structure and sustainable architecture and operations of museums. Other interests include the democratization of collections and the tensions between stewardship and accessibility of collections and their associated data. For 14 years he was the Director of the University of Colorado Museum of Natural History and also was Director of the MS Museum and Field Studies Program. Before joining the faculty at CU Boulder, he was the Executive Director of the California Academy of Sciences.

Irene Korber serves as Head of Library Research, Instruction, & Outreach at Meriam Library at California State University, Chico. Her research and publication interests include access and equity in research and instruction services, critical information literacy and constructivist pedagogies, and student engagement with information literacy concepts. She has served on national committees under the American Library Association Reference and User Services Association, the Association of College and Research Libraries Women and Gender Studies Section, as a reviewer for the American Library Association Annual Conference Poster Session, as a book reviewer for the International Literacy Association Social Justice Literature Awards Committee, and has served as a steering committee member for the California Conference on Library Instruction since 2016. She earned a BA in Geography from California State University, Chico, and a Master of Library & Information Science from San Jose State University with a focus on research and instruction services.

Stephanie Lamson is Director of Preservation Services at the University of Washington Libraries, responsible for developing and managing services to support the preservation and stewardship of materials across the UW Libraries. With Dean Lizabeth Wilson, Lamson was the co-principal investigator of the UW Libraries' Andrew W. Mellon Foundation Award, "Building Conservation Capacity at the University of Washington and in the Pacific Northwest" (2012-2016). She was also project coordinator for two additional Mellon grants, "Collaborative Paper and Photograph Conservation" (2017-2020) and "Sustainable Cooperative Conservation Services" (2020-2026). Prior to joining the UW Libraries in 2001, Lamson worked in preservation at Oberlin College and Cornell University Libraries before earning a Certificate in Preservation Management from Rutgers University and an MLIS from Kent State University. Lamson also earned her BA in English from Cornell University and MA in English from the University of Michigan.

Adriene Lim, PhD, is Dean, University Libraries, and Professor of the Practice, College of Information Studies, at the University of Maryland, College Park, and is co-leader of UMD PACT, a cross-campus group convened to advance sustainable, equitable scholarly publishing, facilitate open research, and promote open education. Prior to joining the University of Maryland, Lim was Dean of Libraries and Philip H. Knight Chair at the University of Oregon. In addition to being active in the Association of Research Libraries (ARL) and the

Association of College and Research Libraries (ACRL), she was elected to serve as American Library Association (ALA) Councilor-at-Large, 2022-2025, and currently is a member of the boards of the Center for Research Libraries (CRL) and the Academic Preservation Trust. She was recently appointed to serve on the U.S. Government Publishing Office's Task Force on a Digital Federal Library Depository Program (FDLP) and is Chair of the University System of Maryland Affiliated Institutions (USMAI). Lim earned her PhD in library and information science (LIS) from Simmons University. A first-generation college student and native of Detroit, she holds a master's degree in LIS and a bachelor's degree in Fine Arts, both summa cum laude, from Wayne State University. She has published numerous articles and book chapters, and given presentations about managerial leadership, technology, diversity, and other topics at the international and national levels.

Cory Lockwood is the Senior Associate Director of the Iowa Memorial Union. In his current role he focuses on strategic planning as well as overseeing the day-to-day operations of the IMU and Iowa House Hotel. Project oversight, ranging from multi-million-dollar flood mitigation and recovery to deferred maintenance and renovation, is also a large part of Lockwood's duties. In the aftermath of the 2008 flood, Lockwood briefly served as the Interim Facility Manager before becoming the General Manager of the University Club. Both of those roles afforded him the training and experience needed in his current high-paced position. Lockwood was recognized in October 2017 with the University of Iowa Outstanding Staff Award. A lifetime Hawkeye, Lockwood earned his BA in Economics from the University of Iowa and was a member of Omicron Delta Epsilon.

Robert H. McDonald is Dean of University Libraries, Senior Vice Provost of Online Education, and Professor at the University of Colorado Boulder. He is responsible for leading the Boulder campus library system in fulfilling its mission to inspire learning, research, and discovery by connecting knowledge, information, and people. In his role as senior vice provost of online and extended education, Robert provides leadership and strategy for online education for the Boulder campus, working with all colleges and schools, and with CU System initiatives.

Simon Neame is the Dean of Libraries at the University of Washington, where he is responsible for a system of seventeen libraries at the Seattle, Tacoma, and Bothell campuses as well as the UW Press. Prior to this role, Neame served as the Dean of Libraries at the University of Massachusetts Amherst, where he was responsible for the W.E.B. Du Bois Library, the Science and Engineering Library, and the Wadsworth Library at the Mount Ida Campus. Before leaving for UMass, Neame served as Associate University Librarian and Director of the Irving K. Barber Learning Centre at the University of British Columbia (UBC) in Vancouver, Canada, overseeing Learning Center programs and services, in addition to several library branches and system-wide programs. Neame is a passionate advocate for accessibility and for using digital tools to preserve and amplify the voices of underrepresented communities. From 2003 to 2010 Neame served as an adjunct faculty member at UBC's iSchool, where he taught courses in collection development and management. Neame holds a bachelor's degree from the University of Victoria and a Master of Library and Information Studies from UBC.

Pamela Nett Kruger is the Institutional Repository Librarian at Meriam Library, California State University, Chico. She previously worked as an archivist in the Special Collections and University Archives department. Kruger earned her BA in Anthropology with a focus on museum studies from California State University, Chico; MA in Anthropology from California State University Northridge; and an MLIS from San José State University with a digital curation emphasis. She has held several roles in art galleries, museums, and historical societies, as well as the National Archives and Records Administration (NARA). Her research interests include information literacy, communities of practice, digital inclusion, tech equity, and inclusive and constructivist pedagogies.

Jessica Nicoll is Director and Louise Ines Doyle '34 Chief Curator of the Smith College Museum of Art. She also serves as the Director of Smith College's Museums Concentration, advising and instructing students in museum history, theory, and practice. Nicoll previously served as the William and Helen Thon Chief Curator and Curator of American Art at the Portland Museum of Art, Maine. A specialist in American art, she has written and lectured on a wide variety of topics ranging from American traditions of portraiture and landscape painting in the nineteenth century to the work of artists including Charles Codman, Robert Henri, and Marguerite and William Zorach. Nicoll holds a bachelor's degree from Smith College in Art History and American Studies and a master's from the Winterthur Program in American Material Culture at the University of Delaware.

Alexandra Regan is Events & Exhibitions Librarian at University of California, Santa Barbara. She selects and manages a rotating schedule of temporary exhibitions in five gallery spaces at UCSB Library. She is professionally active in the Art Libraries Society of North America and the California Association of Museums. She holds a Bachelor's Degree in History and French from Grinnell College and a Masters in Information Studies from University of California, Berkeley.

About the Authors

Leslie Reynolds is a Professor and the Senior Associate Dean of Libraries at University of Colorado Boulder. She plays a leadership role in the formulation and assessment of Libraries-wide services, policies, strategic planning, and diversity initiatives. Leslie has been leading teams, units, and departments in research libraries for over 20 years and has experience leading up, down, and across organizations. She is a past chair of the SLA Academic Division and in 2014 she was honored with the designation of SLA Fellow. Her research interests involve outreach to library users and management of libraries.

Susan Rosenberg, Founding Director of the MA Museum Administration program at St. John's University, New York—where she is Professor of Art History—has over twenty years of museum experience, including as Assistant Curator of Modern and Contemporary Art (Philadelphia Museum of Art 1997-2003) and Associate Curator of Modern and Contemporary Art (Seattle Art Museum 2003-2006). Dr. Rosenberg's writings have appeared in numerous international museum catalogs and academic journals. Her book *Trisha Brown: Choreography as Visual Art* (Wesleyan University Press, 2017) received the College Art Association's summer 2015 Meiss/Mellon Author's Book Award. She was an international fellow in the ART & LAW program (2016 and 2019) and received a Certificate of Completion from the Aspen Institute Seminar on Strategy for Artist-Endowed Foundation Leaders (2019). Dr. Rosenberg currently serves as honorary Consulting Historical Scholar for the Trisha Brown Dance Company.

Hope Saska is the Chief Curator and Director of Academic Engagement at the University of Colorado Art Museum in Boulder, Colorado. In this role Hope works to engage CU students, faculty, and community members with the museum's collections and exhibitions. Before joining CU, she held positions at the Detroit Institute of Art and the Lewis Walpole Library, Yale University Libraries. A specialist in prints and print culture, Hope earned her MA and PhD in History of Art and Architecture at Brown University.

April Sievert is Senior Lecturer Emerita in the Department of Anthropology at Indiana University and Director, retired, of the archaeological research laboratory at the Indiana University Museum of Archaeology and Anthropology (IUMAA) in Bloomington, IN. She holds a PhD in anthropology from Northwestern University. As lead PI on the "Learning NAGPRA" project funded by the National Science Foundation, she has assisted collaborative work on teaching and learning about repatriation with descendant tribal nations. Her work centers on archaeological and industrial heritage in North America, ethics, repatriation, legacy archaeological collections, participatory research, and the scholarship of teaching and learning.

About the Authors 249

Jennifer St. Germain is the Archaeology Collections Manager for the Indiana University Museum of Archaeology and Anthropology (IUMAA) in Bloomington, IN. Jennifer has worked collaboratively on numerous digitization and preservation projects aimed at improving the documentation, accessibility, and use of the extensive artifact and records collections held by IUMAA. She has an MA in Anthropology from Northern Illinois University, an MIS/MLS from Indiana University, and is currently a doctoral candidate in information science at IU. Her research focuses on the intersections of information science and archaeological collections management in museums, with additional interest in digital cultural heritage.

Lynn Teesch serves as Director of the High Resolution Mass Spectrometry Facility, one of the University of Iowa's Central Research Core Facilities under the Office of Vice President for Research, and as Director of Operations for the Metabolomics Core Facility in the UI Carver College of Medicine. She has procured multiple instruments through shared instrument grants from both NIH and NSF. Teesch has trained numerous students and other researchers in mass spectrometry operation and data interpretation. She collaborates on research projects with investigators from multiple departments and colleges across the UI campus and the state of Iowa. Her expertise is mass spectrometry of small molecules, but she also served as director of a precursor facility to the current Proteomics Facility in the UI Carver College of Medicine. Teesch received her BA degree in Analytical Chemistry and Business Administration from Coe College and her doctorate in Analytical Chemistry from Emory University.

Adrienne Scott has served as the Curator of the Valene L. Smith Museum of Anthropology at California State University, Chico (CSU Chico) since 2001. She oversees students in training for all manner of museum work from exhibit installation to educational programming. Adrienne previously worked for the Resident Associate Program at the Smithsonian Institution and in the education department at the Museum of Science in Miami, Florida. Adrienne was selected as a National Endowment of Humanities Scholar for K-12 curricula development at Crow Canyon Archaeology Center in 2013. She received the 2016 California State Superintendent's Award for Excellence in Museum Education for the Museum-in-the-Classroom Project she developed. Most recently, in 2022 she was selected as an external reviewer of the Museum Studies program at CSU San Francisco. She holds a BA in Anthropology from Indiana University at Bloomington and an MA in Curriculum and Instruction from the School of Education at CSU Chico.

Sylvia Wolf is John S. Behnke Director of the Henry Art Gallery, Seattle. Previously she served as a curator of photography at the Whitney Museum of

American Art and The Art Institute of Chicago. Publications include *The Digital Eye: Photographic Art in the Electronic Age* (2010); *Polaroids: Mapplethorpe* (2007); *Ed Ruscha and Photography* (2004); *Michal Rovner: The Space Between* (2002); *Kenneth Josephson: A Retrospective* (1999); *Julia Margaret Cameron's Women* (1998); *Dieter Appelt* (1994); and *Focus: Five Women Photographers* (1994). Wolf is Affiliate Faculty at the University of Washington and has taught undergraduate and graduate courses in studio art, art history, and museum studies at Columbia University, NYU, and School of Visual Arts. Wolf received a BA in French literature from Northwestern University and an MFA in photography from Rhode Island School of Design.